D0443101

RACE AND PLACE

A striking but little recognized change in race relations during the past two decades has been the declining level of racial segregation in most of America's major metropolitan areas. Slowly, more areas of American cities are beginning to have both black and white residents. An integral component of this decline in residential segregation has been the large-scale but under-publicized movement of blacks to the suburbs.

This book focuses on the impact of these changes on the attitudes and behavior of African Americans and whites. Will whites' attitudes about blacks and blacks' attitudes about whites change if they are living in integrated neighborhoods rather than apart from one another? Are black suburbanites more likely to share the views of their fellow white suburbanites or of their fellow African Americans in the central city? Will residential integration and new patterns of race in the suburbs break down divisions between blacks and whites in their views of local public services? These are the central questions of this book.

Susan Welch is Dean of the College of the Liberal Arts and Professor of Political Science at the Pennsylvania State University, positions she has held since 1991. Before joining Penn State, she was the Carl A. Happold Professor of Political Science at the University of Nebraska, Lincoln. Professor Welch is a specialist in American politics, particularly urban, ethnic, and women's politics. She is the author of nearly 150 scholarly articles and six books, two textbooks, and three edited collections. Her most recent books include *Affirmative Action and Minority Enrollments: The Impact of Bakke on Medical and Law Schools,* co-authored with John Gruhl and published in 1998 and *Black Americans' View of Racial Inequality: The Dream Deferred,* co-authored with Lee Sigelman and first published by Cambridge University Press in 1991, and revised in 1993.

Lee Sigelman is the Columbian Professor of Political Science at the George Washington University. He has previously served as department chair at George Washington University and at the University of Kentucky, as dean of social and behavioral sciences at the University of Arizona, as director of the political science program at the National Science Foundation, and as a faculty member at Texas Tech University. He is a former editor of *American Politics Quarterly* and a past president of the Midwest Political Science Association. He was recently named the new editor of the *American Political Science Review.*

Sigelman is a graduate of Carleton College and holds a Ph.D. in political science from Vanderbilt University. His research interests span the fields of American politics, comparative politics, and research methods and cross disciplinary boundaries into sociology, social psychology, and communication. He is the author of numerous articles in leading social science journals and of several books including *Black Americans' View of Racial Inequality: The Dream Deferred* (co-authored with Susan Welch and published by Cambridge University Press).

Timothy Bledsoe is currently Professor of Political Science at Wayne State University in Detroit. He is author of *Careers in City Politics* and co-author with Susan Welch of *Urban Reform and Its Consequences*. His research has appeared in the *American Political Science Review*, the *American Journal of Political Science*, the *American Journal of Sociology*, as well as other leading journals. Professor Bledsoe has been on the faculty of the Department of Government and International Studies at the University of South Carolina and the faculty of Wayne State University. He is currently focusing his studies on judicial elections in the state of Michigan.

Michael Combs is Professor of Political Science at the University of Nebraska, Lincoln. He earned his Ph.D. from Washington University and is a former president of the National Conference of Black Political Scientists. He has published widely on black politics and civil liberties. His recent publications include *Civil Liberties and the Constitution: Cases and Commentaries*, co-authored with Lucius J. Barker, Twiley W. Barker, Jr., Kevin Lyles, and H. W. Perry and published in 1999 and *Police Beatings* for *Political Research Quarterly*, co-authored by the co-editors of this book and published in December 1997.

Cambridge Studies in Political Psychology
and Public Opinion

General Editors

James H. Kuklinski, *University of Illinois, Urbana-Champaign*
Dennis Chong, *Northwestern University*

Editorial Board

Stanley Feldman, *State University of New York,*
Stony Brook
Roger D. Masters, *Dartmouth College*
William J. McGuire, *Yale University*
Norbert Schwarz, *Zentrum für Umfragen, Methoden*
und Analysen ZUMA, Mannheim, FRG
David O. Sears, *University of California,*
Los Angeles
Paul M. Sniderman, *Stanford University and Survey*
Research Center, University of California, Berkeley
James A. Stimson, *University of North Carolina*

This series has been established in recognition of the growing sophistication in the resurgence of interest in political psychology and the study of public opinion. Its focus will range from the kinds of mental processes that people employ when they think about democratic processes and make political choices to the nature and consequences of macro-level public opinion.

We expect that some of the works will draw on developments in cognitive and social psychology and relevant areas of philosophy. Appropriate subjects would include the use of heuristics, the roles of core values and moral principles in political reasoning, the effects of expertise and sophistication, the roles of affect and emotion, and the nature of cognition and information processing. The emphasis will be on systematic and rigorous empirical analysis and a wide range of methodologies will be appropriate: traditional surveys, experimental surveys, laboratory experiments, focus groups, in-depth interviews, as well as others. We intend that these empirically oriented studies will also consider normative implications for democratic politics generally.

Politics, not psychology, will be the primary focus, and it is expected that most works will deal with mass publics and democratic politics, although work on nondemocratic publics will not be excluded. Other works will examine traditional topics in public opinion research, as well as contribute to the growing literature on aggregate opinion and its role in democratic societies.

Other books in the series noted on page following Index

RACE AND PLACE

Race Relations in an American City

SUSAN WELCH
The Pennsylvania State University

LEE SIGELMAN
The George Washington University

TIMOTHY BLEDSOE
Wayne State University

MICHAEL COMBS
University of Nebraska, Lincoln

CAMBRIDGE UNIVERSITY PRESS

PUBLISHED BY THE PRESS SYNDICATE OF THE UNIVERSITY OF CAMBRIDGE
The Pitt Building, Trumpington Street, Cambridge, United Kingdom

CAMBRIDGE UNIVERSITY PRESS
The Edinburgh Building, Cambridge CB2 2RU, UK
40 West 20th Street, New York, NY 10011-4211, USA
10 Stamford Road, Oakleigh, VIC 3166, Australia
Ruiz de Alarcón 13, 28014 Madrid, Spain
Dock House, The Waterfront, Cape Town 8001, South Africa

http://www.cambridge.org

© Cambridge University Press 2001

This book is in copyright. Subject to statutory exception
and to the provisions of relevant collective licensing agreements,
no reproduction of any part may take place without
the written permission of Cambridge University Press.

First published 2001

Printed in the United States of America

Typeface Sabon 10/12 pt.   *System* QuarkXPress™   [HT]

A catalog record for this book is available from the British Library.

Library of Congress Cataloging in Publication Data

Race and place: race relations in an American city/Susan Welch ... [et al.].
    p. cm. – (Cambridge studies in political psychology and public opinion)
    Includes bibliographical references and index.
    ISBN 0-521-79215-0 – ISBN 0-521-79655-5 (pbk.)
        1. Detroit Region (Mich.) – Race relations. 2. African Americans – Michigan –
Detroit Region – Attitudes. 3. Whites – Michigan – Detroit Region – Attitudes.
4. African Americans – Housing – Michigan – Detroit Region. 5. Whites – Housing –
Michigan – Detroit Region. 6. Discrimination in housing – Michigan – Detroit Region –
History – 20th century. 7. Detroit Region (Mich.) – Social conditions – 20th century.
8. Suburban life – Michigan – Detroit Region – History – 20th century.
I. Welch, Susan. II. Series.

F574.D49 A27 2001
305.8'009774'34–dc21   2001025035

ISBN 0 521 79215 0 hardback
ISBN 0 521 79655 5 paperback

Contents

Figures

Tables

Tables

Preface

In 2000, the *New York Times* published a major series based on an investigation of how whites and blacks in America communicate with each other.[1] Featuring individuals as diverse as army drill sergeants, rising Internet entrepreneurs, young Cuban immigrants, elected officials, slaughterhouse workers, antebellum plantation owners, Harlem police officers, and suburban teenagers, the *Times* writers told a story of both progress and setbacks in race relations. According to this series, whites and African Americans are coming into contact with each other with a frequency unprecedented in the twentieth century and in relationships unprecedented in any time in the nation's history. However, for every newly opened line of communication, new misunderstandings arise. For every attempt to understand one another's perspectives, an inclination to blame interpersonal misunderstandings on race develops. The *Times*'s stories are fascinating case studies, which do much to capture the progress, difficulties, and continuing ambiguities of American race relations at the beginning of the twenty-first century.

Many of the *Times*'s stories reflect well-known features of American race relations: the increasingly racially mixed work forces, the difficulties of real integration in supposedly integrated schools, and the struggles and successes of African American candidates for public office. But the stories do not reveal much about a less well known feature of race relations: the declining levels of racial segregation in most of America's major metropolitan areas. To be sure, the pace of this change has been slow and uneven, but the 1990s saw a reversal in the decades-long trend of increasing residential segregation. One indicator of this is a dissimilarity index, a measure indicating the proportion of the population that would have to change locations in order for each neighborhood to reflect the overall racial composition of the city (Massey and Denton,

---

1 These stories ran periodically throughout June and July 2000.

1987; Massey, 2000; see also Sorenson, Taeuber, and Hollingsworth, 1975). With 100 being the highest level of segregation, that index, applied to major metropolitan areas, decreased from 75 in 1970 to 67 in 1990.[2] Slowly, more areas of American cities are beginning to have both black and white residents. Sometimes the residential integration is temporary, as when a neighborhood turns from all white to all black, but other times the mixed-race character of a neighborhood is more permanent.

An integral component of this decline in residential segregation has been the large-scale but underpublicized movement of blacks to the suburbs. This movement has not always been to middle-class or upper middle class suburbs of the sort that grew out of the post–World War II flight of whites from the city. Nonetheless, the exodus of blacks from central cities to suburbs also has a potential for changing the dynamics of race relations in America's metropolitan areas.

This book focuses on the impact of these changes on the attitudes and behavior of African Americans and whites. Will whites' attitudes about blacks and blacks' attitudes toward whites change if they are living in integrated neighborhoods rather than apart from one another? Are black suburbanites more likely to share the views of their fellow white suburbanites or of their fellow African Americans in the central city? Will residential integration and new patterns of race in the suburbs break down divisions between blacks and whites in their views of local public services? These are the central questions of this book.

These questions are important because residential patterns undergird much that is negative about American race relations. From cradle to grave, in hospitals, day care establishments, schools, churches, and funeral parlors, much of America is still largely segregated. Housing patterns shape this segregation.

These questions are interesting, because although social scientists have long been concerned about how residential contexts shape individual behavior, their insights have not been applied very often to questions of race.[3] Thus, we apply understandings gained in other research about the influence of context to the case of race relations in the central city and suburbs. Our guiding principle is that as the racial composition of neigh-

---

2 A second measure of segregation, the *isolation scale,* declined slightly during this time, from 69 to 65. It ranges from 1, designating the lowest possible level of black isolation, to 100, the point at which every black would reside in a neighborhood composed solely of other blacks.

3 There is certainly significant work on how larger racial contexts, such as congressional districts, shape electoral behavior. Although there is little on neighborhood influences, see Huckfeldt (1986), Orbell and Sherrill (1969), Sears and Kinder (1970), Taylor (1998), and Wilson (1971).

borhoods changes, it becomes more and more important to understand what this change might bode for racial attitudes.

Why might we expect changing racial patterns of neighborhood residence to shape racial attitudes and behavior? Attitudes are shaped not only by personal characteristics such as religion, gender, and education, but also by context (see Eulau, 1996, for a general treatment of different levels of analysis). Neighborhoods are an important context. They provide opportunities for forming friendships and close relationships (Huckfeldt, 1986). They also provide settings for more casual interactions, which over time have the potential to influence attitudes in either a positive or conflictual direction (Sprague, 1982). Neighborhoods can be strikingly different: Some subject residents to an existence in which violent crime is an ever-present threat, but others allow residents to enjoy a life in which street crime is something they only read about in the newspaper; in some neighborhoods, schools provide students with excellent educational opportunities, whereas in others the schools are dilapidated and the teachers dispirited. Neighborhoods also provide a spatial focus for structured and unstructured interactions, whether they be school board meetings, sporting events, or casual, spur-of-the-moment conversations on the sidewalk.

We believe that the neighborhood racial context is very important in understanding racial attitudes. We also believe that the difference between living in the suburbs and living in the central city has the potential to affect attitudes. The politics of suburbia are relatively unexplored (see Wood, 1959, for a classic study) and the racial politics of suburbia are almost completely uninvestigated. But no matter how bland the politics of suburbia are, suburbs have their own political structures and organizational and social life. They provide different settings for contact than do central cities. The quality and scope of the public services and the quality of life may also differ dramatically from those found in the central city. All those factors can differentiate the personal and political views of urbanites and suburbanites.

How might these contexts mold attitudes? To date, social scientists have provided few and conflicting answers to these questions. Neighborhoods and city boundaries offer opportunities for both informal social contact and more formal interaction for individuals as members of clubs, churches, schools, and political entities. Prior research, much of which is reviewed herein, indicates that when people of different races have frequent contact with one another, their hostile feelings toward the members of another race often, but not always, tend to decrease. Increasing neighborhood integration offers the potential for more of these contacts. Prior research also indicates, however, that in large geographical units such as counties or metropolitan areas, whites' hostility toward African

Americans is greater where there are more African Americans. Unfortunately, largely ignored in both streams of research have been neighborhood-based relationships, the core of person-to-person interracial contact and the main building block of spatially defined interaction patterns.

This book examines race relations in the city of Detroit and the surrounding metropolitan region, an area often studied by scholars of racial attitudes. The opportunity to study race in the Detroit area offered us the ability not only to examine the effects of residential context on the racial attitudes of both blacks and whites in the early 1990s, when we began this study, but also to compare racial attitudes in the 1990s with those at the time of civil unrest in Detroit a quarter of a century earlier. Our study is nearly unique in its inclusion of black suburbanites as a significant focus of attention and in its comparison of black suburbanites with both their African American central city counterparts and their white suburban counterparts.

Writing about race in America is a difficult task. Emotion can override rationality, and subtlety can lose to simplification. Our own beliefs are that, although the United States has made great progress in moving toward racial equality compared with earlier generations, there is still a very long way to travel. Racism, even in its crudest forms, is not just a historical event but is alive today in some parts of society and perhaps at some times in all parts of society. At the same time, we do not agree with the view that race relations are worse at the beginning of the new century than they were decades ago. Too often, the often harsh realities of race relations at the beginning of the twenty-first century are compared with a sanitized view of the past. Our hope is that this book, by shedding light on conditions that appear to enhance positive attitudes and interactions, will illuminate both areas of progress and areas of stagnation. In all cases, there is much to be done in moving America toward a society where equality of opportunity is an apt description of reality.

This book is the result of a decade of effort. The focus of our analysis is a 1992 survey conducted in metropolitan Detroit. We thank the National Science Foundation for its support for this survey and the Wayne State Center for Urban Studies for conducting the survey. Christian Calientes of Population Research Institute at the Pennsylvania State University kindly prepared the maps in Chapters 1 and 2. David R. Johnson of the University of Nebraska contributed significantly with his sampling design for our survey. The readers for Cambridge University Press were uncommonly insightful and helpful in offering suggestions to strengthen the version of the book that they read.

I

Introduction

RACE AND RESIDENCE

Residential segregation in the United States has proved resilient to change. Residential segregation has been and continues to be the "structural linchpin" of American race relations (Bobo, 1989: 307). This is in striking contrast to the progress that has been made in narrowing the racial divide in public accommodations, the workplace, universities, and the armed forces. The movement toward racially integrated housing has resisted the broader societal sweep of integration, and the residential separation of blacks and whites remains a huge impediment to progress toward racial equality (Farley, Bianchi, and Colasanto, 1978a: 98).

After increasing steadily for most of the 20th century, however, housing segregation finally began to diminish during the 1980s and 1990s (Massey and Denton, 1987; Farley and Frey, 1994; Massey, 2000, see also Taeuber and Taeuber, 1965). During those years, most American metropolitan areas became less racially segregated within the borders of the central city, and many experienced an exodus of African Americans to the suburbs. Indeed, this movement of blacks to the suburbs was a major reason for the small decrease in residential segregation (Schneider and Phelan, 1993).

Although demographers have tracked these migratory patterns (Farley and Frey, 1994; Massey and Denton, 1993, O'Hare and Usdansky, 1992), little is known about the *impact* of such movement on the way blacks and whites think about themselves and one another. Does it matter whether blacks and whites live in mixed neighborhoods or in relatively integrated cities? Does residential integration enhance interracial contact and thereby stimulate more positive views of people of another race? Or does residential integration exacerbate interracial conflict? Do blacks who live in interracial neighborhoods perceive less racial discrimination? Do whites who live close to blacks hold fewer negative stereotypes of blacks than do other whites? Do blacks who live far removed from other blacks identify less as blacks? Do different patterns of interracial contact shape how people judge solutions to racial conflict? In short, do spatial arrangements affect how people think about racial matters? How, and how much?

To the extent that spatial arrangements matter, residential desegregation and black suburbanization may have profound implications for race relations in America. If our perceptions and attitudes are shaped by where we live and who our neighbors are, it becomes crucial to understand how residential patterns matter and whether they have the potential for improving America's tense interracial relations.

In the pages that follow, we use a unique body of data to explore these issues. Our primary source of data is a survey of black and white residents of the Detroit metropolitan area. In 1992, we interviewed blacks who lived in the suburbs as well as those who lived in the central city and whites who lived in the central city as well as those who lived in the suburbs. We interviewed blacks and whites living in mixed-race neighborhoods, whether in the city or the suburbs, and those living exclusively among members of their own race. The resulting data set is, insofar as we are aware, unique, but it also fits comfortably into a series of surveys conducted in Detroit during the quarter-century before we undertook our survey.

In this chapter, we set the stage for our examination of these data. We explore why we believe that the neighborhood environment might affect the attitudes of both blacks and whites about race and about racially charged policy issues. We then provide an overview of our study and the people and neighborhoods that are its base. We conclude by previewing the remainder of the book.

THE OPPORTUNITIES FOR RESIDENTIAL CONTEXT TO MOLD ATTITUDES

Many blacks and whites view the world so differently in part because they live apart from one another. Largely because they live apart, they educate their children separately, shop separately, work separately, worship separately, and socialize separately. From the maternity ward to the funeral home, they are apart from one another in fact, though no longer in law. Much of this separateness is a direct function of residential patterns. Thus, the intermixing of members of different races in residential neighborhoods has long been a source of hope for improving America's troubled race relations. If only blacks and whites lived side by side, the argument has gone, the perceptual and attitudinal gap between them would be narrowed, if not eradicated.

The premise of our research is that indeed, residential context matters in forming perceptions and attitudes. Residential context shapes attitudes and opinion through several mechanisms. First, where people live determines many of the daily informal contacts that they have, in the grocery store, in the liquor store, in the barber shop, or on the street. These frequent, recurring interactions do much to shape a view of the world and the people in it (Sprague, 1982; Huckfeldt, 1986). Second, residence affects friendship patterns. Neighborly contacts often grow into friendships, and friendships influence opinions and attitudes. These continuing informal interactions make a difference.

Third, different residential contexts provide varied settings for social and political organization and communication. Neighborhood schools and social clubs, youth athletics, and neighborhood improvement organizations provide opportunities for people to meet and exchange views about issues from the state of the weather to the state of the nation. Neighborhood differences are amplified when crossing community borders. Certainly not all suburbs have a vibrant community life, replete with a thriving commercial core, a rich network of community groups, a wide array of educational and cultural opportunities, and other urban amenities. However, even industrial suburbs, on the one hand, and bedroom suburbs, on the other, have schools and elected governing boards, both offering the opportunities for community issues to arise that are different from those in other communities. The quality of public services, schools, police and fire protection, street maintenance, and housing code enforcement, to name only a few, varies wildly across suburban boundaries as well, offering additional opportunities for shaping perceptions and opinions.

Finally, differences in neighborhood and community contexts offer different opportunities, which in turn shape opinions. Here we refer not only to the quality of public services but also to a host of other contextual factors, such as opportunities for employment, the probability of becoming a crime victim, the frequency of seeing drug pushers, the amount of peer pressure to stay in school, and differences in economic means to make a college education a realistic possibility: all these factors shape individual possibilities and thus individual attitudes.

This latter point is particularly relevant to our focus on racial attitudes. Sociologists have recently done considerable research on the impact of neighborhoods on individual social conditions. Along with large clusters of poor families, whatever their race, have come increases in such social pathologies as teenage pregnancy, dropping out of school, crime, and abandoned housing (see, e.g., Brooks-Gunn et al., 1993; Massey, Gross, and Eggers, 1991; South and Crowder, 1999). Both middle-class blacks and middle-class whites express more satisfaction with their quality of life the farther they live from poverty-stricken neighborhoods (DeFrances, 1996). This effect is even larger than for their own socioeconomic status (especially for blacks).

Race and Place

The disproportionately high likelihood that black families would live in neighborhoods with higher levels of social pathologies has affected middle-class as well as poor families. Because of residential segregation, in the 1990s it remained more difficult for a black family whose economic status was improving than for a similar white family to move from a poor neighborhood into a better one. Thus, middle-class black families often live in neighborhoods in which the crime rate and the proportion of births to unwed mothers, for example, are much higher than in white middle-class neighborhoods (Massey and Denton, 1993: 152). According to a study of teenage African American girls, living in an integrated neighborhood, even a working-class one, reduces the probability of having a premarital pregnancy by 50%, taking into account the socioeconomic status of a girl's family. The highest pregnancy rates are in the poorest, racially segregated neighborhoods. Accordingly, the authors of that study conclude that living in segregated neighborhoods seals off "participation in mainstream social and economic arenas" (Sucoff and Upchurch, 1998: 581).

Of course, racial segregation has concentrated poverty and the attendant social ills in poor black communities (Hogan and Kitagawa, 1985; Massey and Denton, 1993: 118; see also Wilson, 1987, 1996). In 1980, for example, about 32% of those living in the neighborhood of the average poor black family in Detroit were themselves poor, compared to only about 12% for poor white Detroiters (Massey and Denton, 1993: 129). In a study of black Detroit residents, Cohen and Dawson (1993) found that residents of exceptionally poor neighborhoods were more socially isolated than other blacks and were more isolated than would have been expected on the basis of their individual poverty. Residents of those neighborhoods also were unlikely to participate in politics. Amplifying this picture of isolation, a study of black inner-city residents in Chicago pointed out that many never leave their neighborhood, even to go downtown (Pedder, 1993, cited by Massey and Denton, 1993).

The different social contexts, then, of black and white, rich and poor, and integrated and segregated neighborhoods offer great potentials for affecting attitudes (see Oliver and Mendelberg, 2000). Neighborhood disparities affect individuals' outlooks on the world and their opinions about it.

Thus, residential contexts feature differences in informal contacts, friendship opportunities, formal social and political organizational structures, and economic and social opportunities. It would be amazing if, in a society and a community in which race underlies almost every issue, these residential contexts did not influence perceptions and opinions.

4

Introduction: Race and Residence

WHAT WE KNOW ABOUT RESIDENTIAL CONTEXT AND RACIAL ATTITUDES

The notion that context makes a difference has been an important thread in research on political attitudes since at least the 1950s. Residential context shapes voting choices (Tingsten, 1963; Segal and Meyer, 1974; Butler and Stokes, 1974; Cox, 1974) and political participation (Huckfeldt, 1979). Residential context also structures friendship choices (Huckfeldt, 1986), which in turn affect voting choices (Berelson, Lazarfeld, and McPhee, 1954; Fuchs, 1955; Miller, 1956; Putnam, 1966). Moreover, residential context influences ethnic identity (Pomper, 1966; Kornblum, 1974; Huckfeldt, 1983).

The effect of context on racial attitudes has been noted for more than a half century. In his magisterial study of Southern politics, Key (1949) commented that in that region, "the character of the politics of individual states will vary roughly with the Negro proportion of the population." At the neighborhood level, residence affects racial attitudes both negatively and positively. That is, residential contexts can promote better race relations or can contribute to racial conflict. For example, a social density hypothesis posits that individuals living in spatial proximity to other members of their group will feel a greater sense of identity with that group. This idea is usually applied to racial or ethnic groups. The visibility of the group and the likelihood of contact with other group members are both enhanced by spatial concentration, which encourages the development of institutions that reinforce and perpetuate the group (e.g., Lieberson, 1963; Yancey, Ericksen, and Juliani, 1976). This sense of group identity has the potential to promote hostility toward, and a sense of separateness from, other groups.

A contrary expectation is that it is when individuals are separated from other members of their group that they are most likely to feel antagonistic to other groups. In this scenario, blacks living in suburban and mixed-race neighborhoods would be expected to feel a greater sense of solidarity with other blacks and perhaps hostility to other groups. Race would take on special importance for blacks and whites in mixed-race communities (Lau, 1989; Tajfel, 1981)

Our working hypothesis is that blacks and whites who live in mixed-race communities will be more tolerant of those of the other race. Those who believe that residential integration is a key to ameliorating race relations have pointed to the often reported research finding that interracial contact tends to reduce interracial friction, particularly when people interact under conditions of relative equality (see chapter 3). The type of contact that blacks and whites are likely to have when they share a neighborhood is qualitatively different from the contact that takes place in the workplace or at school (Farley, Bianchi, and Colasanto, 1978).

Prior research provides some basis for our expectation that neighborhood integration has these socially beneficial consequences (although, as we shall shortly see, there is also evidence to the contrary). Research conducted in public housing projects in the late 1940s showed that white tenants of integrated projects were more accepting of close social ties to blacks and held fewer negative stereotypes of blacks than did whites who lived in segregated projects (Deutsch and Collins, 1951). In another study conducted in 18 suburban neighborhoods surrounding New Haven, Connecticut (of which 8 had gained a new black family and 10 had added a new white family), Hamilton and Bishop (1976) observed that when a black family moved into a neighborhood, it was an extremely salient event – much more salient than when a white family moved in. White residents noticed and were concerned about the arrival of black neighbors. However, after a year had passed, the white residents of the newly integrated neighborhoods had significantly lower "symbolic racism" scores than they had previously held, regardless of whether or not they had interacted with their black neighbors. Whites, Hamilton and Bishop concluded, had negative expectations about changing neighborhood conditions prior to the arrival of the black families but altered their beliefs about blacks as time passed without any deterioration of the neighborhood.

More recently, Kinder and Mendelberg (1995), examining survey data, showed that whites who had more exposure to blacks were less likely to express antiblack attitudes. Those whites who had black neighbors, co-workers, and co-worshipers were less likely to convert prejudicial attitudes toward blacks into antiblack policy attitudes. Similarly, Carsey (1995) discovered that New York City voters who lived in neighborhoods with some blacks were more likely than other whites to vote for black candidates.

These findings were consistent with the "mere exposure" thesis first advanced by Zajonc (1968) and subsequently verified in numerous experiments.[1] Exposure to other groups enables people to view the members of such groups as individuals rather than as undifferentiated "others" (members of an outgroup) and can thereby reduce group stereotypes. Thus, for example, Litvak (1969) reported a significant reduction in fear as a consequence of simple exposure to a feared object. Such mere exposure effects have proved to be robust and reliable in a wide array of research settings (Bornstein, 1993). Aside from

---

[1] For reviews of this research literature, see Bornstein (1989), Harrison (1977), and Stang (1974).

controlled laboratory research, field research has suggested that proximity creates better relations between blacks and whites. Ellison and Powers (1994) found that childhood and adult contact with whites helps explain blacks' interracial friendships, which in turn promote more positive views of whites. Sigelman and Welch (1993) also reported that having white friends reduced blacks' hostility toward whites, although casual contact with whites had little effect. These findings build on research undertaken two decades earlier by Schuman and Hatchett (1974), who, in a study of residents of Detroit, found that blacks who socialized with white neighbors were more trusting of whites than were other blacks, but that casual black-white contact had little effect on attitudes.

A different indicator of the effect of proximity is that, after remaining constant for more than a century, interracial marriages between blacks and whites rose dramatically in the 1980s and 1990s (Kalmijn, 1993; U.S. Census, 2000: Table 65).[2] Increased interracial contacts in both residential and work settings were not the only causes of this recent rise, but they unquestionably were contributing factors.

The potential effectiveness of residential integration in healing troubled race relations is far from limitless; indeed, it might lead to increased conflict, as the social salience model would lead one to expect. Coming into contact with those of other groups may be threatening (Blalock, 1967). In the first place, to have a positive effect, exposure to other groups must take place under auspicious conditions, that is, in a positive context, between persons of more or less equal status, and on a voluntary basis (Amir, 1976; Perlman and Oskamp, 1971). Moreover, it is obvious that in our society, nowhere near all interracial contacts take place under these ideal conditions. Ultimately, even these conditions may not be enough to alter deeply ingrained negative impressions of other groups, which are often resistant to contrary evidence (Bornstein, 1993; Hamilton, 1981; Rothbart, 1981).

Thus, early studies of neighborhood effects turned up mostly negative evidence on the impact of racial integration. Orbell and Sherrill (1969) found increased intolerance among low-income whites living in neighborhoods with high proportions of blacks, and Wilson (1971) observed that blacks living in mixed neighborhoods were more alienated than those living in all-black areas.

---

2 In the twentieth century, only about 1% of black marriages involved a white partner until the 1970s. By 1998, more than 1 of every 12 black marriages involved a white partner (*Statistical Abstracts*, 1999: Table 65) and another 1 in 100 involved a partner of another race. Increasingly, African American women are involved in interracial marriages. Given the greater number of whites involved in marriage, this means that fewer than 1 white in 100 marries a black, however.

Moreover, residential integration necessarily involves joining whites and blacks together in the same political jurisdiction, and this can itself heighten the possibility of intergroup conflict. Indeed, one of the ironies of research on contextual factors on racial attitudes is that studies of individual interracial contact have often uncovered positive effects, while studies of larger entities, such as cities or congressional districts, often find increased conflict. Such conflict has been well documented in the South (e.g., Glaser, 1994; Key, 1949; Matthews and Prothro, 1966; Wright, 1977), although Glaser (1994) maintains that even though black–white conflict may harden whites' political attitudes, it is unlikely to make them more racially prejudiced. In other words, whites tend to view blacks as adversaries or competitors in the context of community politics, but this sense of rivalry does not necessarily entail personal animosity. Still, many scholars have argued that putting large numbers of blacks and whites together in the same county or region (let alone the same neighborhood) can create threatening situations and heighten racial animosities (Corzine, Creech, and Corzine, 1983; Huckfeldt, 1986; Giles and Buckner, 1993; Taylor, 1998).

Many attempts have been made to pinpoint the relationship between whites' attitudes and the size of the black population (Blalock, 1957; 1967; Giles and Evans, 1985, 1986; Giles and Buckner, 1993; Fossett and Kiecolt, 1989; Glaser, 1994; Key, 1949; Quillian, 1996; Taylor, 1998). Although much inconsistency runs through the findings, a preponderance of evidence suggests that whites' attitudes toward blacks (and toward policies designed to help blacks) are a curvilinear function of black population size. Whites' attitudes tend to be most favorable in places where the black population is less than 15% or more than 25% (Taylor, 1998).

As we examine different aspects of attitudes about race in this book, we will outline specific expectations about how residential context could shape those attitudes. Our perspective as we began this study was that residential integration may afford a basis of hope for improving race relations and that even though the path toward achieving these payoffs would undoubtedly be rocky, the ultimate payoffs from genuine residential integration could prove substantial. Yet, we would be naïve if we did not also recognize that increased racial interaction can bring enhanced conflict.[3]

Although it would be premature to attempt to describe a precise formula, in general we expect to find that increased residential integration,

---

3 Huckfeldt's (1986) overview of contextual effects (especially Chapter 9) highlights the complex intermix of effects leading to positive acceptance (he labels this assimilation) and effects leading to conflict.

in city and suburb, increases interracial contact. We project that, in turn, for both African Americans and whites, contact results overall in somewhat more positive views of the other race. We emphasize "overall" and "somewhat" because some increased contact will undoubtedly exacerbate stresses and conflict.

Having said that, we should immediately add that the conditions for positive interracial interaction are more in evidence today than they were a half century ago, when some of the first studies of interracial contact were undertaken. White racial attitudes have changed, and the condition of the African American population has changed even more. As many blacks as whites now achieve a high school education, a large proportion go on to college (though not at the same rate as whites), and the size of the black middle class grows each year. To the extent that a positive relationship between contact and positive attitudes presupposes some equality of status, that is much more likely to occur now than it was 50 years ago.

We also expect shared residential location to promote similar views about local public policies. To the extent that blacks and whites live together, they face many of the same challenges that are common in urban environments, such as maintaining safe streets and good schools, to name only two crucial issues.

We believe we are likely to see the most negative attitudes toward the other race in communities where the other race is not present or is barely so (particularly in all-white areas) and conversely, in areas of essentially equal population, where the sense of threat is greatest (Blalock, 1957; 1967).

We also expect suburban residence itself to affect contact and attitudes, beyond the impact of the racial mixture of the neighborhood. This expectation reflects the facts that suburbs are independent of the central city in their governance and to a large extent in the day-to-day circumstances of residents' lives. In particular, we expect suburban whites to be the least positive toward blacks and suburban blacks to be the most tolerant of whites. That is because suburban whites are most able to isolate themselves from African Americans, not only in terms of residence but also in terms of controlling the governance of their towns and schools. Suburban blacks are most likely to be in a minority status in their communities and to have the most contacts with whites.

BLACK AND WHITE DETROITERS

To the extent that racial context shapes racial views, the Detroit area is an extremely useful research site in which to explore the link between residence and attitudes. The Detroit area is unusual, indeed unique, in

the degree of hypersegregation between neighborhood and neighborhood and between city and suburbs (Massey and Denton, 1989). This
hypersegregation resulted from the white flight of the 1960s and 1970s
that we describe in the next chapter. The 1990 census revealed that
Detroit was the second most segregated city in America, trailing only
Gary, Indiana and ahead of Chicago, Cleveland, Newark, and Philadelphia, other cities sometimes known for their racial tensions (Farley and
Frey, 1994).[4] This vast amount of segregation provides a test of amelio-
ration of racial hostility with a stiff challenge; if residential integration
matters in Detroit, it probably does in most American cities as well.

Detroit is also of particular use as a research site because the area contains large populations of blacks and whites. Even though small proportions of Detroit area residents are black suburbanites or white urbanites,
the sheer size of the metropolitan area means that the absolute numbers
of black suburbanites and white central city residents are quite large.

A third reason for our focus on Detroit is that residents of the Detroit
area have been surveyed regularly over the years in the University of
Michigan's ongoing Detroit Area Study (DAS). Indeed, racial attitudes
have been more closely observed in Detroit than in any other American
city (Aberbach and Walker, 1973; Cohen and Dawson, 1993; Farley et
al., 1978a, 1994; Farley, Hatchett, and Schuman 1979; Schuman and
Hatchett, 1974).

The civil unrest of 1967 prompted researchers involved with the University of Michigan's annual survey of metropolitan area residents (the
DAS) to spend the next two years gathering data on racial attitudes, first
with a sample of more than 600 African Americans in 1968 and then
with a sample of more than 600 whites in 1969 (Farley et al., 1978; Farley et al., 1979; Schuman and Hatchett, 1974). Campbell and Schuman
(1968) also included Detroit among the 15 cities in which relatively
large samples of both African Americans and whites were interviewed
following the 1967 rioting (see also Campbell, 1971; Schuman and
Gruenberg, 1970).

OUR 1992 SURVEYS

Building on the richness of these historical data, we conducted an in-
home survey of blacks and whites in the tricounty Detroit metropolitan
area in 1992. Each survey respondent was interviewed by a member of

---

4 On one common measure of segregation, the index of dissimilarity, whereby the
  most segregated city would score 100 and the least 0, Detroit scored 89, with Gary
  scoring 91. The 15 most segregated major cities in America averaged 84 on the
  scale; the 15 least segregated averaged 42 (Farley and Frey, 1994).

his or her own race. Whites living in the city, blacks living in the suburbs, and both blacks and whites living in mixed-race neighborhoods were oversampled. This stratified design enabled us to examine the attitudes not only of black central city residents but also of black residents of the suburbs and not only of blacks who lived in all-black neighborhoods but also of those who lived in integrated neighborhoods. It also permitted us to reach whites who lived in central city areas as well as those who lived in mixed-race neighborhoods. In all, we completed interviews with 466 whites and 658 blacks, with a response rate of 56%. These data provided us with a unique opportunity to probe consistency and change in racial attitudes over a quarter century of remarkable social change. Detailed descriptions of our sampling plan and survey procedures appear in Appendix A, along with brief overviews of the 1968 and the 1969 DAS.

Data from the earlier surveys, combined with our own 1992 survey, enable us to speak with greater authority about trends in race relations in Detroit than we could have about any other city of which we are aware. Even though trend analysis is not the central focus of our study, we have made special efforts to situate patterns of racial attitudes during the 1990s in the context of patterns from earlier decades.

THE FOCUS OF OUR STUDY

Our primary interest, as should be obvious by now, is in the impact of residential context – loosely speaking, where people live – on racial attitudes and experiences. We examine two aspects of residential context especially closely: the racial characteristics of our interviewees' neighborhoods and their residence in the central city or the suburbs. As shown in Table 1.1, these two dimensions yield six types of neighborhoods within the metropolitan area: three in the city and three in the suburbs, four segregated and two integrated. Comparisons among these different types of context enable us to evaluate, to some degree at least, both the idea that residential racial mixing creates conflict and on the other hand the idea that it has ameliorative properties. If group conflict poses a better explanation of racial attitudes, then we should observe more tension and greater sensitivity among numerical minorities – whites in the predominantly black central city (D and G in Table 1.1) and blacks in predominantly white suburbs (F). If residential integration enhances race relations, then racial attitudes should be most tense in segregated settings (A, B, G, and H) and most tranquil in integrated communities (C, D, E, and F).

Table 1.1 also highlights the potential influence of the politics of the larger jurisdiction. Blacks living in Detroit, whether they constitute a

Table 1.1. *Types of residential context*

Neighborhood composition	Political jurisdiction	
	City	Suburbs
Predominantly black	Heavily black neighborhoods where blacks (A) are a politically empowered majority within a major central city	Heavily black neighborhoods where blacks (B) are a politically empowered majority within smaller jurisdictions
Racially mixed	Integrated neighborhoods where blacks (C) are politically empowered, with whites (D) a political minority	Integrated neighborhoods where whites (E) are politically empowered, with blacks (F) a political minority
Predominantly white	Heavily white neighborhoods where whites (G) are a politically weak minority within in a black central city	Heavily white neighborhoods where whites (H) are a politically empowered majority within smaller jurisdictions

majority or a minority in their particular neighborhood, are subject to a predominantly African American mayor–council system. Blacks living in the suburbs, even if they are in a majority in their neighborhoods, are not. Of course, central city whites are a minority living in an African American–led city, and suburban whites, whether a majority or minority in their neighborhoods, live in white-dominated cities. Others have noted the effect of a black city government on increasing blacks' feelings of empowerment (Bobo and Gilliam, 1990). Whether this matters in our setting is a question explored in our analyses.

RESIDENCE AND SOCIOECONOMIC CHARACTERISTICS

Eight different groups of people live in these six settings, for the two types of integrated settings contain both blacks and whites. Table 1.2 provides a variety of information, drawn from census reports and from our survey, about the blacks and whites who lived in these different settings at the time of our survey. The table suggests some of the fundamental differences in context faced by residents of these areas.

The first two rows of the table show, for each type of setting, the percentage of residents who were black and the percentage of all metropol-

itan area blacks or whites who lived there. For example, in suburban settings that were no more than 70% black, the average neighborhood was
43% black. This contrasted sharply with predominantly black neighborhoods in the city of Detroit, where the average percent black exceeded
95%. Table 1.2 illustrates clearly the variety of racial mixes in metropolitan Detroit neighborhoods.

It is important to remember, as the second row of the table indicates,
that nearly all-black neighborhoods in the central city were home to
54% of the blacks in the metropolitan area; only 17% of Detroit-area
blacks resided in the suburbs, and only 10% in mixed-race suburban
neighborhoods. So in Detroit, suburban blacks are a minority within a
minority, and suburban blacks in mixed neighborhoods are even more
so. On the other hand, by our definition about 40% of Detroit's African
Americans lived in mixed-race neighborhoods in the city or suburbs.

Most (86%) of Detroit-area whites, on the other hand, lived in mostly
white suburbs. Only 6% lived in mixed-race suburban neighborhoods
and 8% lived in the city, evenly divided between those in mixed-race and
those in nearly all-white city neighborhoods. These figures illustrate, in
their own way, why Detroit ranks so high in the nationwide listing of city
segregation. They also illustrate that black Detroiters are much more
likely to be part of a mixed-race neighborhood than are their white counterparts.

The next two rows of the table compare change in the racial composition of these neighborhoods, first since 1970 and then since 1980.[5] The
percentage of blacks increased in every type of neighborhood, but
smaller increases occurred in white suburban neighborhoods than elsewhere. Also noteworthy were the sharp increases in the black population
of mixed neighborhoods (C, D, E, and F), up 22 or 30 percentage points
in the city, depending on which definition of "mixed" one prefers, and 9
or 20 percentage points in the suburbs after 1980. Many of these neighborhoods had yet to stabilize their populations and may have been in
transition from predominantly white to predominantly black. Nonetheless, the proportion of blacks grew fastest in these areas. In contrast, a
smaller increase in the black population occurred between 1980 and
1990 in predominantly black portions of the city (column A) or the suburbs (column B); of course, because those areas were already predominantly black, there was little room for further black population growth.

The fifth row shows one last piece of census data about these neighborhoods, the percent living in poverty. Aside from white suburban

---

5 These figures are percentage point increases, not percent increases. That is, in the
table an increase from 1% to 2% would be described as a one percentage point
increase, not a 100% increase.

Table 1.2. *Characteristics of various neighborhood contexts*

Characteristic	Neighborhood Contexts							
	A Blacks in black city areas (90% + black)	B Blacks in black suburban areas (70% + black)	C Blacks in mixed city areas (<90% black)	D Whites in mixed city areas (<65% black)	E Whites in mixed suburban areas (<90% black)	F Blacks in mixed suburban areas (<70 black)	G Whites in white city areas (>65% white)	H Whites in white suburban areas (>90% white)
Percent blacks of neighborhood	97	94	70	40	30	43	9	2
Percent of metropolitan area blacks/whites in these neighborhoods	54	7	30	4	6	10	4	86
Percent point change in black population, 1970–1990	42	28	68	46	17	35	9	2
Percent point change in black population, 1980–1990	4	6	30	22	9	20	4	2
Percent in poverty	35	32	30	20	13	15	25	2
Percent single-adult households	73	60	45	45	48	38	42	26
Percent two-income households	5	10	24	15	28	41	21	33
Percent college-educated	5	11	16	26	16	26	6	34
Mean family income ($000)	16	23	23	24	26	36	24	44
Percent over age 65	26	30	8	19	18	10	18	20
Mean years in area	13	17	8	17	12	8	21	15
Sample size	207	156	95	115	124	200	121	106

neighborhoods (H), poverty was common in all these types of areas, although less so in mixed-race suburbs (E and F) than elsewhere. Poverty levels were higher among African Americans in central-city black areas than in suburban high-density black areas or in central-city mixed areas. For whites, poverty was highest in the city (although less than among city blacks), less widespread in the integrated suburbs, and almost non-existent in the nearly all-white suburbs.

The information in the rest of the table is from our survey. For example, as compared with blacks living in predominantly black areas of the city (A), black residents of integrated suburbs (F) were about half as likely to reside in single-adult households, eight times as likely to reside in two-income households, and five times as likely to have a college degree. They were also younger and had lived in their current residences for less time than blacks in the city. Finally, their average family income was well over twice that of blacks in predominantly black neighborhoods of the city.

The variability among whites was almost as great, though under no circumstances were their social and economic conditions as dismal, on average, as those of blacks. The contrasts between city (G) and suburban (H) whites living in white neighborhoods were especially stark, with city whites lagging behind suburban whites in income and education.

Even more marked than these intraracial differences were some of the interracial differences among those residing in the same type of neighborhood. This was especially true of racially integrated suburbs, where on every measure of affluence blacks (F) were better off than white residents of the same type of neighborhood (E). These marked differences between blacks and whites in mixed-race neighborhoods may reflect the departure from these areas of more affluent, and hence more mobile, whites who moved out to other, less racially mixed suburbs. These differences are also consistent with evidence that lenders and real estate agents continued to discriminate against black buyers (Dedman, 1988 cited in Farley and Frey, 1994; Blossom, Everett, and Gallagher, 1988; Squires, Bennett, McCourt, and Nyden, 1989).

Overall, then, Table 1.2 confirms that residents of Detroit's suburbs differed from residents of the city on several key characteristics, such as income, education, and family composition. The map of the Detroit metropolitan area (Figure 1.1) summarizes the dual realities of life in the Detroit suburbs and the central city, graphically depicting the concentration of low incomes in the city and the progressively greater affluence of the outlying areas. Ze'ev Chafets, a close observer of the Detroit scene, commented only a short time before we conducted our survey that "the suburbs are purring with the contented sounds of post-Reagan America while the city seethes with the resentments of postcolonial Africa"

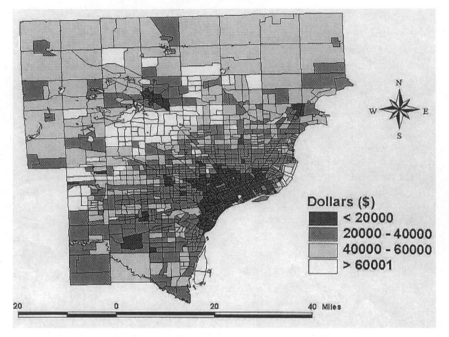

Figure 1.1. Median income by census tract.

(1990: 25). That those two sounds were intermixed with racial differences only compounded the problems of the Detroit metropolitan area.

At the same time, neither the suburban–central city nor the black–white distinction fully captures the different economic conditions of the Detroit metropolitan area's residents. The black suburbanites in our survey were not like their central-city counterparts, and those in mixed-race areas were different from those in nearly all-black neighborhoods. Whites, too, differed by locale and by the racial mix of their neighborhood. These differences are important, especially because they show that black suburbanites in mixed neighborhoods had demographic profiles more like those of their white counterparts than those of their black central-city cohorts.

Earlier we argued that residential contexts have a number of effects on how individuals view racial issues. Our primary purpose is to gauge the extent to which living separately or together affects blacks' and whites' contacts with one another, their perceptions of themselves, of members of their own race, and of members of the other race and their attitudes about public policy. In Table 1.2 we have seen that most of Detroit's blacks and whites live in largely racially segregated neighborhoods, although a significant minority of both races live in integrated settings. This minority is much larger among blacks. There are other vast differences, too, in the residential contexts of Detroit-area citizens, black and white. Some of these differences transcend race and appear to be driven more by central city or suburban location. Others seem to depend more on race than on community. Given this great diversity of contexts, however explained, there is certainly room for an effect on attitudes. But is this potential actualized? Are these residential differences also apparent in attitudes about race and about members of the other race? These are the issues we set out to explore. In estimating the effect of the racial mix, we take account of the demographic differences among residents of different sorts of neighborhoods. We also discuss, at relevant points, the possibility that individuals with different attitudes toward those of the other race choose different residential settings as a consequence – in other words, that racial attitudes are a factor in determining where people live rather than, or in addition to, being shaped by residential location.

THE PLAN OF THE BOOK

Stated most broadly, the expectations guiding our analysis are that residential integration generally enhances interracial contact, and that living in an integrated neighborhood and having contact with people of another race affect people's attitudes toward their own race and other races, their perceptions of group discrimination and hostility, and their opinions on race-related policy issues. Even though a great deal of research has focused on trends in racial integration and racial attitudes, until now little has been known about the impact of residence on race relations and attitudes.

In Chapter 2, we set the stage for our analyses of the impact of residential context by describing Detroit's racial history in the context of larger changes affecting the residential demographics of African Americans in the 20th century. In that context, we then examine changes over a quarter of a century in the attitudes of black and white Detroiters toward residential segregation and toward members of the other race as neighbors. In Chapter 3, we consider whether and to what extent residential integration has increased contacts between black and white residents of the Detroit area. If residential context matters in softening hard-line attitudes about race, it must do so by increasing contact between members of different races. In Chapter 4, we consider various aspects of the link between residential context and racial discrimination. How does living in an integrated neighborhood affect both blacks' and whites' perceptions of discrimination against blacks, against whites, and against themselves?

In Chapter 5, we focus on the impact of residential context on race consciousness among blacks. Does living in an integrated neighborhood promote greater feelings of racial identity or does it begin to dissolve those feelings? Chapter 6 turns to an exploration of racial prejudice among whites, focusing on whites' belief in black inferiority and their need to distance themselves from blacks. Are whites who live in more integrated settings more tolerant, or does an integrated neighborhood help kindle feelings of hostility?

In Chapter 7, we analyze the effects of residential context on blacks' and whites' satisfaction with local public policies, focusing on two major local government services, criminal justice and education. Are the views of blacks and whites similar when they live in similar communities and neighborhoods, or do racial differences transcend this commonality? Finally, in Chapter 8 we summarize and assess the major implications of our findings and return to our central question: How does where one lives affect one's views of race?

2

Race Relations in Detroit, 1968–1992

"All of America's major cities are on greased skids," one urban analyst has said. "What differentiates one from another is the angle of descent. You may slow the descent but unless there's a major shift in public policy, America will lose all its major cities" (quoted in Russakoff, 1994: 9). Once the industrial heart of the nation, Detroit is a city whose angle of descent has been steep, and whose probability of loss remains great. In this chapter we review that angle of descent in light of historical national patterns of residential segregation.

RACE IN DETROIT

In 1990, Detroit had 777,000 African American residents, more than any other city except New York and Chicago (O'Hare and Frey, 1992). It had the highest proportion of blacks of any major American city, with Atlanta, Washington, and New Orleans lagging considerably behind. It was also one of the most residentially segregated cities in the nation (Farley and Frey, 1994) and one where residential segregation had not significantly decreased, although it was not totally immune to the national trend toward declining segregation in the workplace and public facilities.

The population of Detroit peaked at approximately $2^1/_2$ million residents in the mid-1950s, a decade when the auto industry boomed. By 1990, Detroit's population was less than 1 million, whereas its suburbs had swollen to 3 million people as a result of the tidal wave of whites that washed to the suburbs during the 1960s and 1970s. Between 1970 and 1990, the city of Detroit lost 32% of its population, second among major cities only to Cleveland's 33% drop (Russakoff, 1994). This white wave transformed the racial composition of the city from 20% black in the mid-1950s to over 75% in 1990. As a consequence, Detroit in the 1990s was, in the words of one observer, "an impoverished island surrounded by prosperous suburbs" (Chafets, 1990). Noting that there were few links between the city and its suburbs besides a common water system and major media, Chafets (1990: 25) observed further that Detroit-area blacks and whites most frequently came together on radio talk shows that "offer a steady diet of racially loaded charges and countercharges."

In his pioneering study, *An American Dilemma,* Gunnar Myrdal (1944: 568) judged Detroit to have had uniquely poor race relations relative to other Northern cities because of the strength of its Ku Klux Klan and its large Southern-born population. Myrdal, of course, was basing his assessment on the city's long history of racial tension. Nonetheless, the history of race relations in Detroit is but a slightly worse version of patterns throughout the nation.

Like most other large cities, at the beginning of the 21st century Detroit had areas at its core that were largely black and poor, and these areas were surrounded by higher-income suburbs composed mostly of whites. These patterns of residential segregation, which were largely products of the 20th century, greatly complicated almost every major issue of life in a major metropolitan area, whether it was the quality of the public schools, the provision of other public services, or the control of crime.

THE BEGINNINGS OF URBAN RACIAL HOSTILITY

Until partway through the 20th century, black Americans were overwhelmingly a Southern, rural population.[1] Residential segregation was much less pronounced in both the North and the South than it would become later. In the South, residential integration was encouraged in order to prevent the formation of cohesive black communities (Massey and Denton, 1993: 24). Very few blacks lived in the North, but where they did live, many whites lived among them, and many blacks lived among whites.

Of course, considerable discrimination in housing did exist, foreshadowing the norm of the 20th century. For example, in the early 1830s, when one black family tried to move into a white area of Boston, local residents threatened to demolish the house (Curry, 1981: 49). Between 1830 and 1850, residential segregation increased in both northern and southern cities, although it remained minimal by modern standards; the *index of dissimilarity,* an often employed measure of segregation, ranged from 20 to 60.[2] Housing was generally more segregated in the North than in the South and more segregated in larger than in smaller cities.

---

1 Outside the South, they were primarily urban, even a century ago (Price, 1969: 12).
2 The index indicates the proportion of the population that would have to change locations in order for each neighborhood to reflect the overall racial composition of the city. Housing segregation was highest in Boston and Philadelphia, lowest in Washington, Charleston, Baltimore, and Louisville (Curry, 1981: 56).

Race Relations in Detroit, 1968–1992

The first black person in Detroit was brought there in the early part of the 18th century when Detroit was part of New France. Detroit's 1750 census, its first, noted 33 slaves in a population of 483.[3] The African American population grew slowly to 100 by the end of the century (McRae, 1975).

As was the case in other northern cities, Detroit's 19th century African American population continued to be very small. Yet the city's first race riot occurred in 1833, 4 years before slavery was abolished in Michigan. Kentucky slave hunters came to Detroit to capture an escaped couple who were considered respectable, industrious members of the Detroit community (Katzman, 1973: 9). Detroit's blacks, who at that time numbered only 150 in a population of 5,000, armed themselves with clubs, stones, and pistols, surrounded the jail where the fugitives had been taken, attacked and severely wounded the sheriff, and threatened to burn the city. With the help of the black community, both ex-slaves escaped to Canada. Federal troops were mobilized, 30 blacks were arrested, and later a special commission issued a report, "probably the first race-riot commission report" (Katzman, 1973). The report concluded, in words that foreshadowed the views of later generations of Detroit whites toward black Detroiters, that "neither their habits, nor their morals, with a few exceptions, make them a safe or desirable addition to our population" (quoted by Katzman, 1973: 11).

Detroit's black community grew slowly through the 19th century, largely on the east side of the city, and developed a rich variety of churches, schools, and literary, social, and benevolent organizations. Nonetheless, the black population before World War I totaled only 6,000.

Indeed, blacks remained a predominantly rural, southern population through the 19th century, although both blacks and whites began migrating to cities after the Civil War. Still, more than 90% of all blacks lived in the South at the turn of the 20th century, and in 1910 only 27% of blacks lived in cities, as compared with 49% of whites (Price, 1969: 11). Nationwide, residential segregation was still low by modern standards. For example, before 1915, blacks lived in almost every part of Chicago, many in areas that were less than 10% black (Abrams, 1965: 515). The idea, now common, that black residents devalued a neighborhood was not widely accepted. Jacob Riis commented in 1902 that "where the Negro pitches his tent, he pays more rent than his white neighbor next door and is a better tenant" (Abrams, 1965: 515). Of course, part of this belief stemmed from self-interest on the part of whites. In both the North and the South, blacks were frequently

---

3 Some of these slaves may have been American Indians. For an interesting account of the early African American presence in Detroit, see McRae (1975).

employed as personal servants of middle- and upper middle-class families. Integrated neighborhoods helped ensure that maids, handymen, and butlers would be close to their employers.

THE GREAT MIGRATIONS AND HOUSING POLICIES

The great migration of blacks to northern cities began during World War I, as millions of African Americans sought a better life, more economic opportunities, and greater freedom. It continued thereafter, as about 2 million blacks moved North between the wars, one of the major demographic changes of the century (Price, 1969).

Detroit was the destination for thousands of these immigrants. During the war several thousand African Americans settled in Detroit, and black neighborhoods expanded. These immigrants were lured by jobs, as some (but far from all) of Detroit's industries began to hire black workers. The Ford Motor Company, for example, had only 50 black employees in 1916, but 5,000 by 1923 (Boyle and Getis, 1997).

By 1920, over 40,000 black Detroiters lived in a densely populated section of the city's east side. In addition, a few pockets of black population were scattered around other parts of the community (Sugrue, 1996: 23–25). Racial tensions over housing were intense, and further exacerbated Klan activity (Widick, 1989). In 1925, white crowds responding to Klan incitement sought to prevent a black doctor, O. H. Sweet, from moving into a white neighborhood. After gunfire killed a white member of a mob gathered around the house, Dr. Sweet, his brother, and some friends were arrested and charged with murder. In a stroke of good luck, the presiding judge at the trial was Frank Murphy, a liberal who later became governor and then a justice of the U.S. Supreme Court. The National Association for the Advancement of Colored People (NAACP) persuaded the most prominent defense attorney of the time, Clarence Darrow, to defend Sweet. After 46 hours of deliberation, the jury deadlocked, thus freeing the defendants. Later, Sweet's brother was prosecuted again but acquitted (Franklin, 1967: 484; Widick, 1989: 5–22).

Detroit's racial tensions were echoed in other major cities. During the 1910s and 1920s, violence against blacks who lived in integrated neighborhoods was endemic in most major cities as a tactic to drive blacks out. According to one report, in Chicago between 1917 and 1921 an average of one black home was bombed every 20 days (Spear, 1967: 35).

Violence was far from the only tactic used to deny African Americans access to most housing stock. Restrictive covenants (contracts committing a property owner to sell only to whites [Vose, 1959] were used frequently during the interwar period.⁴ Zoning laws were another method of limiting the access of people of moderate means to affordable housing. Moreover, real estate agents steered blacks away from certain neighborhoods and toward others, practicing "blockbusting," frightening whites with threats of plummeting property values if any blacks moved into the area, and at the same time selling at high prices to black families in search of better housing (Danielson, 1976).

The federal government's lending policies were perhaps the greatest promoter of residential segregation (see, e.g., Farley and Frey, 1994). From 1935 to 1950, more than 11 million houses were built and sold in the United States, most of them in the suburbs and most purchased with government-sponsored Federal Housing Authority (FHA) or Veterans Administration (VA) loans. Loans for purchases in the suburbs favored the "ideal family" type, leaving behind in the central city older people, working-class or lower-income families, single people, and smaller families. Most of all, left behind were African American families, who had trouble getting loans to buy suburban houses (Grier and Grier, 1966: 531; Barker and McCorry, 1980: 20) and who, when they obtained such loans, were limited to buying homes in black neighborhoods. In 1938, the FHA even provided directions for constructing "effective restrictive covenants" and "effective zoning" regulations to maintain neighborhood racial homogeneity, or as the policy labeled it, "Protection from Adverse Influences" (Farley and Frey, 1994). Whites, by contrast, received more liberal terms for houses in the suburbs than in the central city; down payments were smaller, monthly payments lower, and repayment periods longer. Indeed, whole areas of the central city were typically "redlined," which meant that loans on properties in those areas would not be made at all. Thus, the federal government sanctioned overt racial discrimination. As blacks moved in expanding numbers to northern cities, the government financed the moves of more and more white families out of those cities.

In Detroit as in other major northern cities, job opportunities during World War II spawned an even larger increase in the African American population despite poor and segregated available housing. Between 1940 and 1950, the black population doubled, from about 149,000 to about 300,000, as tens of thousands came to work in Detroit's booming war industries (Sugrue, 1996: 23). Prompted by the shortage of workers, many firms hired blacks for the first time. Even though many of these jobs were menial and low-skill, they paid more than was available in the South.

---

4 They were declared unenforceable in 1948 by the Supreme Court in Shelly v. Kraemer.

Race and Place

The increased black population, the presence of blacks in large numbers in the factories, and the pressure for housing all contributed to further racial tensions. Violent clashes between African Americans and working-class whites over access to limited housing during the war were harbingers of racial tensions to come. In 1942, whites protested the placement of public housing for blacks in a racially mixed neighborhood. Police helped white mobs try to keep blacks out of houses for which they had already paid rent (Myrdal, 1964: 678). A year later, a fight between a white and a black turned into the largest race riot of World War II (Capeci and Wilkerson, 1991; Franklin, 1967: 597). Whites roamed the streets, burning cars and beating blacks. President Roosevelt proclaimed a state of emergency and sent 6,000 soldiers into the city. In all, 25 blacks and 9 whites were killed.

THE POST-WORLD WAR II ERA

After the war, blacks continued their journeys North by the tens of thousands. By 1960, barely half of all black Americans lived in the South, and African Americans were becoming an urban population. More than 70% lived in urban areas, and 25% lived in the 12 largest cities alone.[5] Indeed, in all regions except the South, over 90% of blacks were urbanites. Blacks accounted for 30% of Detroit's population, 35% of Baltimore's, 25% of Cleveland's, and 55% of Washington's.

Postwar housing policies shaped race relations for the ensuing decades as blacks were confined to the central cities. As blacks moved into cities, whites moved out. The crowds that rushed to the suburbs in growing numbers after World War II had mostly white faces, reflecting the pull factor of new suburban housing opportunities subsidized by government and the push factor of the reluctance of many whites to live in proximity to increasing numbers of urban blacks. By 1960, less than one-third of urban and suburban whites lived in central cities (Abrams, 1965: 515). The National Commission on Civil Disorders (Kerner Commission) was reflecting reality, not a possibility, when it warned in 1968 that trends were leading to a "white society principally located in the suburbs, in smaller central cities and in the peripheral parts of large cities, and a Negro society largely concentrated within large cities" (National Advisory Commission on Civil Disorders, 1968: 407).

In Detroit, housing continued to be a major problem for the black population. Even in the city, not enough good housing was available because of rigidly segregated patterns. By 1947, fewer than 10% of the

5 Virtually the same proportion of whites (69%) lived in urban areas.

Race Relations in Detroit, 1968–1992

Table 2.1. *Increasing racial isolation in Detroit*

Year	Index of black isolation
1890	5.6
1900	6.4
1910	6.8
1920	14.7
1930	31.2
1970	77.1
1980	77.3
1990	82.0

Note: For 1890 to 1930, isolation is measured by ward; for 1970, isolation is measured by tract-level census area and reflects the proportion of other blacks among whom a given black in a ward lived. A score of 100 means that the average black lived totally among other blacks, a score of 1 means that the average black lived in a tract with 1% blacks. The data are from Massey and Denton (1993: Tables 2.2, 2.4, and 3.1); Lieberson (1980: 266, 288); Massey (2000).

city's 545,000 housing units were open to blacks (Sugrue, 1996: 43) at a time when blacks constituted about 15% of the population. Moreover, only 1% of the new single-family homes constructed in Detroit during the 1940s were open to blacks (Sugrue, 1996: 43).

According to a survey of Detroit residents conducted in the late 1940s, only 18% of whites were supporters of nondiscriminatory policies. More than two-thirds agreed that the remedy for problematic race relations was more segregation (Kornhauser, 1951: 85). The few blacks who were interviewed in that survey (less than 100) viewed housing and the police as the major problems facing them, but they were remarkably optimistic about race relations in Detroit.

Table 2.1 illustrates patterns of black isolation in Detroit. The isolation scale used in the table ranges from 1, designating the lowest possible level of black isolation, to 100, the point at which every black would reside in a neighborhood composed solely of other blacks. As the table indicates, levels of racial isolation were very low at the turn of the century. Segregation began to increase with the migrations of the 1920s and 1930s, and skyrocketed in the post-World War II years. This pattern was matched in most major cities of the East and Midwest. The racial patterning of residence in the Detroit area is obvious in the 1990 census data shown in Figure 2.1, which shows a predominantly (in some areas,

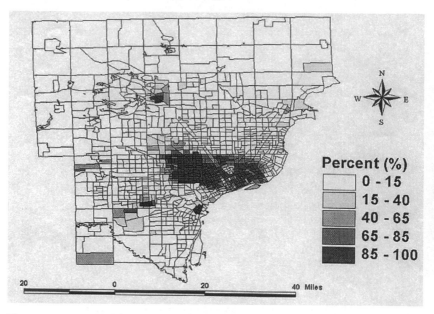

Figure 2.1. Percent African American population by census tract, Detroit 1990.

entirely) black central city surrounded, with very few exceptions, by areas that become progressively whiter (in some areas, exclusively so) the farther out into the suburbs one looks.

Racial friction, largely caused by conflict over residential location, persisted throughout the 1950s and 1960s. Attacks against black families seeking to flee overcrowded black neighborhoods were common. These attacks peaked in the mid-1950s, slowed, and then increased again in the early 1960s. Violence organized by homeowner associations involved thousands of whites, although whites residing beyond the transitional neighborhoods may not have known about the violence because it was not publicized by the white Detroit press (Sugrue, 1996: chapter 9). As one observer noted, whites unable or unwilling to move from their place of residence viewed black movement into their neighborhood as "the moral equivalent of war ... [N]eighborhood groups demarcated racial boundaries with great precision, and, abetted by federal agencies and private real estate agents, divided cities into strictly enforced racial territories ... [Whites] spoke of 'invasions' and 'penetration' and planned 'resistance'" (Sugrue, 1996: 246).

By the 1960s, African Americans constituted nearly 40% of Detroit's population, but whites still controlled the city, which had a white mayor, a majority white city council, and a white police force. Only 5% of the city's police officers were black. Blacks had also lost the economic battles, for just as many whites abandoned Detroit, so too did jobs. Whereas in the 1940s and 1950s, workers could expect to find jobs in Detroit's factories, even though most jobs were at the bottom of the scale, by the 1960s there were few jobs to be found. The decline of the auto industry and the migration of jobs to the suburbs left an economically deteriorating central city. Unemployment among young blacks skyrocketed to 30% (Sugrue, 1996: 261).

THE VIOLENCE OF 1967 AND WHITE FLIGHT

The battles over housing and jobs culminated in the violence of 1967. Sparked by a police raid on an after-hours night club, several days of violence and destruction destroyed parts of the city, leaving 43 dead, thousands injured or homeless, and $200 million in property damage. The police were the focal point of black antagonism rooted in a variety of grievances, from brutality to lack of jobs and poor services. Detroit's riot was not, of course, an isolated instance. Black communities throughout the United States exploded in violence in 1967, 1968, and 1969 (National Advisory Commission on Civil Disorders, 1968).

Whites and African Americans differed markedly in their understandings of the unrest that spread through the nation, even to the point of disagreeing about what to call it. Many African Americans saw it as a rebellion against a brutal and oppressive white regime – a payback of sorts for the countless insults, indignities, and exclusions heaped upon them by white society. Many whites, by contrast, viewed it as rampant lawlessness and found in this looting and burning reinforcement for their negative stereotypes of African Americans.

The deaths, injuries, and property damage that resulted from the Detroit riots were easier to measure, but the damage to race relations was no less real. Detroit had been losing population to the suburbs for years, mostly because whites were leaving the city for more space, better services, lower taxes, and white neighborhoods. After 1967, what had been a gradual white exodus turned into a stampede. Sizable portions of the city (especially the parts with large concentrations of African Americans) were never rebuilt, and the area was dealt another harsh blow by the deterioration of the American auto industry. Unemployment soared, social pathologies multiplied, and blacks were hit hardest of all. Between 1960 and 1980, the city's white population declined from more than 1.1 million to 360,000, a drop of two-thirds. No American city of comparable size has ever been abandoned so quickly by whites. In just 20 years, overwhelmingly white Detroit became overwhelmingly black Detroit. By 1990, 9 of every 10 whites in the Detroit metropolitan area lived in the suburbs.

Race and Place

Race relations did not improve much after 1967, even though African Americans became an ever larger proportion of the city. The Detroit Police Department's STRESS (Stop the Robberies, Enjoy Safe Streets) squad was an especially sore spot for African Americans in the early 1970s. The excesses of STRESS peaked in an incident in December 1972. In the course of searching for a suspect in the shooting of a Detroit police officer, police retaliated against innocent members of the African American community. One African American was killed, several were beaten, and the entire community was terrorized. The resulting outrage helped propel Coleman Young into office in 1974 as Detroit's first black mayor (Rich, 1989). Within 3 months, Young dismantled STRESS.

Although Young's election led to a surge of pride among Detroit's blacks and although he instituted many changes benefiting blacks (including affirmative action in city jobs), he could not halt the downward spiral of Detroit's economy. Nor did he improve race relations. In the mid- and late 1990s, blacks controlled the mayor's office and the city council, and constituted 55% of the police force. However, the election and appointment of black city officials had not brought economic equality or racial peace to the city, underscoring the limitations of black (or any) local leadership in bettering the conditions of black urbanites. By 1990, Detroit had a higher poverty rate (32%) than any other major city, substantially higher than Cleveland and Chicago's 22% or Washington's 17% (Russakoff, 1994).

Relations between the police and citizens continued to be poor, the most widely publicized flare-up being Detroit's own version of the more renowned Rodney King incident. In November 1992, several members of the Detroit Police Department repeatedly kicked, punched, and bludgeoned Malice Green, a black Detroit resident, who subsequently died from blunt force trauma to the head. Seven officers (six whites and their black supervisor) were suspended for their roles in the beating, and three were subsequently tried. In the days and weeks following the conviction of two of the three officers, further incidents heightened the tension. The acquitted officer filed suit, accusing the Detroit Police Department of racial discrimination; a fund-raising event for the two convicted officers in the largely white suburb of Warren drew 2,500 participants; and county commissioners in white suburban Macomb County offered a motion asking the governor to pardon the convicted officers (see Bledsoe, Combs, Sigelman, and Welch, 1996).

Other frictions continued. The changing racial composition of neighborhoods periodically led to cross burnings and spray-painted racial epithets. Occasionally, these acts of racial anger culminated in gunshots and led to police arrests. During just the first half of 1990, the Detroit chapter of the NAACP reported 40 to 50 complaints of racial harassment (Marchetti 1990). Most of these incidents occurred after African American or interracial families moved into previously all-white neighborhoods.

During the 1990s, rarely a week passed in the Detroit area without the occurrence of an event or incident that either had racial overtones or was a manifestation of overt racial conflict. In a widely publicized case in 1993, the U.S. Department of Justice negotiated a record $350,000 housing discrimination settlement against the owners and manager of a Detroit-area apartment complex. The basis for the suit was the differential treatment accorded testers who were sent to the complex to seek housing. One day a white person seeking lodgings would be told that units were available, but the next day an African American with similar background and credentials would be told that there would be a 6 month wait. The complex was visited by four different pairs of testers, and each time the result was the same: Housing was available for whites but not for blacks. Housing discrimination lawsuits also were filed against three other suburban apartment complexes (Gordon, 1993).

These events said a good deal about underlying racial tensions and frustrations in the Detroit area. The racial conflict that boiled over during the summer of 1967 simmered thereafter, usually staying just below the surface but occasionally erupting in violent incidents. These incidents were conveyed to the public by the media, which, for example, carried intense coverage of the trial of the police officers in the Malice Green case, and the media coverage of these situations may itself have further undermined racial harmony. Thus, the events described above were simultaneously indicators of the racial climate in Detroit and influences on it.

CHANGING HOUSING POLICIES AND THE BLACK FLIGHT TO THE SUBURBS

With the civil rights era in the late 1950s and 1960s came changed attitudes about federal housing policies that either promoted segregation or looked the other way when racial discrimination in housing occurred. Thus, new federal legislation of the 1960s, especially the Fair Housing Act of 1968, slowed the increase in residential segregation and curtailed some of the most overtly discriminatory selling and lending practices (Massey and Denton, 1987; McKinney, 1989; Jakubs, 1986). The black middle class expanded (Landry, 1987), swelling the number of blacks whose resources enabled them to consider a broader range of housing choices. Consequently, blacks began increasingly to relocate to the suburbs. By 1980 the national trend toward housing segregation stopped. It is obvious that integrated housing did not suddenly become a universal reality or anything close to it, but the proportion of blacks and whites living in segregated housing began slowly to decline (Lee, 1985, 1991; Massey and Denton, 1987).

Residential segregation declined at different times and rates in different parts of the country. Integration occurred in both cities and suburbs, but it was most evident in the suburbs and in newer cities. The suburbanization of blacks was both a cause and an effect of the decline of residential segregation. New suburban housing and new urban areas were less likely to be defined as white or black and thus were more integrated than older, more established neighborhoods (Farley and Frey, 1994).

Although some blacks had always lived in the suburbs (Blackwell and Hart, 1982; Farley, 1970; Wiese, 1993), the suburbanization of blacks began in earnest during the 1960s (Clay, 1979; Rose, 1976).[6] In the 1970s, the black population increased faster in the suburbs than in the cities, as large numbers of blacks moved to the suburbs and as migration from the rural South slowed (Galster, 1991; Long and DeAre, 1981; Rose, 1976). Some have characterized this demographic change as no less significant in scope than the earlier suburbanization of the white population (Frey, 1985).

By 1990, 27% of all blacks in the United States lived in the suburbs – a substantial proportion, although still far smaller than the 50% of whites who were suburbanites (O'Hare and Frey, 1992). As Figure 2.2 shows, the proportion of blacks living in the suburbs grew considerably from 16% in 1970, while the proportion of whites living in the suburbs also increased.

Early predictions that black suburbanization would bring an end to racial segregation proved greatly overblown. The cities with the largest black populations did not become less segregated during the 1970s, and some even become more segregated. Much integration occurred in suburbs with few blacks (Massey and Gross, 1991). Some integration was temporary, occurring in areas that were in transition between all-white and all-black (Smith, 1991). Many blacks who did move to the suburbs

---

6 Northwood and Barth (1965: 25) found that black "pioneers" (those who were the first to move into all-white neighborhoods or suburbs) in the Seattle area tended to move into neighborhoods that were somewhat more prosperous than the city as a whole, and bought houses that cost more than the average in their neighborhood. On average, the pioneers were themselves more prosperous and better educated than their neighbors and much more prosperous than other blacks. Most had extensive interracial contact before moving: At least a third lived in mostly white worlds, a sixth had white spouses, and many had other family members who were white.

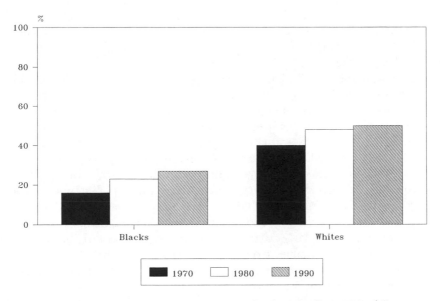

Figure 2.2. Proportions of black and white suburban dwellers, United States, 1970–1990.

moved to aging suburbs that were close to the central city and already had large black populations (Galster 1987, 1991; Stahura, 1988). In those suburbs, the segregated housing patterns of the city continued largely intact.

During the 1980s, however, black suburbanization accelerated, as did its impact on desegregation (Schneider and Phelan, 1993). This impact reflected both the civil rights laws of the 1960s and changes in the racial attitudes of whites. By 1990, only 20% of the white interviewees in a national survey claimed that whites had a right to keep blacks out of their neighborhoods, as compared with the 84% of the public who had agreed in 1942 that there "should be separate sections in towns and cities for Negroes to live in" and the 60% who had agreed in 1964 that "white people have a right to keep blacks out of their neighborhoods if they want to" (National Opinion Research Center, 1942, 1990; Farley and Frey, 1994).

In the 1980s, considerable progress was made for the first time toward integrating metropolitan areas that had very large African American populations. The black suburban population grew substantially (Schneider and Phelan, 1993), and in the 100 largest metropolitan areas more than 8% of the suburban population was black by 1990, an increase from 6% in 1980 (Schneider and Phelan, 1993). Virtually every suburb had some black residents by 1990, although one in three still had fewer

than 1%, and two out of three had fewer than 5%.[7] Still, blacks constituted at least 15% of the suburban population in about 14% of all suburbs. On the other hand, 5% of the suburbs had a majority black
population (Phelan and Schneider, 1996).

Increasing black suburbanization certainly did not usher in the end of
segregation in the suburbs (Phelan and Schneider, 1996). Race rather
than income remained the major predictor of residence (Darden, 1990;
Farley, 1995). However, segregation continued to be less marked in the
suburbs than in the central cities (Alba and Logan, 1991). The suburbs
with the largest black populations at the end of the 1980s tended to be in
the South, to lie close to the central city, and to have lower median
incomes, relatively old housing stock or multiple family units, and
higher proportions of black residents in 1980 (Stahura, 1986; Alba and
Logan, 1991). Suburbs with significant African American minorities also
had higher tax rates, larger expenditures on housing, welfare, health and
police, and larger revenues from state and federal aid than comparable-
income, all-white suburbs or those with large Asian or Hispanic minorities (Phelan and Schneider, 1996).

Detroit was part of this national trend, though the extent of African
American movement to the suburbs lagged behind many other cities. By
1990, 130,000 Detroit-area blacks were living in the suburbs, a growth
of 28% during the preceding decade. Every one of Detroit's 59 suburbs
with more than 1,000 population had some black and some white residents. Even so, blacks constituted only 4% of the total suburban population, compared to the national average of 8% (O'Hare and Frey, 1992).
Moreover, as Figure 2.1 shows, nearly half of these suburban communities had only about 1% African American population and the next
largest group of communities had between 1% and 5%. Only 11 of the
59 communities had more than 5% and less than 50%.

Black migration was concentrated in a few suburbs, most of which
were adjacent to the central city. The largest suburb to experience rapid
black population growth was Southfield, in 1990 30% black, with a
strong commercial base that offered generous municipal services with
modest tax rates. Even within Southfield, there were clear patterns of res-

---

7 Still, black suburbs, on the whole, are poorer than white ones and have relatively
fewer jobs and higher taxes (Galster, 1987; Schneider and Phelan, 1990). The same
migratory patterns that offer some faint hope of eventually leading to a more thoroughly integrated suburbia may threaten the social fabric of existing African American neighborhoods in the city. As Wilson (1987) has argued, blacks who depart the
central city for suburbia effectively deprive their former neighborhood of its most
successful citizens, who would be role models and community leaders. This may
perpetuate the cycle of poverty and despair that grips many of these neighborhoods.

idential segregation, with the southern section adjacent to Detroit being overwhelmingly black whereas the northern section was overwhelmingly white. However, in Southfield and several other cities in the metropolitan area, there were several areas with thoroughly integrated neighborhoods, although many of these were changing from white to predominantly black.

The Detroit area also contained several suburbs (Pontiac, Mt. Clemens, Romulus, and Ecorse) that had substantial black communities prior to the civil rights movement, and a few subsequently emerged as predominantly black cities.

HOUSING INTEGRATION TODAY

Changes in government policies and in the economic base of African Americans have promoted housing integration, but obviously residential segregation persists. Long-ingrained attitudes and practices make overcoming residential segregation a struggle. Negative white attitudes remain a barrier. Those attitudes stem both from racism and from widespread fear of declining property values with black neighbors. An early study found that whites living in the most integrated neighborhoods were the most resistant to residential integration (Bradburn, Sudman, Goekel, and Noel, 1971), apparently because of their concerns about declining housing values in neighborhoods undergoing racial change. In part for the same reason, white flight from the central city to the suburbs is a function of the proportion of blacks in a neighborhood (Huckfeldt, 1986). Fear of declining property values when black neighbors arrive may partly be a racist response, but it is also partly a response to the contextual factors that often make this a reality. Realtors practice scare tactics to encourage whites to sell at low prices and blacks to buy at high ones.

Indeed, many homeowners, landlords, and real estate agents have continued practicing outright discrimination. As a barrier to discrimination, the Fair Housing Act of 1968 was more symbolic than substantive; not until amendments to the act were passed in 1988 did it pose a real threat to those who practiced discrimination (Massey and Denton, 1993). The housing discrimination case involving testers that we described earlier would have been impossible to pursue prior to the 1988 amendments to the Fair Housing Act (Turner, 1992).

Cost to African Americans can also pose a barrier to residential integration. Blacks incur these costs when they move into predominantly white neighborhoods. Many blacks are understandably reluctant to serve as pioneers in a previously all-white neighborhood (Farley, Schuman, Bianchi, Colasanto, and Hatchett, 1978b), a reluctance that presumably springs, in large measure, from apprehension about the reception they might receive from their new neighbors. In many instances, black families that are integrating a neighborhood are separated from other blacks, which results, perhaps, in a lowered sense of belonging. Pioneering blacks have faced, at worst, overt discrimination, hostility and violence, and at best, points of view insensitive to blacks (Dent, 1992). The children in these families have often been the only blacks in classrooms and social and recreational activities. Blacks generally desire neighborhoods that are evenly divided between blacks and whites, presumably in part so their children will not feel isolated. Being the only black can affect a child's self-concept and self-esteem.

Finally, some African American political, religious, and business leaders have not shown the same enthusiasm for residential integration that they exhibited in working to abolish other forms of segregation. To a large extent, black politicians have depended on black voters, black clergy have relied on black parishioners, and black businesses have needed black customers or clients. Beyond self-interest, these black leaders have understood the need to maintain strong black institutions, given the unwillingness of many whites to vote for black politicians, attend largely black churches, or patronize black-owned businesses (Jones, 1994). Hence, the rhetoric of confrontation seems to have been relatively muted in the case of residential segregation. Indeed, some African Americans have argued that the black community itself is ill served by residential integration. Carmichael and Hamilton (1967: 54) denounced integration as "a subterfuge for the maintenance of white supremacy," and Piven and Cloward (1980: 110) contended that the social cohesiveness that would be required for minorities to influence the major institutions of American society would be thwarted by "the mingling of bodies in school and neighborhood." Similar sentiments were expressed by black leaders in Detroit during the 1980s and 1990s (Gillmor and Prater, 1991).

In sum, the Detroit metropolitan area has had a long history of racial conflict, reflecting in extreme form that which has occurred in most American cities. That conflict resulted in white flight to the suburbs when the inroads of African Americans into formerly all-white neighborhoods could not be stopped. The resulting poverty-stricken black inner city and the moderate-income and well-off, largely white suburbs were especially striking examples of the pattern found in most American major cities. As elsewhere, the decades-old pattern of ever increasing residential segregation began to reverse during the 1980s, but that progress was slower in Detroit than elsewhere. Despite this slow progress, even in Detroit housing integration is slightly increasing and, as we shall see in chapter 3, some other sorts of interracial contact are increasing substantially.

Race Relations in Detroit, 1968–1992

RACIAL ATTITUDES IN DETROIT, 1968 TO 1992

With this historical context as background, we now explore racial attitudes in the Detroit area during the 25 years between 1968, immediately
after the riots and the onset of the mass white exodus to the suburbs, and
1992, by which time black political control of the black-majority city
had been established. We focus in the remainder of this chapter on attitudes about race relations in housing and the residential context, for
these were the attitudes that shaped the residential patterning of Detroit,
which in turn has molded other attitudes about race.

Our analysis is based on a comparison of the attitudes Detroit-area residents expressed in the 1968 and 1969 Detroit Area Survey (DAS) and in
our own 1992 survey, which repeated many questions from the 1960s surveys and also introduced several similar, though not identical, questions.

First, however, we must sound a note of caution about identifying
trends with only two time points as references. With interview data for
the late 1960s and the early 1990s, we cannot say with any certainty
where matters stood in the 1970s or 1980s. Certainly we cannot, for
example, simply interpolate between the beginning and ending points by
assuming that attitudes changed at a constant rate over this long period.
This would be especially foolish for attitudes that are subject to short-
term fluctuations based on current events, such as assessments of may-
oral performance. On the other hand, people seldom change their
perceptions of the racial environment overnight, nor do their basic views
concerning race ordinarily change even in response to some significant
event. Thus, although racial views and experiences undoubtedly did not
unfold linearly from the 1960s to the 1990s, it seems equally unlikely
that they took a roller coaster ride.

The expectation underlying our analysis was that despite dramatic
changes in the population of the Detroit area during this quarter century,
we would uncover relatively few changes in attitudes about race. Despite
their political empowerment in the city, we expected African Americans'
frustrations regarding racial discrimination and race relations to have
remained high. Indeed, the isolation of African Americans in the city
could even have increased their sense of being targets of discrimination.
We also expected that although white anxiety about black neighbors
may have softened somewhat, no sea change in sympathy with the plight
of African Americans would have occurred among whites.

BLACKS' VIEWS ABOUT INTEGRATION

At the time we undertook this study, data from national surveys indicated
that black and white Americans perceived race and racial issues very dif-

ferently (Bobo, 1988; Brink and Harris, 1966; Campbell, 1971; Feagin, 1991; Kluegel and Smith, 1986; Schuman, Steeh, Bobo, and Krysan 1997; Sigelman and Welch, 1991). Whereas white Americans perceived great progress in race relations, black Americans were not very positive in assessing their gains since the 1960s. Whites were optimistic about the future of race relations, blacks less so (Kluegel and Smith, 1986; Sigelman and Welch, 1991). African Americans perceived discrimination as being widespread, although many did not attribute all of blacks' problems to discrimination by whites (Sigelman and Welch, 1991).

After the late 1960s, did Detroit-area blacks become more eager to live in integrated neighborhoods, or even in predominantly white ones? Did the notion of integrating into white society rather than focusing on the black community win wider favor? Did blacks view whites as generally more supportive of black interests and causes in the early 1990s than they had a quarter of a century earlier? And did blacks believe that opportunities for them to buy housing had improved?

Our interviewees' responses to our 1992 survey convinced us that the answer to all four of these questions was, in a word, no.[8] As can be seen in Figure 2.3, there was essentially no change in the proportion of blacks who preferred an integrated or mostly white neighborhood rather than a mostly or exclusively black one. In 1992, as was true in the late 1960s, most blacks preferred that a neighborhood be equally shared by blacks and whites. Relatively few wanted to live in a predominantly black neighborhood, and still fewer preferred a predominantly white one. Blacks were no more eager to live in neighborhoods where they were in the minority than they had been 30 years earlier, but they were just as eager to live in fully integrated neighborhoods. Thus, even though there was no sign that integrationist sentiment had broadened, neither was there any sign that it had lessened. Black support for housing integration continued at more or less the same high level as in the late 1960s.

When we asked black Detroiters more generally to counterbalance the values of integrating versus concentrating on development of the black community, they placed a higher priority on community development. More than two-thirds agreed that "blacks should be more concerned with developing the black community than with working for integration" (Figure 2.4.) This sentiment was about seven percentage points more widespread than in 1968. Thus, racial integration per se was, at the

8 Except as noted in the text, comparisons for blacks are with items from the 1968 DAS that were replicated in our 1992 survey exactly as they had originally appeared, except that "Negro" was replaced by "black."

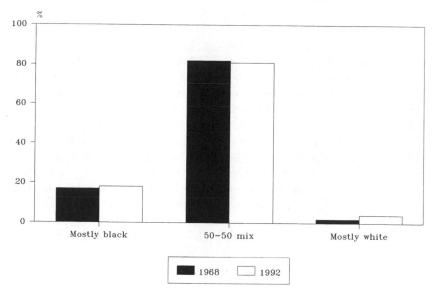

Figure 2.3. Neighborhood preferences of African Americans in Detroit.

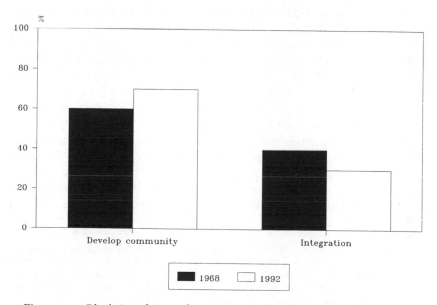

Figure 2.4. Blacks' preference for community development or integration.

very least, no more popular among blacks than it had been in the 1960s, and perhaps somewhat less so.

Were housing opportunities for blacks seen as having improved? In 1968, about 70% of the black respondents in the DAS perceived discrimination in housing. The same was true 24 years later. Approximately 34% reported that they themselves had been discriminated against, and 71% perceived that Detroit blacks in general suffered discrimination in obtaining decent housing.

We also asked black Detroiters a bottom-line question about whether whites wanted to give blacks a "better break." The results revealed a dramatic shift in black Detroiters' perceptions of whites.[9] In 1968, many blacks viewed whites as people of good will: almost half (47%) felt that whites wanted to see blacks "get a better break"; another 31% saw whites as indifferent; and only 22% took the view that whites wanted to "keep blacks down." By 1992, though, only 22% of blacks perceived whites as sympathetic, whereas an absolute majority (52%) saw whites as indifferent and 26% considered them antagonistic to black interests (Figure 2.5.) This shift in black attitudes was especially pronounced among those of lower social and economic status, whereas upper-status blacks were neither so positive in their original assessments nor so negative in their later assessments.

We have only tentative explanations for these changing perceptions. To some extent, these views reflect a certain reality. That is, by 1992, nearly 30 years had passed since the passage of the Civil Rights Act, and although significant changes had occurred, they were much less dramatic than optimists had expected. Because white resistance has been part of the reason for the slow progress, it makes sense that many blacks would question whites' commitment to their cause. At the same time, African Americans' sense of empowerment may have increased since 1968, leading to a decline in their faith in whites' willingness to support efforts toward equality. And, not unreasonably, blacks expectations of whites may have increased.

In sum, these comparisons provide no evidence of positive change and some signs of deterioration over a quarter of a century in blacks' views of

---

9 It is unusual for survey researchers to be able to corroborate their findings at any point in time, but this is a rare instance when we can corroborate results at both points in time. At the same time that the 1968 DAS asked this question, it was also included in Campbell and Schuman's (1968) Kerner Commission–sponsored survey, which was administered to approximately 200 black residents of Detroit. At the same time the question was included in our 1992 survey, it was also used in the 1992 DAS. Hence, we can place considerable confidence in the reliability of this particular change.

Race Relations in Detroit, 1968–1992

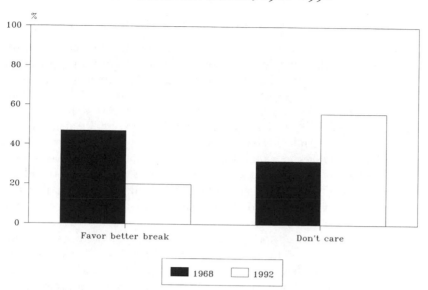

Figure 2.5. Blacks' views of whites' attitudes toward blacks.

integration in Detroit and in their broader orientations toward whites. As compared with the late 1960s, in the early 1990s blacks in Detroit were slightly less supportive of the concept of racial integration and less sanguine about white good will. Although they reported as much discrimination in housing as had their counterparts in 1968, they remained eager to live in neighborhoods with an even mix of blacks and whites – the type of neighborhood that is harder to find in the Detroit area than in almost any other metropolitan area in the nation. Anyone who had expected black political empowerment in the city of Detroit to foster more positive black views of race relations would have been disappointed by these results. So would anyone who had assumed that the relative quiet of the past decade in the civil rights field represented an easing of racial tensions.

On the other hand, we should not close this discussion without commenting that there may or may not be a close relationship between optimism and actual conditions. In 1942, 69% of a small sample of black Detroiters thought race relations in Detroit were good and 67% thought they were improving, views that we now recognize as at great variance with the actualities of the situation (Kornhauser, 1951: 82–83). It may be simply that the African Americans have grown more realistic about the nature of race relations and the potential for change at more than a snail's pace.

Race and Place

Because blacks represent only one side of the black–white equation, we also considered the changing situations and outlooks of Detroit's whites. Over the past 50 years, whites across the nation have expressed growing support for the principle of racial integration (Brink and Harris, 1966; Campbell, 1971; Condran, 1979; Farley, Steeh, Jackson, Krysen, and Reeves, 1994; Greeley and Sheatsley, 1971; Hyman and Sheatsley, 1956; Taylor, Sheatsley, and Greeley, 1978). However, white support for specific policy initiatives in policy areas such as busing, affirmative action, and housing has often been less strong. Moreover, recall that the black population of the Detroit metropolitan area fell into the 15 to 25% range, exactly where white opinions have been shown to be the most hostile.

With the data at our disposal, we have only a limited ability to explore trends in whites' acceptance of residential integration. This is largely because, even though surveys conducted in the Detroit area have routinely asked blacks about their neighborhood composition preferences, whites were not asked such questions in the late 1960s or early 1970s, presumably because it was taken for granted that they would not want black neighbors. The data do reveal a modest softening of white opposition to the prospect of having a new black neighbor of similar income and education, from one-third opposed in 1971 to one-fourth opposed in 1992; this trend is paralleled by the lessening of incidents of intimidation and violence against new black residents of previously all-white neighborhoods from the 1960s to the 1990s, although such incidents did continue to occur. However, we must look elsewhere for a detailed account of trends in whites' attitudes toward residential integration.

Fortunately, the 1992 DAS replicated an elaborate series of questions about race-of-neighborhood preferences, which was first asked in 1976 (Farley et al., 1978; Farley et al., 1993). Interviewees were shown a series of cards picturing 15 houses, some colored black to represent black homeowners, others colored white to represent white homeowners. On the cards, the number of black homes varied from one to eight. Interviewees were asked to imagine that their home was in the middle of this neighborhood, and then to indicate whether they would feel comfortable in the neighborhood, whether they would be willing to move into it, and whether they would try to move out of it.

In every respect, whites appeared more accepting of black neighbors in 1992 than they had been during the mid-1970s (Table 2.2.) In 1976, most whites said they would be uncomfortable living in a 15-home neighborhood with 5 black families. By 1992, most whites raised no objection to the prospect of living in a one-third black neighborhood, a

Race Relations in Detroit, 1968–1992

Table 2.2. *Housing preferences of whites in Detroit (%)*

Neighborhood composition	Would not move in		Not comfortable in	
	1976	1992	1976	1992
3 of 15 families are black	50	31	42	30
5 of 15 families are black	73	59	57	44
8 of 15 families are black	84	73	72	65

Note: The data are from Farley and Frey (1994).

significant increase in acceptance of having some black neighbors. Nearly two-thirds of whites, however, expressed discomfort about the prospect of living in a neighborhood where 8 of the 15 families were black, only a small improvement from 1976. When queried about whether they would move into neighborhoods with various proportions of blacks, half in 1976 said they would not consider moving to a neighborhood that was 20% black, but by 1992 only 31% of whites gave this response. However, in 1992 nearly 60% of whites said they would avoid a neighborhood where 5 of the 15 families were African American. As Farley et al. (1993: 27) concluded, although whites had become significantly less resistant to residential integration, appreciable resistance to integration remained, especially when more than a few black families were moving into a neighborhood. In other words, white acceptance of residential integration tended only to extend to a token presence of blacks. This, of course, was in direct conflict with the vision of residential integration that prevailed among blacks, which involved near parity of the races.

According to our own survey, about one white in four preferred a neighborhood with an even mix of blacks and whites, but three whites in ten stated a preference for an all-white neighborhood, rejecting the middle option of "mostly white." That "only" 3 whites in 10 preferred an all-white neighborhood may at first seem encouraging, for it meant that 7 of 10 of whites were willing to accept some degree of residential integration. In practical terms, however, this figure is hardly encouraging. Imagine that a single black family moved into a previously all-white neighborhood of 20 households. If 30% of the whites acted on their preferences for an all-white neighborhood, six "For Sale" signs would immediately go up. (Indeed, if the opposition from these six families were strong enough, it could have prevented the black family from moving in in the first place.) Of the six homes that went on the market, perhaps one or two would be sold to black families, further altering the racial composition of the neighborhood and perhaps nudging it to the

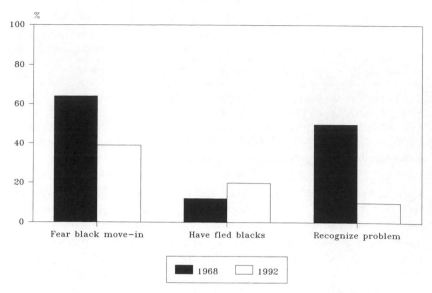

Figure 2.6. Whites' opinions about blacks and toward blacks.

point where other whites would decide to sell. In other words, the 30% of whites who preferred to live in an all-white neighborhood could have a dramatic, snowballing impact on the racial composition of a neighborhood if they chose to act on their preferences and if their preferences did not change as they became accustomed to having black neighbors (see Schelling, 1973).

Of course, the decision to move is a major one, involving potential financial loss, abandonment of neighborhood friends, uprooting of children, and various other types of stress. Whatever their ideal preferences may be regarding the racial composition of a neighborhood, it hardly seems credible that many whites would care so intensely as to uproot their families and flee a neighborhood simply because a few black families were moving in. Or does it?

In 1969, relatively few whites (approximately 12%, as can be seen in Figure 2.6) reported having changed residence at least partly because black families were moving into their old neighborhood. However, by 1992 this phenomenon was no longer rare, at least among some types of whites. Overall, 20% of Detroit whites reported in 1992 that they had changed residence partly because blacks were moving into the neighborhood. If accurate, this estimate would imply that about 600,000 of the 3 million whites in the Detroit area had changed residence partly because of blacks' migration to their neighborhoods. Even this 20% figure may be an underestimate, however, for presumably some people would not have admitted to these motives for moving and others, although they may have recognized these motives, would have "sugar-coated" them by emphasizing their desire to live close to good schools or in a safe neighborhood. Having moved to avoid blacks was especially common among those who had lived in the area 25 years or more. More than one-quarter of these long-term white residents reported having fled neighborhoods changing in racial composition.

It is even more revealing to consider just those whites who were long-term residents of the Detroit area – let us say those who had lived in the area since 1965 – and who changed their address at some time after 1967, when rioting swept the city. One out of every three whites who changed neighborhoods after 1967 mentioned race as a reason for having done so. Thus, many whites obviously were willing to act on their preferences concerning the racial mix of their neighborhood. The costs of relocating are substantial, both monetarily and personally, but many whites revealed by their actions that they considered these costs worth paying.

Fear that problems will ensue when African Americans move into one's neighborhood is another potential indicator of racial hostility, although given racial redlining and steering practices, this fear can sometimes be based on genuine threats of changing socioeconomic conditions. In 1969, nearly two-thirds of whites harbored such fears, but by 1992 most (61%) thought problems would not arise if black families moved into the neighborhood. This confirmed the earlier evidence that whites were more accepting of African American neighbors than they had been a few decades before.

Another indicator of troubled race relations in metropolitan Detroit is white denial of the discrimination that blacks face in the housing market. In 1969, when whites were asked whether housing discrimination was a major or minor problem in Detroit, half said it was a major problem (10% volunteered that it was not a problem at all). In 1992, responding to a differently worded question, few whites acknowledged the existence of widespread housing discrimination. Only 11% agreed that blacks, in general, were discriminated against. When we recall that about one-third of the 1992 African American interviewees reported discrimination against them personally and over 70% perceived general housing discrimination, the magnitude of this perceptual gap becomes clear. The passage of fair housing acts that made housing discrimination illegal may have led many whites to assume that such discrimination no longer existed. Most blacks think otherwise.

These findings are consistent with national trends that show a sharp decline after 1964 in the proportion of whites who see whites as responsible for blacks' disadvantaged situation in America (Schuman and

Krysan, 1999). For example, in response to a question about who is primarily to blame for blacks' disadvantage, the proportion responding "whites" declined from 43% in 1963 to 23% in 1968 and then to the mid-teens in the 1980s and 1990s. The proportion holding blacks responsible rose correspondingly.[10] At the same time, the proportion agreeing that blacks have just as good a chance as whites in their community to "get any kind of job for which they are qualified" rose sharply from 51% in 1963 to a peak of 82% in 1979 and then declined to the low 70s in the 1990s (Schuman and Krysan, 1999: 5).

Schuman and Krysan believe that whites' attribution of blacks' difficulties to whites was probably a short-lived phenomenon stimulated by the civil rights movement of the 1950s and 1960s, which highlighted severe injustices to blacks perpetrated by (usually) southern lawmakers, judges, and police officers. Survey data in the early 1960s captured that brief historical moment. They argue further that the passage of the civil rights laws of 1964 and 1965 ended the most blatant legal discrimination, and the riots of the late 1960s portrayed, to many whites, blacks as the perpetrators rather than the victims of crimes. Thus, willingness to blame whites for the problems of blacks declined precipitously and has remained fairly low.

Overall, then, whites' experiences with race relations in the Detroit area are as mixed as blacks' experiences. Compared with the late 1960s, whites in 1992 were more accepting of black neighbors in racially integrated neighborhoods, at least if their black neighbors were of the same social status. This was a clear sign of improving white racial attitudes, in spite of the troublesome racial experiences described above. But there were less positive developments as well. Whites in 1992 seemed less aware of housing discrimination than they had been in 1969, even though Detroit was still among the most segregated areas in the nation.

GAPS IN PERCEPTIONS OF REALITY

Despite huge changes in the demographic composition of Detroit and its suburbs and in the political control of Detroit itself, in this chapter we have observed remarkable stability in attitudes. African Americans were less likely in 1992 than they had been in 1968 to believe that whites wanted them to get ahead but expressed about the same preferences for housing integration for themselves and about the same sense that housing discrimination was a problem. As in 1968, in 1992 they gave somewhat more weight to community development than to racial integration

---

10 Adjusting for question wording results in a less steep but still pronounced decline.

when asked to choose between the two, but their descriptions of their own housing preferences suggested that most were firmly committed to integration.

The picture for whites is mixed. Many (20%) admitted that they had fled their neighborhoods because of the presence of African Americans. Whites seemed stubbornly resistant to the idea that housing discrimination had persisted in Detroit despite the fair housing laws. Most denied the existence of such discrimination, even though in 1968 half had considered it a major problem. Unlike blacks, who perceived discrimination as common in their daily lives and those of their family members and friends, whites seemed content to believe that legislation had brought about the change it was designed to achieve. On the other hand, whites were considerably more accepting than they had been in the late 1960s of small amounts of racial integration in their neighborhoods. Though still threatened by and fearful of proportions approaching half, most found black–white ratios in the range of 20% to 80% acceptable.

Thus, large black–white gaps persisted in perceptions and attitudes about housing segregation and discrimination. Majorities of both groups favored or accepted housing integration, but the ideal ratio of blacks to whites differed widely between the two groups. Whereas blacks were most comfortable with a 50–50 split, to whites integration was least threatening when the presence of African Americans was 20% or below. Likewise, the racial gap in perceptions of the existence of housing discrimination was dramatic. With views so different, it is not difficult to see why blacks and whites have so much difficulty talking to one another about race.

In the late 1960s, Detroit-area African Americans voiced both positive and negative assessments of trends in racial discrimination, and in retrospect, their ambivalence seems to have been highly appropriate. They were overwhelmingly positive about the progress that had been made toward eliminating discrimination over the previous 10 to 15 years, the period of the civil rights movement. But when asked whether there would always be a good deal of racial prejudice and discrimination in America, most said yes.

Why are African Americans and whites so far apart in their assessments of the problems African Americans faced? An example based on the incident, already discussed, in which a Detroit-area apartment owner was sued by the Department of Justice for discrimination against African Americans may be enlightening. We can speculate about how African Americans and whites may have interpreted this affair. For blacks, incidents of this nature presumably serve as reminders of how rampant housing discrimination is in Detroit, reinforcing a broader sense that racism is alive and well. Most African Americans would probably treat this incident of housing discrimination as notable not because it occurred, but only because the authorities decided to do something about it.

By contrast, the lesson most whites learn from this incident would probably center less on housing discrimination itself than on the successful prosecution of those responsible. Unlike the situation of the 1960s, by the 1990s laws existed and were enforced to promote equal access to housing. Whites may understand such an incident as involving an isolated landlord who had been practicing discrimination but has now been ferreted out and brought to justice, teaching a lesson to any other similarly inclined landlords and ensuring color-blind housing opportunities throughout the metropolitan area. Whites might assume that because discrimination is against the law, it must have been virtually eliminated, and that on those rare occasions when housing discrimination does occur, the perpetrator is apprehended and punished.

In sum, hearing the same media account of the same incident, blacks and whites would be predisposed to draw very different conclusions about what it indicates about the broader racial environment and the plight of African Americans. Where many whites see the removal of legal barriers as the end of racism, many African Americans see a system of racism, with such an incident serving only as a rare example visible to non–African Americans. If whites later recall this incident, it would be as an affirmation that the system works. If blacks later recall it, it would be as yet another affirmation that racism is pervasive.

When Detroit area residents spoke of the realities of race in their community in the 1990s, they talked about such incidents of housing discrimination as well as more notorious incidents of police beatings or shootings, neighborhood violence between persons of different races, and, of course, the remarkable degree of residential segregation. These racial realities shape or frame the racial perceptions of both African Americans and whites. People's perceptions differ in large measure because their realities differ, and their perceptions are unlikely to grow more similar until their realities converge.

That is the idea that stimulated this study. Integrated neighborhoods, whether in the city or the suburbs, shape a different reality than segregated neighborhoods. The realities of life differ in many ways in integrated and segregated areas and in the city and the suburbs. For our Detroit-area interviewees, how were these different realities translated into experiences with members of the other race, views about them, and indeed, views of one's own race? It is to these issues that we now turn.

3

Black–White Social Interaction

Black and white America have been described as two separate, hostile, and unequal nations (Hacker, 1992). The appropriateness of the latter two adjectives has been documented in study after study of racial attitudes and of the legal, economic, and social status of African Americans, but far less attention has been paid to racial separateness and its consequences.

Several unanswered but fundamental questions about interracial contact are central to our study. Context can be crucial in reshaping blacks' and whites' attitudes toward each other in more positive directions only if in interracial neighborhoods blacks and whites actually have contact with one another. Thus, we believe that context affects attitudes through informal interactions and friendships and by shaping the composition of political, sports, religious, social, and other neighborhood organizations that provide opportunities for interactions involving a range of people (Huckfeldt, 1986). So neighborhood context is not just a "black box" into which people enter who happen to live in houses in some proximity to those of another race and from which they emerge with changed attitudes. What happens inside the box – how and how frequently people come into contact with each other – is the key to attitude change. Sheer proximity of the races to one another (Alba and Logan, 1993) will matter little without this intervening step.

In this chapter we ask whether mixed residential neighborhoods promote interracial contact, ranging from casual encounters to intense personal relationships. In areas where many members of both races live, how much black–white contact occurs? As legal barriers have fallen, has social contact between the races become more widespread? Is relatively casual contact now common but close friendship still rare? What conditions facilitate or impede interracial contact?

In the past, researchers have by no means ignored interracial contact. Indeed, they have conducted dozens of studies of its impact. Most of these

47

studies, though not all (see, e.g., Demo and Hughes, 1990), have tested the proposition that interaction between blacks and whites undermines negative stereotypes and builds positive attitudes – that "to know them is to love them" rather than "familiarity breeds contempt." The idea that positive attitudes follow from interracial contact has often been sustained (see, e.g., Aberbach and Walker, 1973; Amir, 1976; Ellison and Powers, 1994; Meer and Freedman, 1966; Schuman and Hatchett, 1974; Robinson, 1980; Sigelman and Welch, 1993; Tsukashima and Morton, 1976; Williams, 1964), particularly when attention has centered on people interacting under conditions of relative equality (Desforges et al., 1991; but see Ford, 1973; Jackman and Crane, 1986; Robinson and Preston, 1976). Unfortunately, scant attention has been paid to the prevalence of interracial contact or the conditions under which it is likely to occur. In this chapter, we analyze contact between blacks and whites in the Detroit area. Our purposes are to probe the prevalence of various sorts of contact, contrasting the situation in 1992 with that of a quarter-century earlier, and to probe the conditions that facilitate or impede such contact, especially the impacts of where blacks and whites live and work – in the city or the suburbs and in racially homogeneous or heterogeneous settings.

THE CHANGING RACIAL ENVIRONMENT

Prior to the enactment of the Civil Rights Act of 1964 and the Voting Rights Act of 1965, social contact between blacks and whites was severely limited throughout the United States. In the South, every aspect of life was segregated by law (Baker [1908], 1964). In the North, the separation of the races was not legally mandated, but segregated housing patterns and white racial prejudice had much the same effect.

The civil rights revolution of the 1960s helped open new educational and economic doors for blacks, at least for those with sufficient resources to take advantage of these opportunities. Many of these policies promoted interracial contact on the job and in neighborhoods, classrooms, and public accommodations as a by-product of attempts to ensure equal opportunity, and proponents also argued that increased contact among black and white children would promote future racial harmony (Orfield, 1993).

Partly as a consequence of these policies, residential segregation slowly declined in major cities throughout the United States, as we noted in chapter 1. Sharply defined black and white residential districts continued to exist in most metropolitan areas, but in both cities and suburbs there were neighborhoods, often transitional but sometimes more stable, in which many blacks and whites lived close to one another. Occupational segregation also decreased (Farley, 1984; Simms, 1987). Because spatial isolation tends to produce social isolation (Massey and Denton, 1993: 161), diminishing levels of residential and occupational segregation provided more opportunities for interracial social interaction. At the same time, when we undertook our study, the Detroit metropolitan area was one of 16 "hypersegregated" metropolitan areas in the United States (Massey and Denton, 1993). In a hypersegregated area, the spatial separation of the races makes it unlikely that blacks or whites will encounter members of another race in their own neighborhood or in surrounding neighborhoods. As we have seen, the city of Detroit does have some white enclaves, but most whites live in the suburbs, which run the socioeconomic gamut from grimy downriver communities through exclusive Grosse Pointe. Suburban whites tend to make little use of the central city.

Even so, white people do live and work in the central city, African Americans do live and work in the suburbs, sports teams and local media outlets do feature both blacks and whites, and some churches and other civic groups do work to bring people together. Does any of this promote greater interracial contact?

TRENDS IN INTERRACIAL CONTACT

On the assumption that broad societal changes have facilitated social contact between blacks and whites (Blau, 1977), we expected interracial contact to have increased over the quarter-century spanning the late 1960s and the early 1990s. The eradication of legal barriers to integration and the opening up of middle- and upper-echelon jobs to blacks were both expected to facilitate greater interracial contact, although continuing residential segregation would have limited it.

Our expectation proved accurate. Figures 3.1 through 3.4 show the prevalence of four different forms of interracial contact for blacks and whites in the Detroit area, first as of 1968–1969 and then as of 1992.[1] According to Figure 3.1, during this quarter-century span the proportion

---

1 Question wording was as follows, for (a) the 1968 DAS (blacks only), (b) the 1969 DAS (whites only), and (c) our 1992 survey. (1) Contact in school: (a) Were there any white students in the schools you attended? (b) In all the years you went to school, did you ever go to school where there were Negro students too? (c) In all the years you went to school, did you ever go to a school where there were [black/white] students too? (2) Workplace contact: (a) On your job, do [did] you work with only Negroes, only whites, or with both Negroes and whites? (b) Of the 10 or 12 people you work most closely with on your job, are there any Negroes? (c) On your job do [did] you work with only blacks, only whites, or with both blacks and whites? (3) Neighborhood presence: (a), (b), and (c) In the two or three blocks right around here, how many of the families are [black/white]: none, only a few, many but less than half, or more than half?" (4) Home visits: (a), (b), and (c) Do

(footnote continues)

49

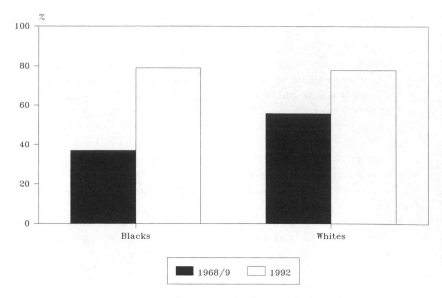

Figure 3.1. Percent who attended school with the other race.

of blacks attending integrated schools more than doubled. As a consequence, the once wide racial gap in the likelihood of having experienced segregated schooling vanished; by 1992, almost four out of five adults less than 70 years of age, black and white alike, had attended school with at least one member of the other race.

Most blacks who went to school with whites had numerous white classmates. Indeed, almost 60% of those who attended grade school with whites and almost 70% of those who attended junior high and high school with whites had more than a few white classmates. By contrast, most whites who went to an integrated school had only a few black classmates; only 40% of those who had black classmates in grade school and only 30% of those who had black junior high and high school black classmates recalled having more than a few. Only 6% of whites were in

(footnote continued)
you and the [blacks/whites] that live around here visit in each other's home, or do you only see and talk to each other on the street, or do you hardly know each other? As noted above, interviewees in the 1968 and 1969 DAS were less than 70 years of age. Thus, in comparing frequency estimates between 1968–1969 and 1992, we excluded respondents aged 70 or above from the 1992 data. All 1968 DAS interviewees were residents of the city of Detroit. It made virtually no difference whether suburban blacks in our 1992 survey were included in or excluded from comparisons with the 1968 black interviewees, as response frequencies for 1992 black interviewees varied by no more than one percentage point depending on how we treated black suburbanites; we did include them in the comparisons.

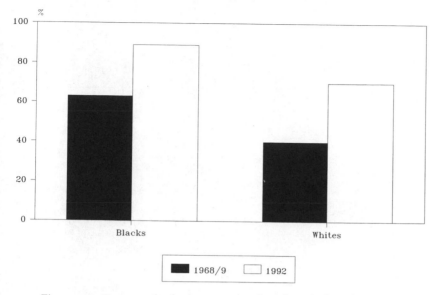

Figure 3.2. Percent who had contact on the job with the other race.

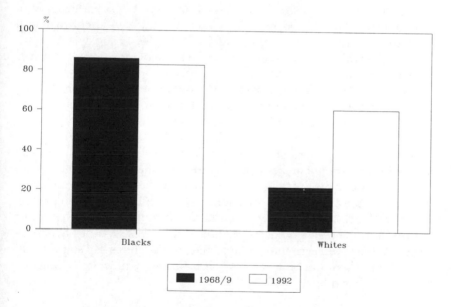

Figure 3.3. Percent who had neighbors of the other race.

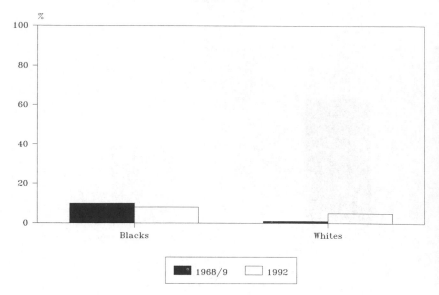

Figure 3.4. Percent who visited in the homes of neighbors of the other race.

the racial minority in either grade school or junior high and high school (as against 20% of blacks in grade school and 25% in junior high and high school). In this respect, Detroit's blacks were roughly similar to blacks throughout the Midwest, 30% of whom attended majority-white schools (Orfield, 1993: 239).

Even in 1968, most blacks had some contact with whites on the job, and thereafter the trend continued apace (Figure 3.2.) For whites, job contact with blacks was still the exception in 1969, but by 1992 more than two whites in three had job-related contacts with blacks.[2]

Blacks were no more likely in 1992 than they had been in the late 1960s to have white families living nearby, but the percentage of whites with at least one black family living in the neighborhood almost tripled, from 22% to 61% (Figure 3.3.) Though still well below the comparable figure for blacks, this represents substantial change in a relatively short period. It is an especially surprising figure in light of Detroit's hypersegregation. However, even though most blacks and whites had some neighbors of the other race, only 26% of blacks and 13% of whites claimed to have more than a few.[3]

2 This is much higher than in a 1990 national sample, in which only about 40% of whites reported having black co-workers (Kinder and Mendelberg, 1995).
3 This again is higher than reported from a national sample surveyed in 1990, in which only 52% reported having African American neighbors within eight blocks (Kinder and Mendelberg, 1995).

Black–White Social Interaction

Thus, from the late 1960s through the early 1990s, Detroit area blacks became much more likely to have attended school with whites and to have job-related contacts. If anything, though, they became somewhat less likely to have white neighbors. For whites, every trend was toward greater exposure to blacks, and yet such exposure was largely superficial, for example, going to school with only a handful of black students or living near a single black family in a primarily white neighborhood. Nonetheless, continuing casual contact has the potential to affect attitudes. Contact can be important not only because it is intense but also because it is frequent (Sprague, 1982).

The frequency of casual rather than intense contact also comes through in Figure 3.4, which focuses on a more personal form of contact. Because blacks are generally more likely than whites to visit with neighbors (Lee, Campbell, and Miller, 1991) and because in Detroit blacks are more likely to have white neighbors than whites are to have black neighbors, our survey uncovered a black–white imbalance in visiting neighbors of the other race. That gap may have closed slightly between 1968–1969 and 1992, but far more salient is the sheer infrequency of interracial association with neighbors. As we have seen, in 1992 approximately one black in five and two whites in five had no neighbors of the other race. Of those who did, only about 1 in 10, black or white, claimed to have the type of relationship in which visiting in one another's home played any part; 57% of blacks and 66% of whites hardly knew their neighbors of the other race. (Of course, visiting in the homes of neighbors of any race may not be the norm in modern urban societies.)

In general, then, whites in metropolitan Detroit had more personal contact with blacks in 1992 than they had had 25 years earlier, but they did not have contact with many blacks.[4] Blacks' daily exposure to whites changed considerably less over the years, and blacks still found themselves, for the most part, interacting with whites in situations in which whites were numerically predominant. This, of course, is the situation that whites prefer but that blacks do not. At least when referring to housing choices, African Americans prefer settings in which the numbers of blacks and whites are about equal; whites, on the other hand, are open to integration as long as whites are in a clear majority. This clash of perspectives, often unrecognized, lies at the heart of many difficulties in trying to achieve true racial integration.

4 It may have been more socially desirable in 1992 than it was 25 years earlier to report interracial contact. Even so, it seems unlikely that this would explain the increases identified in Figures 3.1 through 3.4. If social desirability had prompted a significant number of responses, presumably these effects would have been more uniform across items rather than showing the vast range evident in the figures.

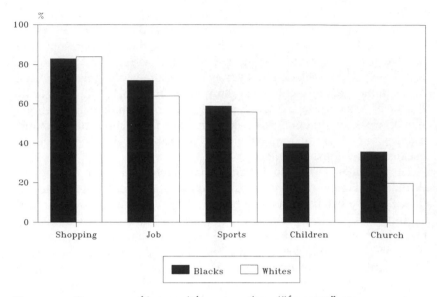

Figure 3.5. Frequency of interracial conversations ("frequent" or "sometimes").

Over time, close personal contact between blacks and whites, as indicated by having neighbors of the other race in one's home and as distinct from mere exposure or casual contact, underwent little change. Rare in the late 1960s, close personal contact remained rare in the early 1990s.

This is as far as our trend analyses can take us, but it is not as far as we can go. Figure 3.5, based on questions in our 1992 survey about how often interviewees had conversations with members of the other race in various settings, conveys a more complete picture of personal contact between blacks and whites.[5] Although in most instances blacks were involved in more interracial conversations than were whites, most of these differences were not large. There was exactly the same gradation among the settings for blacks and whites, ranging from settings in which conversations between blacks and whites were most likely to take place to those in which they were least so. Comparing the totals of frequent

5 The questions were as follows: How often do you have conversations with [members of the other race] ... on the job? ... at places where you shop? ... at events involving your children (day care, school, youth sports, etc.)? ...at church or religious activities? ... at sports events or other entertainment? The three response categories were: Never, occasionally, and frequently. It is conceivable that blacks and whites differ in their perceptions of what "frequently" means. Although we know of no reason to believe that differences in these perceptions are racially based, hindsight suggests that it would have been preferable to ask the question using a more concrete metric, perhaps referring to contact within a given time period.

and occasional ("sometimes") conversations, we see that conversations while shopping were most common, followed by conversations on the job, at sporting events, and at children's events. Least common were conversations in church or other religious activities. If we confine our attention to occasions with frequent interracial conversations, then discussions on the job were by far the most common. Blacks and whites also talked frequently while shopping, but the other settings offered fewer opportunities for interracial conversation.

Most adult Americans (about 90% of whites and 82% of blacks, according to one national survey) consider at least one person as a friend.[6] Of course, the proportion who have friends of a different race depends on what "friend" means. According to one study, 20% of whites said they had at least one black friend in 1964, but by 1974 the figure had risen to 40% (McLemore, 1980). In a national survey conducted in 1989, 82% of blacks and 66% of whites claimed to have friends of the other race (Sigelman and Welch, 1993). In the 1979 National Survey of Black Americans, which defined a friend as "someone to whom you can say what you really think," 57% said they had at least one white friend (Ellison and Powers, 1994).

We asked the interviewees in our 1992 Detroit survey how many good friends they had of the other race.[7] Of the African Americans, 43% said they had a good friend who was white, and 27% of the whites said they had a good friend who was an African American. These percentages were considerably higher than those obtained in a 1975 national survey that used the same definition (Jackman and Crane, 1986); in that survey, only 21% of blacks claimed to have a close white friend.[8] Unfortunately, there is no way to determine how much of the difference between the 1975 and 1992 estimates is attributable to the difference between Detroit and the rest of the country and how much stems from change over time. Surely some of it reflects the greater opportunities in Detroit than in the nation as a whole for whites to have black friends, since

---

6 From a national survey of 1,768 married adults conducted by Alan Booth, David Johnson, Paul Amato, and John Edwards. Unfortunately, only 98 blacks were in the sample (personal correspondence from Alan Booth).
7 The question was: I would like to ask you some questions about the people you consider your good friends. By good friends, I mean adults you enjoy getting together with at least once a month and any other adults who live elsewhere that you try to keep in close touch with by calling or writing. Are any of these good friends [members of the other race]? [If Yes] "Would you say that only a few, about half, or most of your friends are white?" Response categories ranged in four steps from "none" through "most."
8 Even more stringently than the 1975 survey, Usui (1984) asked adults 60 years of age or older in Louisville to name their three closest friends; 97% of blacks and 99% of whites named only members of their own race.

approximately one Detroit-area resident in four is an African American, as compared with only one in eight in the nation as a whole. One would hardly expect as many whites to have close black friends in Bangor, ME or Missoula, MT as in Detroit, where interracial friendships, if not highly probable, are at least possible though blacks in Bangor or Missoula might well be expected to have more white friends than those in Detroit). It is possible that a genuine change in the likelihood of interracial friendships occurred after the mid-1970s, but this must be seen merely as a possibility, not an accomplished fact. Even if we assume that genuine change did occur, we would have to take care not to exaggerate it. In 1992, 73% of our white interviewees claimed to have no black friends at all, and of those who had any, the great majority (89%) said they had only a few. Among blacks, the counterpart figures were only slightly lower (57% and 84%, respectively).

THE CONDITIONS OF INTERRACIAL CONTACT

Now we begin to consider the conditions that facilitate or impede both casual and close interracial contact. Drawing on Blau's (1977) structural analysis of heterogeneity, we probe the impacts of several aspects of the social structure, especially physical propinquity brought about by integration of the neighborhood, workplace, schools, and church.

The Influence of Propinquity

A simple premise informs our analysis: The greater the physical propinquity of two groups, the greater the likelihood of social interaction between them (Blau, 1977: 9091). Being surrounded for most hours of the day and most days of the week primarily, or even exclusively, by members of one's own race limits one's opportunities for interracial social contact, but spending substantial time in a racially heterogeneous environment increases the chances for such contact. Indeed, it may almost mandate it.

Sheer propinquity increases informal interaction and eventually promotes friendship (Blau, 1977; Hallinan, 1982; Hallinan and Williams, 1989; Verbrugge, 1983). People make friends with others who are available to be friends, and neighbors and co-workers generally fit that description better than anyone else (Berscheid and Walster, 1969; Festinger, Schachter, and Back, 1950; Vander Zanden, 1984). Most people's primary daily activities occur within the neighborhood where they live and the place where they work. Almost everyone ventures outside his or her own neighborhood at least occasionally, but most people spend a great deal of time at home, at work, or somewhere nearby. One study concluded that the two principal determinants of friendship patterns within neighborhoods are the distance between houses and the direction the houses face (Festinger et al., 1950),[9] and casual contacts tend to be even more localized than close friendships.

How does propinquity affect contact between blacks and whites? Those who live in a racially diverse area have more opportunities to interact with members of the other race than do those who live in an all-black or an all-white area, who are racially isolated for a major portion of each day. Accordingly, racially mixed neighborhoods should stimulate interracial friendships and promote interracial contacts in church, school, and civic activities and in casual, everyday endeavors such as shopping (Jackman and Crane, 1986). According to one study, low-income blacks who move to white suburbs are just as likely to have friendly contacts with neighbors as are low-income blacks who relocate inside the largely black inner city and are more likely to have white friends (Rosenbaum, Popkin, Kaufman, and Rusin, 1991). Racially mixed neighborhoods are also more likely to have integrated schools, enabling interracial friendships to develop at an early age and promoting cooperative interactions between black and white parents (DuBois and Hirsch, 1990).

It has also been established, however, that white acceptance of blacks as neighbors becomes strained when blacks come close to constituting a majority of the population (Farley et al. 1994). It follows that interracial contact might rise as a function of the percentage of blacks in the population only until that percentage reaches a tipping point, after which interracial contact might decline. Moreover, the simple likelihood of coming into contact with members of another group increases more rapidly as group numbers initially rise from zero than after the group has achieved substantial size. If, for example, the probability of one white person's contact with any other individual in the population under completely random circumstances conforms to a binomial distribution and if the person meets 20 people on some outing, the probability of meeting at least one minority group member increases from .64 to .99 as the minority share of the population grows from 5% to 20%; however, another 15 percentage point increase in the size of the minority population, from 20% to 35%, raises the probability of meeting at least one minority group member by only .01. In short, there could well be a ceiling above which a group's sheer size does little to promote contact with members of another group. Indeed, given the racial climate in American cities, added numbers may at some point even have an intimidating, and

9 About one good friend in four comes from one's own neighborhood (Connerly 1985; Oliver 1988; Wellman 1979).

therefore negative, impact on the perceived desirability of contact with minority group members. And for the minority, added numbers may mean that it is less necessary to interact with the majority.

An example of these dynamics lies in the frequency of black and white marriages in America. In six of the nine states where the black population is extremely low (less than 2% or so), a majority of the blacks who marry marry whites, and in the other three states nearly 40% do so (Kalmijn, 1993: p. 128). The principles of propinquity suggest that most of the available marriage partners for African Americans in these states are white – never mind America's racial obsessions. For their part, whites can hardly feel threatened by a black population so small. As the proportion of blacks in a state increases, the rate of intermarriage declines. However, once the black proportion in the state is above 12% or so, further increases in the black population have little impact on rates of intermarriage with whites.

The likelihood of interracial contact should also be affected by where one works. For many white suburbanites and black city dwellers, the workplace may be the main or even the only site of regular contact with members of the other race, whether as co-workers, customers, bosses, or employees. At the very least, having a job outside the home brings one into contact with more people than one would encounter if one stayed home all day. Under certain conditions (as when a black city dweller makes the daily trek out from the predominantly black city to work in a predominantly white suburb or when a white suburbanite commutes in the opposite direction), working outside the home can increase not only the number but also the variety of the people with whom one comes into regular contact (Fischer, 1982). Moreover, with the passage of time, work-based relationships can be transformed into social relationships and even enduring friendships.

Another opportunity for interracial contact is provided by church attendance, especially if it is regular and is generalized to other church-related activities. For many blacks and white ethnic group members, the church is the center of social and community life. America, it has been said, is at its most segregated at 11 a.m. on Sunday. Yet some churches in the Detroit area have led the campaign for racial harmony, and several major churches in the city have long had multiracial congregations. Moreover, it is possible that the predilection for active church attendance is linked to an interest in other forms of group membership, including service groups linked to the church or even groups unrelated to the church, that lead participants to interracial contacts.

Nor is present-day physical propinquity to members of another race the only consideration, for childhood contact with members of the other race could also affect current interracial contact. Those who grew up in a racially diverse environment might be expected to view black–white contact as relatively normal and thus to have greater contact with members of the other race. Indeed, many of the social policies of the 1960s were based on the assumption that race relations would improve if ways could be found to bring blacks and whites together as children. The movement to desegregate public schools was premised in part on the belief that educational opportunities could be equalized only by eliminating single-race schools, but also on the belief that something of value would occur if blacks and whites began to interact with one another at an early age (Orfield, 1993). The same dual rationale propelled the desegregation of other public facilities and of previously all-white residential areas. Harmful racial stereotypes would be reduced, it was assumed, and children who sat together in the same classroom, played on the same team, and swam in the same public pool would be more prepared to maintain positive relations with one another as adults.[10]

In Detroit, events have sometimes seemed to suggest that propinquity breeds negativity. But as we will see, our interviewees' reports of their behavior suggest that that this is not always true. Because basic attitudes and behaviors tend to be acquired early in life and because children spend most of their time at school or at home, the character of the schools one attended and of the neighborhood where one grew up can hardly fail to have shaped one's adult attitudes and behaviors. Thus, if there is a carryover effect from youth to adulthood, those who lived in a neighborhood or attended school with children of the other race should be more likely to seek out, or at least accept, interracial contact as adults and to regard such contact as normal.

The Influence of Personal Attributes

Regardless of where one grew up or currently spends time, personal attributes might also shape contact with members of the other race. To understand the influence of propinquity on interracial contact, we have to take these personal attributes into account. Personal attributes affect tastes, or preferences, for interracial contact. Some whites who live in all-white areas and some blacks who live in all-black areas are motivated, at least in part, by a desire to be surrounded by others of their own race; as noted earlier, 30% of our white interviewees said they

---

10 Many also recognized that propinquity must be reinforced by other conditions. Thus, for example, Singleton and Asher (1979) observed that the additional years of interracial contact between third and sixth grade did not improve relations between black and white students; supportive curricula, they argued, were required for school integration to improve relations between students of different races.

would prefer to live in an all-white neighborhoods and nearly 20% of our black interviewees say they preferred an all-black one. Of course, for present purposes we could have tapped preferences for interracial contact directly by looking at the pertinent survey responses, but that would have begged the issue of whether preferences lead to contact or vice versa. Accordingly, we stepped back to look at the impact of three personal attributes that we suspected might shape such preferences: age, sex, and socioeconomic status.

Age. Middle-aged people play more numerous and more varied social roles than either the young or the elderly, for during middle age one is especially likely to function simultaneously as a spouse, parent, worker, and member of various informal groups and community, civic, and recreational organizations (Riley, 1985). This surfeit of social roles provides extra opportunities for contact with others, including people of another race. People of different ages have undergone different socialization experiences and may have learned different attitudes and values, including racial attitudes, as a consequence. Those who grew up during or after the mid-1960s, for example, are likely to have more liberal racial and social attitudes than their parents (Greeley and Sheatsley, 1971; Hyman and Sheatsley, 1956; Schuman, Steeh, and Bobo, 1985; Taylor, Sheatsley, and Greeley, 1978).

A socialization-based interpretation would lead us to anticipate greater interracial contact among the young and middle-aged than among those who grew up prior to the mid-1960s. An opportunity-based interpretation, on the other hand, would suggest greater interracial contact among middle-aged people than among either their younger or their older counterparts. If both interpretations are correct, interracial contact should rise as a function of age, peak in middle age, and then decline at a steeper rate than it rose.

Sex. Men have sometimes been shown to have more interracial contact than women (Blackwell and Hart, 1982), apparently owing to the greater frequency with which men work outside the home and thereby come into contact with a variety of people. Once working outside the home is taken into account, though, we know of no particular reason to anticipate any sex-based difference in interracial contact.

Socioeconomic Status. Because prejudice against blacks is more widespread among less educated, lower and working-class whites and because estrangement from whites is more intense among less educated, lower and working-class blacks (Sigelman and Welch, 1991), interracial contact may vary according to gradations in socioeconomic status.

Moreover, those higher on the status ladder are likely to have more opportunities for contact with members of the other race. Whereas the very poor may travel little outside their own neighborhood, education and affluence lead to greater involvement in a range of social activities that bring blacks and whites into contact with one another. Because of the ghettoization of very poor blacks, there is reason to expect socioeconomic status to be an even more crucial determinant of interracial contact among blacks than it is among whites.

In one study, blacks with the most education and highest incomes were the most likely to prefer neighborhoods where whites are numerous, and whites with the most education were the least likely to hold negative stereotypes of blacks and to be uncomfortable living near them (Farley et al., 1994). However, income did not affect negative stereotyping among whites, and displayed a curvilinear relationship with whites' discomfort about living in neighborhoods with blacks. Whites in the $60,000 to $80,000 annual income range expressed the greatest reluctance to live in a racially mixed neighborhood; those with lower or higher incomes were less resistant to the idea (Farley et al., 1994). Because education appeared to have a somewhat different relationship with both the opportunity and the preference for interracial contact than did other aspects of socioeconomic status, we keep it separate in our analysis.

Measures

Using data from our 1992 survey, we test these interpretations for two measures, one of casual interracial contact and the other of close interracial friendship; detailed descriptions of these measures and all the other measures employed in this chapter and the ensuing chapters are presented in Appendix B. In brief, the casual interracial contact scale combines each interviewee's responses to the five-part series of questions on interracial conversations summarized in Figure 3.5. The close interracial friendship scale is based on the question about interracial friendships that we also described earlier.

Many of the predictors in our model pertain to propinquity, tapping various aspects of spatially based opportunities for interaction with members of the other race. These include whether an interviewee lived in Detroit or in the suburbs; the African American percentage of the residents of the interviewee's neighborhood; whether the interviewee worked in Detroit, worked in the suburbs, or did not work outside the home; the frequency with which the interviewee attended church services; whether the interviewee grew up in a racially mixed area; and the racial composition of the elementary, junior, and senior high schools that the interviewee attended.

Race and Place

The personal attributes in the model, which we view as underlying differences in preferences for interracial interaction, include age, sex, level of education, and financial status (a composite measure based on annual household income, receipt of government aid, self-described financial stringency, and home ownership).[11]

PREDICTING CASUAL CONTACT

The Impact of Propinquity

For blacks, where one lived had no bearing on how often one interacted casually with whites (Table 3.1.) Neither living in the suburbs nor living in a racially heterogeneous neighborhood contributed to contact with whites. For whites, though, the racial mix of the neighborhood was an important determinant of casual contact, although whether the neighborhood was in the central city or the suburbs made no further difference.

The effect of the racial mix of whites' neighborhoods on their contact with African Americans was curvilinear. For whites, simple calculations based on the two racial composition coefficients reveal that casual contact with blacks topped out when blacks reached 50% to 60% of the residents of a neighborhood and then declined at an ever-increasing rate; in fact, the expected level of casual interracial contact for whites living in a neighborhood that was 80% black is somewhat lower than the expected level for whites living in a neighborhood that was 40% black. Thus, the more blacks who were living nearby, the more common was white contact with blacks, but not beyond the 50% to 60% ceiling. Overall, residential considerations affected blacks and whites altogether differently.

11 Although we expected certain predictors to register different effects for blacks than for whites, we first tested a pair of simple additive models (one for casual contact, the other for close friendship) for the combined sample of black and white respondents, using race as one of the predictors. We then compared the performance of the additive models to that of fully interactive models, which specified interactions between race and every other regressor. For casual interracial contact, the fully interactive specification achieved a significantly better fit than the simple additive model ($F = 2.62$, $df = 13$, 1021, $p < .01$); for close interracial friendship, the fully interactive model also fit the data significantly better than the simple additive one ($\zeta^2 = 92.3$, $df = 13$, $p < .001$). These differences were consistent with the idea that these factors did not affect blacks and whites in the same way. Because of the awkwardness of presenting statistical results for models with 13 interaction terms, we decided to present separate results for blacks and whites. This amounted to purely a difference in mode of presentation, for the two approaches are statistically equivalent. The intervallike properties of the casual contact scale permitted us to employ ordinary least squares regression, but because close friendship was measured on an ordinal scale with only four categories, we analyzed it with an ordered probit model.

Black–White Social Interaction

Table 3.1. *Predicting casual interracial contact*

Predictor	Blacks b	Blacks (s.e.)	Whites b	Whites (s.e.)
Detroit residence	−.12	(.09)	.13	(.09)
Percent black in neighborhood	.01	(.01)	.02^a	(.01)
Percent black in neighborhood (squared)	−.0001	(.0001)	−.0002^a	(.0001)
Work in the city	.17	(.11)	.37^a	(.13)
Work in the suburbs	.34^a	(.11)	.20	(.11)
Church attendance	.12^a	(.04)	.18^a	(.04)
Early life neighborhood composition	.37^a	(.08)	−.06	(.10)
Early life school composition	.06^a	(.02)	.09^a	(.03)
Age	.04^a	(.01)	.05^a	(.01)
Age (squared)	−.0005^a	(.0001)	−.001^a	(.0001)
Sex	.02	(.08)	.11	(.09)
Education	.03	(.05)	.02	(.05)
Financial status	.07	(.05)	.01	(.05)
Constant	−1.33^a	(.35)	−1.47^a	(.36)
R squared	0.25		0.25	

Note: b is the unstandardized regression coefficient; next to it in parentheses is the standard error of *b*.
$^a p < .05$.

Where white people lived strongly affected their contact with blacks, but where black people lived had little effect on their contact with whites.[12]

More consistent patterns emerge for whether blacks and whites worked in the city or suburbs. Among neither blacks nor whites did working outside the home per se lead to more frequent casual interracial contact: There is no significant difference between blacks who did not work outside the home and those who had a job in the city, nor is there a significant difference between whites who did not work outside the home and those who worked in the suburbs. What matters is not that one worked outside the home, but where one worked. As compared with

12 The racial composition of one's neighborhood affected virtually every type of casual interracial contact more decisively for whites than for blacks. For example, whites' church-related contact with blacks was strongly affected by whether whites lived in Detroit or the suburbs and whether they lived in a predominantly white or racially mixed neighborhood. However, these factors played no role in shaping blacks' church-related contact with whites.

blacks who did not work outside the home, blacks who worked in the suburbs had significantly more casual contact with whites (a difference of .34 on the contact scale), and compared with whites who did not work outside the home, whites who worked in the city had significantly greater contact with blacks (a difference of .37).

Church attendance affected blacks and whites in the same way. In each case, but more for whites than for blacks, casual interracial contact was more common among those who attended church more frequently. Attending church more often, it would seem, offered at least an opportunity for members of the two races to interact.

For blacks, exposure to whites during the formative years carried over to adult life. Compared with other blacks, those who had lived near whites while growing up reported significantly more casual contact with whites as adults, the difference amounting to approximately $^1/_3$ of a point on the contact scale. Blacks' adult contacts with whites were also shaped by whether they had attended racially integrated schools. For every 1-point increase on the 6-point school integration scale, blacks scored approximately .06 higher on casual interracial contact; thus, the contact score for a black who attended all-black elementary and secondary schools would be expected to fall .36 below that of a black who had had mostly white classmates in elementary and secondary school.

For whites, having grown up in the same neighborhood with black children was unrelated to casual interracial contact as an adult.[13] However, as was true for blacks, having attended an integrated school as a child increased whites' adult contact with blacks. Each 1-point increment on the school integration scale translates into an increment of almost .09 on the casual contact scale, so that from the bottom to the top of the 6-point school integration scale, whites' interracial contact scores as adults rose by approximately .50.

The Impact of Other Personal Attributes

For both blacks and whites, casual interracial contact varied as a function of age, although, as expected, not in a linear fashion. Rather, casual contact rose with age at a steadily decreasing rate until it topped out, at

---

13 The negative sign of this coefficient warrants comment. The simple correlation for whites between adult interracial contact and having grown up in a neighborhood where black children lived was actually positive, although the relationship was weak (r = .10). The sign reversal in the multivariate analysis stemmed from the inclusion in the model of the extent of racial integration in the schools a white person attended. This variable was strongly related to the presence of blacks in the neighborhood during the same period (r = .51). With the school integration variable removed from the model, the estimated impact of neighborhood racial composition turned positive, although it still fell short of statistical significance.

which point it began to fall at a steadily increasing rate. For blacks and whites alike, the turning point came for 40- to 45-year-olds.

No significant male–female difference emerged for either blacks or whites. Although the mean score on the casual contact scale is significantly higher for white men (.36) than for white women (–.53), once working outside the home is taken into account, no difference remains.[14] In contrast to the pattern for whites, the mean interracial contact score is about the same for black men (.65) as for black women (.64).[15] Nor did more affluent and highly educated blacks or whites interact significantly more with members of the other race than did their poorer, less educated counterparts.

In sum, our findings concerning casual contact between blacks and whites generally bear out our expectations. The extent to which blacks and whites interacted casually is, as anticipated, a function of current and childhood propinquity and certain personal attributes. Not all these factors affected blacks and whites in the same manner or to the same degree, but for members of each race our analyses highlight conditions that shaped and constrained casual interracial contact.

THE LINK BETWEEN CASUAL AND CLOSE INTERRACIAL FRIENDSHIP

Before we turn to the determinants of close interracial friendship, let us briefly consider the link between casual interracial contact and close interracial friendship. We do not view either of these as a cause of the other, for just as casual contacts can blossom into close friendships, close friendships can beget new casual contacts. However, we do note that among our interviewees, casual and close contact were differentially linked according to race and sex. Among whites, both men and women who had more casual contact with blacks also had more black friends.[16] Similarly, black women who had more casual contact with whites had more white friends, but among black men casual contact with whites was unrelated to friendship with whites.[17] An implication is that fostering conditions for interracial contact may do little to enhance black males' friendship with whites in the absence of other changes in the

---

14 Only 51% of white women worked outside the home, compared with 75% of white men.
15 For blacks, our control for working outside the home did not explain the lack of a male–female differential in casual interracial contact. The male–female difference in outside-the-home employment was smaller than among whites in any event.
16 The correlations were .44 and .48, respectively.
17 The correlations were .35 and .09, respectively.

social environment that would lessen the subordination of African Americans, both real and perceived.

PREDICTING CLOSE FRIENDSHIP

Turning now to the determinants of close interracial friendship, Table 3.2 displays the estimates for blacks and whites. The major message of Table 3.2 is that interracial friendship is much less predictable for blacks than for whites. For blacks, the only significant predictor is having attended a more highly integrated school in one's youth. For whites, though, several factors stand out, including living in a racially mixed neighborhood, having attended school with blacks, and being middle-aged. Whereas the racial heterogeneity of one's neighborhood increased casual interracial contact up to a point and then turned in the opposite direction, for close interracial friendship there was no tipping point. Rather, the higher the proportion of African Americans in a neighbor-

Table 3.2. *Predicting close interracial friendship*

Predictor	Blacks b	(s.e.)	Whites b	(s.e.)
Detroit residence	−.07	(.11)	.14	(.13)
Percent black in neighborhood	−.02	(.01)	.02[a]	(.01)
Percent black in neighborhood (squared)	.0001	(.0001)	−.00004	(.00008)
Work in the city	.04	(.14)	.24	(.18)
Work in the suburbs	.23	(.13)	−.06	(.16)
Church attendance	.02	(.05)	.13[a]	(.06)
Early life neighborhood composition	.20	(.12)	−.29	(.15)
Early life school composition	.07[a]	(.03)	.08[a]	(.04)
Age	−.01	(.02)	.04[a]	(.02)
Age (squared)	.0001	(.0002)	−.01[a]	(.0002)
Sex	.07	(.11)	.01	(.13)
Education	.01	(.06)	−.08	(.07)
Financial status	.03	(.06)	−.13	(.07)
Constant	.56	(.48)	−1.00	(.53)
Pseudo-R squared	0.11		0.23	

Note: b is the unstandardized regression coefficient derived from an ordered probit analysis, followed in parentheses by the standard error. Pseudo-R squared is the Aldrich-Nelson (1984) approximation.
[a] $p < .05$.

hood, the more common were white residents' interracial friendships. However, other factors fall by the wayside as determinants of whites' friendships with blacks. Conspicuous among these is having a job in the city, which significantly increased whites' casual contacts with blacks but not their close friendships. That is, working in the city brought whites into greater contact with blacks, but apparently these working relationships did not intensify into close personal relationships. Whites' friendships with blacks were also shaped by church attendance, with regular churchgoers being more likely than others to have black friends.

DISCUSSION

Earlier we suggested that context has the potential to improve racial attitudes by stimulating casual interracial contact, facilitating interracial friendships, and providing a common ground where individuals of different races can join together in community organizations ranging from churches to sports teams. Our findings suggest that even in hypersegregated Detroit, the neighborhood context produces some, but not all, of these effects on interracial contact.

Many of these findings are open to different, and often contradictory, interpretations. On the one hand, by 1992 whites had become much more likely to interact with African Americans than had been the case a quarter-century before, and African Americans had become somewhat more likely to interact with whites. By these standards, Detroit became more integrated in fact as well as in law. Indeed, very few Detroit-area residents (only about 1% of the blacks and 6% of the whites in our survey) had no contact with members of the other race, and most had considerable, albeit casual, contact. Moreover, in this hypersegregated area, where media reports of racial hostility appeared almost every day during the 1990s, the fact that approximately one person in three had one or more close friends of the other race may be welcomed as unexpectedly good news. Some will undoubtedly take heart from the findings reported in this chapter, buoyed by the progress that recent decades have ushered in.

On the other hand, much interracial contact consists purely of brief, superficial encounters while shopping, attending sporting events, and the like. Nearly half of our black interviewees who lived in the city reported not having a single white friend, and almost the same proportion of white interviewees from the suburbs reported having no black social acquaintances, let alone any black friends. These findings will undoubtedly strike some as bleak corroboration of the separateness of black and white America. Moreover, some of the increased interracial contact since the late 1960s is undoubtedly of a negative character. Both the popular

67

press and scholarly studies have extensively documented instances of hostile treatment of African Americans who were simply trying to gain service in restaurants or stores or to walk in or drive through predominantly white neighborhoods (Feagin, 1991).

These findings should convey fresh insight into the realities of interracial contact in a hypersegregated city. Indices of hypersegregation are based on aggregate racial housing patterns. Individual patterns of interracial contact are probably correlated positively with indices of housing segregation. Still, considerable interracial contact can occur in the presence of hypersegregation, for example, if white neighborhoods have at least some black residents even though most blacks live in segregated neighborhoods, or if such contact occurs in workplaces, whether among fellow employees or between employees and customers. Thus, we have noted extensive and increasing interracial contact in Detroit, even in the context of a hypersegregated environment. The other side of the coin is that although integrationist policies have the potential to promote interracial contact, they can do relatively little to promote close interracial ties. Nor can increased interracial contact, or even close interracial ties, guarantee that blacks' and whites' attitudes toward one another will change.

Still, mixed-race residential settings do indicate a potential for improved race relations. This is particularly true because they stimulate casual contact and because they seem to provide organizational settings where people come into contact with others of different races. Looking in particular at churches and schools, we have observed some impact on casual contact. Interracial friendships, another mechanism, are much less common, but for whites both the neighborhood racial context and church attendance do stimulate such friendships.

Our findings about the conditions under which interracial contact occurred are straightforward. For whites, propinquity – where one lives, works, studies, and worships – was the key to the quantity and the quality of contact with African Americans. However, for African Americans, spatial considerations hardly mattered. Those who worked in the suburbs had more contact with whites than did those who did not work outside the home, but other spatial considerations were irrelevant. Living in the suburbs, living in a racially integrated neighborhood, and working in the city did not bring blacks into more frequent contact with whites. Spatial factors were clearly secondary to early life experiences and personal attributes as influences on blacks' interracial contact.

This black–white difference in the impact of the racial environment has close parallels in research on friendship networks among young children. According to Hallinan and Teixeira (1987), the higher the proportion of black children in an elementary school classroom, the more likely a white child is to choose a black peer as a friend, but the racial composition of the classroom has no bearing on whether a black child chooses a white classmate as a friend.

Thus, the differential impact of propinquity that we have observed for black and white Detroit-area adult residents may extend beyond the realm of adult interracial contact in the Detroit area. How might we account for this racial difference? Part of the answer would be that although within each race, people have different preferences for interracial contact, African Americans as a group have less of a free hand than do whites to live where they want to live.[18] Most blacks in the Detroit area, as we noted in chapter 2, prefer to live in a racially integrated neighborhood. However, whereas most blacks want a more or less even mix of black and white neighbors, most whites want at most just a few black neighbors. Blacks tend to see integration in terms of numerical equality, but whites are concerned about maintaining their majority status.

As we pointed out earlier, this is a difficult paradox; satisfying the desires of whites to have integrated settings but only token integration means that most blacks are likely to remain in all-black settings. Satisfying the desire of blacks in this respect likely leads to a tipping point that resegregates an area, again leaving both blacks and whites in near single-race settings (Schelling, 1973).

Because blacks are often unable to put their residential preferences into practice, their friendship choices are less likely than those of whites to reflect the racial character of their neighborhood. A different explanation would be based on opportunity rather than preference. Other things being equal, members of a minority group should be expected to have more contact with the majority than members of the majority have with the minority. Many white residents of a predominantly white neighborhood have extremely limited opportunities for contact with blacks, but many black residents of a predominantly black neighborhood still have numerous opportunities for contact with whites. Furthermore, most whites who attended an integrated school had very few black classmates, but many blacks attended predominantly white schools and had many white classmates. In the example of interracial marriages that we discussed earlier, we noted that in states with few blacks, most blacks marry whites, but of course in those same states almost all whites also marry whites.

For both blacks and whites, interracial contact in general and interracial friendship in particular also reflect early life contact with members of the other race. To the extent that black–white contact and friendship

---

18 Recall that 81% of Detroit-area blacks would prefer to live in a neighborhood that is 50% black and 50% white. Almost none do.

have grown over the years, the greater frequency of early-life contact with members of the other race is undoubtedly part of the reason for this, and the consequences of such contact should continue well into the future. However, blacks are more likely than whites to be affected by these early-life experiences, particularly by the racial composition of the neighborhood in which they grew up. This difference, we believe, largely reflects parental social class. For many blacks, having grown up in a racially mixed neighborhood means that their family belonged to the middle class or at least was upwardly mobile. For many whites, though, having grown up in a racially mixed neighborhood could mean just the opposite.

Earlier we pointed out that the increased interracial contact that has developed since the late 1960s has not been a purely spontaneous development. Rather, policies such as school integration, equal employment opportunity, and affirmative action have shaped behavior. Even fair housing laws, though largely ineffectual, may have had some effect, as suggested by the fact that approximately 60% of the whites in the Detroit area and more than 80% of the African Americans live in neighborhoods that have at least some residents of the other race. Thus, civil rights policies seem not only to have reduced the sorts of outright discrimination that once kept blacks and whites physically apart but also to have enhanced many blacks' prospects for earning higher wages in better jobs and to have opened up a wider range of choices concerning places to live, activities in which to engage, and people with whom to interact.

Finally, high levels of residential segregation continue to pose a major impediment to social contact between the races. We have seen in this chapter that residential proximity is the major predictor of whites' contact with blacks. Accordingly, more intensive efforts to implement fair housing laws could increase interracial contact, especially among whites.

We have argued that the impact of residential context on attitudes about race cannot be understood without considering the impact of that context on interracial contact. Now that we appreciate the extent and limits of that effect, we turn to an examination of the impact of context and contact on attitudes about race.

4

Perceptions of Racial Discrimination

"If I outrank a person and he gets a job because of his color, then there's something wrong" (Holmes, 2000). This complaint by a white sergeant in the U.S. Army about his black counterpart who got the promotion that both desired could even more likely have been spoken by African Americans throughout the military or in civilian life. However, it is also the voice of many whites who believe they have been passed over for jobs, promotions, or admission to elite universities because of perceived preferences given to African Americans. In twenty-first century America, race relations are rife with such resentment – resentment by blacks of both historical and contemporary antiblack discrimination and resentment by whites of attempts to remedy that history of discrimination through affirmative action.[1]

Perceptions of racial discrimination lie near, if not at, the center of America's troubled race relations. These perceptions play a key role in people's views of the world around them, the community in which they live, and the potential remedies they favor for social, economic, and political problems (Sigelman and Welch, 1991). Building bridges between people of different races will depend, at least in part, on whether the realities of day-to-day racial contact can undermine a belief that others are getting special treatment based on their race. In this chapter, our focus is on perceptions of discrimination and how the neighborhood context helps shape them. We probe Detroit-area residents' perceptions of discrimination against blacks and whites in general and against themselves in particular. We are especially interested in the extent to which and the manner in which our interviewees' perceptions were shaped by their race, by whether they lived in the city or the sub-

---

[1] We are using the term *racial resentment* in a general sense and not in the specific sense used by Kinder and Sanders (1996) as a term measuring how whites think about black disadvantage.

urbs, and by the racial composition of their neighborhood. Unlike most prior treatments of perceptions of discrimination, we examine discrimination against whites (so-called reverse discrimination) as well as discrimination against African Americans.

HOW THE NEIGHBORHOOD MIGHT SHAPE PERCEPTIONS OF DISCRIMINATION

Many scholars have examined the impact of countywide, metropolitan-area-wide, and even statewide racial composition on the attitudes and behavior of whites. In his classic study, *Southern Politics in State and Nation,* V.O. Key (1949) found that Southern whites' attitudes toward blacks and racial segregation were strongly influenced by the racial composition of the county in which they lived. Because Key's research stimulated a myriad of other investigations, we now know that the black share of the population at the metropolitan or county level is strongly linked to white prejudice (Pettigrew, 1959; Quillian, 1996; Taylor, 1998); white support for segregationist candidates (Giles and Buckner, 1993); white opposition to busing (Olzak, Shanahan, and West, 1994); inequalities in housing, educational status, and labor markets (Blalock, 1957; Burr, Galle, and Fossett, 1991; Frisbie and Neidert, 1977; Tienda and Lii, 1987; Wilcox and Roof, 1978); the frequency of crimes against African Americans such as lynching (Corzine, Creech, and Corzine, 1983); and policies intended to ameliorate the status of blacks (Fossett and Kiecolt, 1989; Glaser, 1994; Giles and Evans, 1986; Taylor, 1998). However, as we shall see, little is known about the impact of these or indeed of any contextual effects on perceptions of discrimination. Nor is much known about the impact of contextual factors on black perceptions and attitudes.

Our focus continues to be on neighborhood effects, and we posit that mixed-race populations at the neighborhood level may have more positive effects than those just mentioned. Of course, on a very indirect level, the competitiveness and threat factors that seem to shape the attitudes of whites living in metropolitan areas and counties with large black populations might operate at the neighborhood level, too. Indeed, decades of white flight from the central city seem to be reactions to neighborhood as well as citywide African American populations. Whites living in areas with large black populations felt threatened and fearful, and race relations were most problematic in those areas. Certainly feelings of competition and threat could heighten resentment and lead to feelings that one's own group was discriminated against and that other groups were given special treatment.

Perceptions of Racial Discrimination

The neighborhood also has the potential, however, to shape perceptions of discrimination in more positive ways. There is a difference between the anonymous, amorphous threat that may be posed by large populations of the other race living nearby and the effects of closer, more personal associations at the neighborhood level. The neighborhood may shape perceptions directly. We have already seen that neighborhood context does much to define the amount and content of both casual and more intimate contacts with people of the other race. How one is treated in these contacts certainly contributes directly to shaping perceptions of discrimination. Then, too, in daily activities within the neighborhood, individuals observe how others are treated as well. Do shopkeepers wait on whites first and shun blacks? Do landlords declare fewer vacancies when potential black tenants are looking for housing? Do teachers treat all children fairly and with respect regardless of race?

Indirect information is important, too. One reason that interracial friendship tends to diminish racial prejudice is that by having friends of the other race, one can begin to see the world, at least a little bit, through their eyes. Part of the reason why blacks and whites tend to see the world differently is the wall of separation between them. As mixed neighborhoods promote interracial contact, these walls may be eroded. On the other hand, this same empathy may enable whites to perceive more accurately the discrimination that African Americans do face, so that mixed neighborhoods may actually increase whites' perception of discrimination against blacks.

The social and civic organizational settings of the neighborhood also play a role. Interracial competition and conflict in community groups, as contrasted with smooth working relations, could shape perceptions of discrimination in mixed-race neighborhoods.

Although prior studies of perceptions of discrimination have largely ignored place of residence, Taylor (1998) has found that, other factors being equal, the black proportion of the population of a metropolitan area has little impact on whites' perceptions that blacks are victims of discrimination or deserve special help because of past discrimination. However, according to Taylor, the proportion of African Americans in a metropolitan area is related to traditional antiblack prejudice, opposition to policies to provide extra opportunities for blacks, and the belief that blacks are worse off because they lack the requisite motivation and ability rather than because of any shortcomings of the system.

Analyses of the link between the black proportion of the population and the attitudes and behavior of African Americans are also rare. We know almost nothing about attitudes of African Americans in different racial contexts (but see Wilson, 1971), although one recent study finds a greater incidence of rioting in metropolitan areas where the African

American population is more highly segregated (Olzak, Shanahan, and McEneaney, 1996; Massey and Denton, 1993).

How, then, should neighborhood racial composition be expected to affect residents' perceptions of discrimination? The studies we have just been considering suggest that whites in highly integrated neighborhoods might perceive greater discrimination against whites than do other whites and that blacks in the same neighborhoods might perceive greater discrimination against blacks. However, in mixed-race neighborhoods, both races should be more aware of discrimination against the other group as well as against their own group. Mixed-race neighborhoods, then, should heighten the salience of race for both groups. It may also be that, despite casual and closer personal ties, both blacks and whites feel more threatened in more mixed neighborhoods, where conflict, and consequently perceptions of discrimination and victimization, are likely to be more common.

Perceptions of racial discrimination should also be expected to be more widespread in the city of Detroit than in the suburbs. Among blacks, city dwellers seem likely to have personally experienced more discrimination and more often to have witnessed discrimination against other blacks. Among whites, those living in the city, with its palpable racial tensions, should be expected to perceive more discrimination against both blacks and whites.

CONTINUITY AND CHANGE IN PERCEPTIONS OF DISCRIMINATION

Before probing the impact of residence, it is useful to examine trends in Detroiters' perceptions of discrimination. Were Detroit-area residents more or less likely to perceive racial discrimination in 1992 than they had been 24 years before? Did white and black perceptions of discrimination converge or diverge over that period? Although our ability to answer these questions is limited by the data at hand,[2] the evidence at our disposal contains indications of both continuity and change.

Discrimination against Blacks

Returning to issues raised in the 1968 and the 1969 Detroit Area Survey (DAS), we asked our 1992 interviewees about discrimination against

---

2 Perceptions of discrimination were tapped in both the 1968 and 1969 DAS and our own 1992 survey. However, the wording of these questions differed between the earlier and later surveys and between the 1968 DAS (administered only to blacks) and the 1969 DAS (administered only to whites), and the DAS did not explore all the aspects of discrimination about which we inquired.

Perceptions of Racial Discrimination

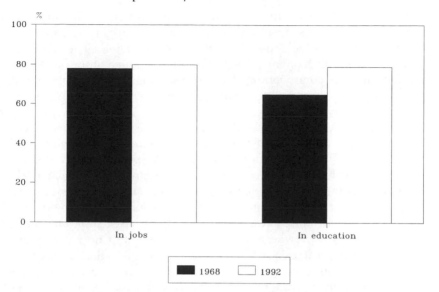

Figure 4.1. Blacks' perceptions of discrimination against blacks, 1968 and 1992.

blacks in the workplace and in education. The 1968 interviewees (all African Americans) were asked how many places in Detroit – many, some, or just a few – they thought would hire a white person before they would hire a Negro even though both have the same qualifications; 78% replied many or some (Figure 4.1). In our 1992 survey, we asked: In this city or community, are blacks in general discriminated against, or not, in getting a job? Of the African American interviewees, 80% perceived that blacks in general were discriminated against in getting a job. Even though "in general" does not necessarily translate into "many places," we were struck by how widespread the perception of job discrimination was in 1992 – at least as widespread, we would argue, as it had been in 1968, despite the implementation of civil rights laws and the introduction of affirmative action procedures in the interim.

We can compare these responses with those of national samples asked a similar but unfortunately not identical question. In 1963 and 1991, respectively, 77 and 63 percent of national samples responded "not as good a chance" when asked whether "blacks have as good a chance as white people in your community to get any kind of job for which they are qualified, or don't you think they have as good a chance?" (Schuman, Steeh, Bobo, and Krysan, 1997: 261–263). The national samples suggested both lower levels of perceived discrimination than in our Detroit sample (although we must be mindful of the difference in question wording) and some decline in the proportion perceiving discrimination. However, the decline was measured from a pre-Civil Rights Act baseline, whereas our survey had a post-Civil Rights Act baseline.[3] The depressed state of the Detroit economy, the ghettoization of much of the black population, and the continuation of racial discrimination undoubtedly all contributed to the persistence among blacks of widespread perceptions of racial inequity in hiring.

The 1992 black interviewees also cited more personal experience with job discrimination than had their 1968 counterparts.[4] In 1968, 26% answered "yes" to the question: Do you think you were ever refused a job or laid off from a job because of being Negro? Approximately the same number (28%) agreed that they had personally missed out on getting the kind of job they wanted and were qualified for. However, in 1992, almost half (47%) responded yes when asked, somewhat more broadly: Have you ever been discriminated against, or not, in getting a job? Reports of greater discrimination in 1992 might reflect the scope of the 1992 question, which interviewees could have construed as referring to discrimination in promotions or work assignments as well as to being refused a job or laid off from a job. At the very least, though, these responses do not point toward a lessening of perceived discrimination against blacks in employment since the late 1960s.

Although the evidence available to us is not nearly as extensive as we would like, we would hazard the conclusion that among blacks, neither the likelihood of having personally experienced discrimination nor the perception of widespread discrimination in the Detroit area diminished much, if at all, after 1968.

In Chapter 2 we observed that whites perceived less housing discrimination against blacks in the 1990s than in the late 1960s. The same was not true of employment discrimination. In 1969, when asked whether they would say there's a lot of or little discrimination against Negroes when they look for a job in the Detroit area, only 12% of whites answered "a lot." In 1992, an almost identical 11% of whites perceived that blacks in general are discriminated against in getting a job (Figure 4.2). Not only did whites' perceptions remain essentially unchanged from 1969 to 1992, but in neither year did whites consider employment discrimination against blacks to be at all widespread. In general, Detroit whites were less likely than the national white population to believe that blacks are discriminated against in jobs. About 20 to 30% of whites in

---

3 Sixty-eight percent of national samples of blacks in 1981 and 1989 also perceived blacks as discriminated against for managerial positions.
4 Recollections of being a victim of discrimination in education were not elicited in the 1968 DAS.

Perceptions of Racial Discrimination

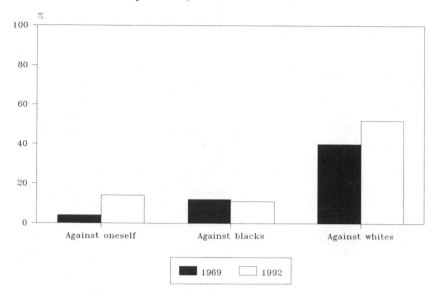

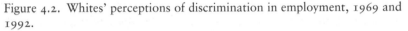

Figure 4.2. Whites' perceptions of discrimination in employment, 1969 and 1992.

national samples during the 1980s and 1990s responded that blacks in their communities do not have as good a chance as whites for jobs for which they are qualified and that blacks are discriminated against in finding managerial jobs (Schuman, Steeh, Bobo, and Krysan, 1997: 158–160).

Perceptions of discrimination in education at least persisted and may even have spread from the 1960s to the 1990s. In 1968, 65% of the African Americans interviewed in the DAS responded "not as good" when asked: Do you think Negroes get as good an education as whites in Detroit schools, or not as good an education? Twenty-four years later, 79% said black children were not getting as good an education and 65% agreed that in general, blacks are discriminated against in getting a quality education. Here again, then, blacks were no less likely, and perhaps were more likely, to feel discriminated against in 1992 than in 1968.

Discrimination against Whites

In the 1969 DAS, only 4% of the white interviewees recalled encountering difficulty in obtaining a job or advancing in a job because blacks had been given an advantage over them, and only about 12% said this had happened to someone they knew personally. However, 40% claimed that such reverse discrimination occurred "fairly often" in the Detroit area.

Race and Place

We repeated these questions in our 1992 survey. Compared with 1969, in 1992 somewhat more whites characterized themselves as victims of reverse discrimination (14%), about the same proportion (14%) said they knew someone who had been a victim of reverse discrimination, and still more (52%) perceived reverse discrimination as happening "fairly often" in the Detroit area.

In sum, while massive changes were transforming the Detroit area between the late 1960s and the early 1990s, Detroit-area residents' perceptions of discrimination against both blacks and whites remained surprisingly stable. In spite of heightened black political power in the city, increased job opportunities for educated African Americans, and increasing interracial contact in a variety of areas, blacks continued to perceive discrimination by whites as common. If anything, blacks were more likely to report discrimination in the early 1990s than in the late 1960s. Whites mirrored national patterns, seeming to become somewhat less sensitive to the occurrence of discrimination against blacks (Schuman and Krysan, 1999). Perhaps they assumed that in the decades since civil rights legislation outlawed discrimination in employment and housing, equality in those areas had become a reality. So from 1968 through 1992, the racial gap in perceptions of discrimination against blacks, if anything, widened. At the same time, more whites came to perceive whites as victims of discrimination, although they saw reverse discrimination as being aimed more at other whites than at themselves personally.

A Closer Look at Perceptions of Discrimination in the 1990s

Most survey information on perceived racial discrimination touches on only a few aspects of daily life, namely, items similar to those we have just examined, pertaining to employment, housing, and education. Though very important, these elements capture only portions of the reality of discrimination. Our 1992 survey, therefore, contained a much more extensive battery of questions tapping perceptions of discrimination (see Appendix B for the exact question wordings). Figure 4.3 shows the responses to the first of these sets of questions, in which we asked both blacks and whites whether they, as individuals, had been victims of racial discrimination of various types, including discrimination in jobs, schools, and housing, and also in various locations where they shopped and received services.

With one exception, the discrimination reported by blacks far outran that reported by whites. In general, one-quarter to one-half of African Americans reported discrimination against themselves in the various settings. Because we asked whether discrimination had "ever" occurred, it

Perceptions of Racial Discrimination

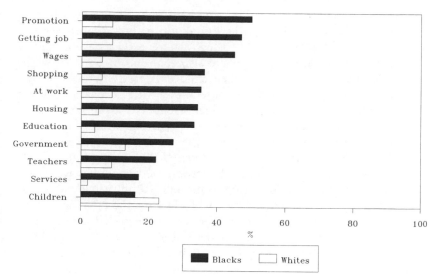

Figure 4.3. Percent of blacks and whites experiencing discrimination.

might be considered surprising that these proportions were not even higher. It should hardly be taken as a cause for celebration, however, that as many as half of the African American interviewees in a major U.S. city in the 1990s would claim to have been personally victimized by a given form of racial discrimination.

The largest proportions of African Americans reported discriminatory treatment in job settings. Fully half said they had been discriminated against in getting promoted, and nearly that many saw themselves as victims of discrimination in getting jobs in the first place and getting equal wages thereafter. On the next lower level were the 32% who perceived discrimination against themselves where they shopped regularly. About the same proportions reported discrimination against themselves in education and in getting decent housing. One in three (35%) also said they had heard racial slurs from a boss or co-workers.

Blacks reported less frequent discrimination against themselves in government offices (27%) and in other places where they received services, such as dentists' and physicians' offices (17%). We also asked those with school-age children whether their children had experienced racial discrimination. About one in five said their children were treated worse by teachers and staff members (22%) or by other children (16%) because of their race.

By contrast, whites perceived little discrimination against themselves. In most instances, fewer than 10% of our white interviewees reported being victims of racial discrimination. The only settings where more than 10% of whites reported discrimination against themselves were government offices (13%) and places where services were received (17%). Antiwhite slurs at work were also reported by 21% of whites, and 23% of white parents said their children were sometimes or often treated badly by other students because of their race. The latter item was the only one on which more whites than blacks reported discrimination.

Given the frequency that one hears about reverse discrimination in daily conversations and media reports, it may seem surprising that so few whites reported experiencing it in this racially polarized area. Yet, in comparison with whites around the nation, Detroit whites were more likely to report such discrimination. Nationally, about 7% of whites said this had happened to them personally. In Detroit the figure was about twice that high. Moreover, about a third of those polled nationwide in the National Opinion Research Center's General Social Survey in the early 1990s considered it "very likely" that "these days" a white person "won't get a job or promotion while an equally or less qualified black person gets one instead." In our survey, a much larger percentage of whites (52%) agreed that whites in Detroit very often encounter difficulty in getting a job or advancing in a job because blacks are given the advantage.

Now, what about perceptions of discrimination, not against oneself, but against blacks and whites more generally? Table 4.1 shows our black and white interviewees' perceptions of discrimination against blacks in the Detroit area and, for comparative purposes, blacks' perceptions of discrimination against themselves personally. Three points stand out in the table. First, the order of perceived discrimination is similar across the three columns. The most common forms of discrimination against blacks, as seen by both blacks and whites, were in getting promoted, getting a job, and getting equal wages. Perceptions of discrimination against blacks in housing and in opportunities for a quality education were somewhat less widespread.

Second, echoing a pattern uncovered by Sigelman and Welch (1991), blacks were much less likely to report discrimination against themselves than against blacks in general. The incidence of blacks' reports of discrimination against themselves, although high (with one-third to one-half of the black interviewees saying they had been victims of a given form of discrimination), was considerably lower than that of reports of discrimination against blacks in general.

Third, whites saw things very differently than did blacks. On average, blacks perceived almost four of the five types of discrimination against blacks that we asked about, but whites perceived less than one. Nearly one white interviewee in five did perceive discrimination against blacks

Perceptions of Racial Discrimination

Table 4.1. *Perceptions of discrimination against blacks (%)*

	Perceptions held by		
	Blacks	Whites	Blacks
	of discrimination against		
In getting ...	Blacks	Blacks	Themselves[a]
Promoted to better positions	82	18	50
A job	80	11	47
Equal wages for a job	79	11	45
Decent housing	71	11	34
A quality education	65	8	33

Note: Question wording: In this city or community, are blacks in general discriminated against or not ... ? Have you yourself ever been discriminated against or not, on the basis of your race?
[a] "Themselves" means as individuals.

in getting promoted, but only about one in ten perceived any other type of discrimination. The great majority of whites, therefore, viewed discrimination against African Americans as an historical artifact rather than a present-day reality.

Reflecting the extreme racial polarization of the Detroit area, the differences shown in Table 4.1 between blacks' and whites' perceptions, which ranged from 57 to 69 percentage points, were much larger than those reported in national surveys. For example, Sigelman and Welch (1991) found differences of 30 to 40 percentage points between blacks' and whites' perceptions of discrimination against blacks, as ascertained in ABC/*Washington Post* surveys – differences comparable to those found by Hochschild (1995: 76–77) in Harris survey questions.

That our interviewees' responses were affected by the polarized and often tense Detroit racial setting becomes all the more obvious in light of the difference between black Detroiters and blacks nationwide in reports of discrimination against themselves. Nationally, about 40% of blacks claimed to have been victims of job and wage discrimination, compared with about 50% in Detroit; about 25% nationally perceived discrimination against themselves in education and housing, compared with about 33% in Detroit (Sigelman and Welch, 1991: 55).

Not surprisingly, perceptions of discrimination against whites were entirely different. As Table 4.2 shows, few whites and few blacks – fewer than 10% of either group – perceived reverse discrimination in any form. Unlike the huge racial gap in perceptions of discrimination against blacks,

Race and Place

Table 4.2. *Perceptions of discrimination against whites (%)*

	Perceptions held by		
	Blacks	Whites	Blacks
	of discrimination against		
In getting ...	Whites	Whites	Themselves[a]
Promoted to better positions	9	9	4
A job	7	4	9
Equal wages for a job	6	6	9
Decent housing	6	2	5
A quality education	6	2	6

Note: Question wording: In this city or community, are whites in general discriminated against or not ... ? Have you yourself ever been discriminated against or not, on the basis of your race?
[a] "Themselves" means as individuals.

African Americans were no less willing than whites to acknowledge some discrimination against whites. For some categories of discrimination, more whites reported discrimination against themselves than against whites in general, although these differences were so small that it would be unwise to make much of them; the more important point is that this is a very different pattern than for blacks, who were more likely to report discrimination against blacks in general than against themselves.

To simplify our analyses of our interviewees' perceptions of discrimination, we constructed three separate scales based on the responses we have just been considering, one of perceived discrimination against blacks generally, one of perceived discrimination against whites generally, and one of perceived discrimination against oneself, simply by totaling each interviewee's yes responses to these items. Scores on the resulting scales ran from 0 (for those who perceived none of the five types of discrimination whatsoever) to 5 (for those who perceived all five types of discrimination). Figure 4.4 shows the mean scale scores separately for blacks and whites. The differences between blacks' and whites' mean scores provide further evidence (as if any were still required) of the racial divide in perceptions of the reality of discrimination. What stands out above all else is that whites perceived whites as almost as victimized by racial discrimination as blacks were – a telling commentary, indeed, on black–white differences in perceptions.

Of course, this pattern is very consistent with the fact that most whites, nationally and even more in Detroit, believe that blacks' failures

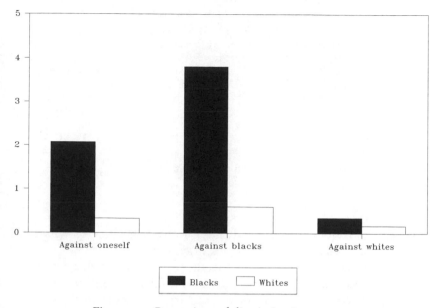

Figure 4.4. Perceptions of discrimination, 1992.

to move ahead in society are their own fault (Schuman and Krysan, 1999). Many whites close their eyes to instances of discrimination or interpret acts of discrimination in other ways, believing that laws forbidding discrimination indeed reflect reality. No doubt, the existence of affirmative action laws and the controversy over these laws reinforce whites' views that if anything, blacks receive an extra benefit, not a penalty, for their race.

THE IMPACT OF PLACE OF RESIDENCE

White residents of the Detroit area have fought long and hard against the perceived threat of blacks moving into their neighborhoods, and these neighborhoods have sometimes been the sites of war-to-the-death racial turf battles. On the other hand, as we have described, interracial contact has increased significantly in the Detroit area, and such contact can lead to better interracial relations.

Table 4.3 shows the differences in perceptions of discrimination between city dwellers and suburbanites of each race. As expected, city dwellers perceived more discrimination than did suburbanites. Both blacks and whites who were city dwellers perceived more discrimination against blacks than they would have if they were suburbanites. Of course, blacks saw more discrimination against blacks than did whites in

83

Table 4.3. *Mean number of types of discrimination perceived by race and residence*

Perceived Discrimination	Blacks		Whites	
	City	Suburbs	City	Suburbs
Against blacks	3.9	3.1[a]	1.3	0.5[a]
Against whites	0.3	0.4	0.6	0.1[a]
Against oneself	2.1	1.8	0.5	0.3

[a] $p < .05$ comparing city dwellers and suburbanites of each race.

both city and suburbs, but clearly city residence heightened whites' as well as blacks' awareness of antiblack discrimination.

There was no significant difference in perceptions of discrimination against themselves between city dwellers and suburbanites of either race. However, among whites but not blacks, city dwellers were significantly more likely than suburbanites to perceive discrimination against whites. As the city's minority group, whites were clearly more aware of antiwhite discrimination, or were at least more likely to interpret certain outcomes as evidence thereof.

These findings fit comfortably with our expectations, illustrating again the salience of racial conflict in the city of Detroit. As a racially mixed, heavily African American city, Detroit offers its residents opportunities for racial conflict and discrimination on a daily basis, and these conflicts, widely publicized by newspapers and the electronic media, are staples in the daily diet of public dialogue in the city.

Besides expecting Detroit residents to perceive more discrimination than residents of the suburbs, we expected blacks to report more discrimination in racially mixed areas than in areas where they constituted either a large majority or a small minority. Opportunities for discrimination abound in interracial settings. So, of course, do opportunities for constructive interaction, but we suspected that when we asked our interviewees to characterize their area in terms of the incidence of racial discrimination, it would be the absolute rather than relative level that mattered to them.

As expected, blacks living in mixed-race neighborhoods were the most likely to perceive discrimination against themselves and against blacks in general. (Table 4.4) These were the very neighborhoods that were likely to have the most interracial tension, including transitional neighbor-

Perceptions of Racial Discrimination

Table 4.4. *Mean number of types of discrimination perceived by race and neighborhood type*

Perceived discrimination	Blacks in nearly all-black	Blacks in mixed	Blacks in largely white	Whites in nearly all-white	Whites in mixed	Whites in largely black
Against blacks	2.9	3.6	3.4	0.5	0.9	1.6
Against whites	0.5	0.3	0.1	0.1	0.5	0.7
Against oneself	1.8	2.2	1.6	0.3	0.8	0.5

Note: All differences are statistically significant, comparing same-race residents of different neighborhood interracial mixtures.

hoods where turf battles were being fought. They were probably also the neighborhoods where whites felt most threatened.[5]

Blacks living in largely white neighborhoods were, in fact, the least likely to perceive racial discrimination against themselves. This could have been an artifact of the affluence of these areas, for majority-white neighborhoods with some black residents were likely to be middle-class and upper middle-class areas. On the other hand, it could be, as research cited earlier in this chapter suggests, that discrimination is less common in areas where blacks pose less of a numerical challenge to whites (although the racial history of Detroit neighborhoods suggests the acute sensitivity of whites to even a handful of black neighbors). Blacks in nearly all-black settings perceived neither as much racial discrimination as those in mixed-race areas nor as little as those in predominantly white areas.

As is consistent with the threat-based hypotheses discussed earlier in this chapter, we also expected whites to report greater discrimination against themselves in mixed-race settings. That expectation, too, was borne out by our survey data.

In sum, blacks' and whites' perceptions of discrimination varied according to place of residence, both in terms of city versus suburbs and in terms of the racial composition of the neighborhood. It remains possible, though, that these perceptual differences might be reflections of other differences, such as individual disparities in age, education, financial status, and the like. Because, as we saw in chapter 1, people with different sociodemographic characteristics live in the city and sub-

5 Mixed-race neighborhoods were defined as 21% to 90% black for our African American sample and 6% to 30% for our white sample.

urbs and in racially mixed and single-race neighborhoods, we need to take account of these other sociodemographic differences before drawing conclusions about neighborhoods. Thus, we need to probe more deeply to see whether these residential differences would remain when we take the effects of other pertinent factors into account.

PREDICTING PERCEPTIONS OF DISCRIMINATION

To make this determination, we test models of perceived discrimination against blacks generally, whites generally, and oneself personally, focusing on each interviewee's scores on the three 0–5 scales. The key predictors in these models are the interviewee's race, residence in the city or the suburbs, and the racial composition of the neighborhood; with respect to the latter, we expected perceptions of discrimination to be highest in the most racially mixed areas and lower in neighborhoods where either only a few blacks or only a few whites lived. We also expected those who had grown up in an integrated neighborhood or who had attended integrated schools to perceive less discrimination than those who had grown up in a single-race setting or had attended nonintegrated schools.

Among the remaining predictors, which we had to select on the basis of scanty prior research, are first, the age and sex of the interviewee. We expected younger blacks to perceive more discrimination than older ones, who we thought would be more likely to compare current conditions with those of prior decades. We also expected younger whites to perceive more reverse discrimination than their older peers. Women are less likely than men to perceive discrimination against themselves (Crosby, 1982), and we generalized this finding to a broader expectation that women would perceive less discrimination in general. Sigelman and Welch (1991) found that for whites, awareness of discrimination against blacks was more widespread among younger people, women, and those with less education; among blacks, awareness of discrimination against oneself was greatest among men, older people, those with more education, and those in difficult financial circumstances. Accordingly, we include the interviewee's level of education and financial status in the model, even though Taylor (1998) concluded that few socioeconomic factors affect whites' perceptions of discrimination against blacks. According to Taylor, only education has a significant bearing on those perceptions, increasing one's chances of perceiving discrimination against blacks. Sigelman and Welch, too, found that blacks with more education are more likely to perceive discrimination (see also Hochschild, 1995), although those lower in other aspects of socioeconomic status are also more likely to perceive discrimi-

Perceptions of Racial Discrimination

Table 4.5. *Predicting perceptions of discrimination against blacks*

Predictor	Blacks		Whites	
	b	(s.e.)	b	(s.e.)
Detroit residence	.90	(.18)[a]	.44	(.17)[a]
Percent black in neighborhood	.03	(.02)[a]	.03	(.01)[a]
Percent black in neighborhood (squared)	−.0003	(.0001)[a]	−.0002	(.0001)[a]
Work in the city	.49	(.23)[a]	.13	(.24)
Work in the suburbs	.34	(.22)	.33	(.21)
Church attendance	.48	(.30)	.12	(.27)
Early-life neighborhood composition	−.25	(.18)	.05	(.19)
Early-life school composition	.06	(.04)	−.04	(.05)
Interracial contact	−.14	(.09)	.05	(.09)
Age	.02	(.01)[a]	−.01	(.01)
Sex	−.47	(.17)[a]	.10	(.16)
Education	.10	(.03)[a]	.03	(.03)
Financial status	−.36	(.12)[a]	−.19	(.12)
Constant	.27	(.71)	.23	(.55)
R squared	.11		.09	

Note: b is the unstandardized regression coefficient, derived from an ordinary–least squares regression analysis, and s.e. is the standard error of the coefficient.

[a] $p < .05$

nation. Among both blacks and whites, those who are not homeowners and those in difficult financial circumstances perceive more discrimination against blacks.

We also include church attendance and interracial contact in the model. We had no firm expectation concerning church attendance, although we suspected that regular churchgoers might perceive less racial discrimination. More importantly, we expected perceptions of discrimination to increase as a function of interracial contact. For one thing, greater contact increases the opportunities for discrimination to occur, and presumably the recognition that discrimination does occur would expand as those opportunities are actualized. For another, those who interact more frequently with members of another race might be predisposed toward empathy with them or might come to empathize with them as a consequence of such contact; in either case, greater interracial contact should be associated with a better understanding of the discrimination that members of another race confront. So, albeit for altogether different reasons, we expected greater interracial contact to be associated with perceptions of more widespread discrimination.

Table 4.5 indicates that among blacks, men and older persons perceived more discrimination against blacks as a group, as expected. Level of education and financial status worked in opposite directions: holding income constant, more highly educated African Americans were more likely to perceive discrimination against blacks; holding education constant, the less affluent perceived more discrimination. The impact of financial status is not difficult to understand, given the natural tendency of those who are struggling to make a living to look for external explanations. By contrast, the more highly educated presumably have a relatively sophisticated grasp of societal problems, and this might account for their increased perception of discrimination.

We saw in Tables 4.3 and 4.4 that blacks living in the city of Detroit and in racially mixed neighborhoods perceived more discrimination against blacks than did suburban blacks and those living in segregated neighborhoods. The same patterns are evident in Table 4.5. Other factors being equal, African Americans who lived in the city outscored their suburban counterparts by almost a full point (.90) on the 0–5 scale of perceived discrimination against blacks. Some simple calculations based on the regression coefficients for the two neighborhood racial composition variables reveal that, also as predicted, blacks living in racially mixed neighborhoods perceived greater antiblack discrimination than blacks living in predominantly black or predominantly white neighborhoods. In fact, the tipping point for perceptions of discrimination against blacks came exactly at a neighborhood composition of 50% black and 50% white. Below that point (i.e., at less than 50% black), perceptions of discrimination rose as a function of the African American percentage of a neighborhood's residents; above that point, they fell.

Thus, as predicted, blacks living in predominantly black neighborhoods or in predominantly white neighborhoods perceived less discrimination against blacks than did blacks living in racially mixed neighborhoods. We view this as reflecting a tendency for blacks in well-integrated neighborhoods (that is, neighborhoods where both blacks and whites have a substantial presence) to be more threatening by their very presence to whites who do not want to live in a racially mixed neighborhood. Whites in such neighborhoods may express their hostility quite overtly, and as we have seen, Detroit's neighborhoods have historically been racial battlegrounds. It is somewhat ironic that, as we discussed earlier, blacks prefer racially mixed neighborhoods to those where they constitute a small minority or an overwhelming majority. Of course, in expressing their ideal, African Americans probably are assuming reason-

Table 4.6. *Predicting perceptions of discrimination against oneself*

Predictor	Blacks		Whites	
	b	(s.e.)	b	(s.e.)
Detroit residence	.29	(.17)[a]	.02	(.10)
Percent black in neighborhood	.05	(.02)[a]	−.01	(.01)
Percent black in neighborhood (squared)	−.0004	(.0001)[a]	.0001	(.0001)
Work in the city	.34	(.23)	.01	(.14)
Work in the suburbs	.23	(.21)	−.32	(.12)[a]
Church attendance	−.05	(.29)	.17	(.15)
Early-life neighborhood composition	−.15	(.18)	.05	(.11)
Early-life school composition	.05	(.04)	.03	(.03)
Interracial contact	.14	(.09)	.12	(.05)[a]
Age	.02	(.01)[a]	−.004	(.003)
Sex	−.84	(.16)[a]	−.19	(.09)[a]
Education	.05	(.03)[a]	.03	(.02)[a]
Financial status	−.38	(.11)[a]	−.17	(.07)[a]
Constant	−.25	(.72)	.46	(.31)
R squared	.09		.09	

Note: b is the unstandardized regression coefficient, derived from an ordinary–least squares regression analysis, and s.e. is the standard error of the coefficient
[a] $p < .05$.

able neighbors no matter what the racial configuration of the neighborhood may be.

According to Table 4.3, whites living in the city of Detroit were more likely to perceive discrimination against blacks than were other whites. That finding, too, is reconfirmed in Table 4.5, though the impact is only half as large as that recorded for African American interviewees (.44 versus .90). Again, living in the city seems to have heightened the salience of racial issues and racial slights, for whites as well as blacks. Whites' perceptions of discrimination against blacks were also affected by residential integration. As was true for blacks, whites in racially mixed neighborhoods were the most likely to perceive discrimination against blacks, and those in more homogeneous neighborhoods were progressively less so. We interpret this as meaning that although racial tensions are often strongest in mixed-race neighborhoods, the increased interracial contact in those settings means that whites living there have opportunities to observe racial discrimination and to hear about instances from their acquaintances. Whites sheltered in all-white neighborhoods have neither opportunity.

However, whereas blacks' perceptions were affected by several factors contained in the model, for whites nothing else mattered – even place of work, age, sex education, or financial status.

Table 4.6 shows the results for parallel analyses of perceptions of discrimination against oneself personally. For blacks, the results so closely resemble those we have just been discussing for perceptions of discrimination against blacks in general that an extensive presentation of results would be redundant. It should suffice to note: (1) For blacks, living in the city (rather than the suburbs) and the racial composition of the neighborhood continued to have major impacts; (2) city versus suburban residence had less of an impact on perceptions of discrimination against oneself than against blacks in general; and (3) African American women perceived substantially less discrimination against themselves than did African American men (–.84 versus –.47).

As for whites' perceptions of discrimination against themselves, Table 4.6 reveals that some of the same factors that shaped African Americans' perceptions of discrimination against themselves influenced whites as well. Those who were better off financially were less likely to consider themselves victims of discrimination, which is consistent with our expectation that the least economically secure would feel the most threatened by the other race; as with African Americans, when financial status was held constant, more highly educated whites perceived more discrimination against themselves. Unlike black women, who perceived less discrimination than black men, among whites men were less likely to perceive discrimination against themselves than were women. Whites who interacted more with African Americans also reported more discrimination against themselves. If interracial contact is assumed to ameliorate harsh race relations, this should come as a surprise. However, interracial contact obviously opens new opportunities for unpleasant as well as pleasant contact.

According to Tables 4.3 and 4.4, city whites were slightly more likely than suburban whites to perceive discrimination against themselves, and whites in mixed neighborhoods perceived substantially more discrimination against themselves than did those living in areas where one race was numerically predominant. Neither of these differences, however, persists when other factors are taken into account in the analyses summarized in Table 4.6, although whites working in the suburbs did perceive less discrimination against themselves than those not working or working in the city.

Finally, Table 4.7 shows the results for perceptions of discrimination against whites in general. Because few interviewees of either race per-

Table 4.7. *Predicting perceptions of discrimination against whites*

Predictor	Blacks		Whites	
	b	(s.e.)	b	(s.e.)
Detroit residence	-.09	(.11)	.33	(.11)[a]
Percent black in neighborhood	-.01	(.01)	.01	(.01)
Percent black in neighborhood (squared)	.0001	(.0001)	-.0001	(.0001)
Work in the city	-.04	(.14)	.04	(.15)
Work in the suburbs	-.08	(.14)	.10	(.13)
Church attendance	-.08	(.18)	.22	(.17)
Early-life neighborhood composition	-.14	(.11)	.18	(.12)
Early-life school composition	.04	(.03)	-.002	(.03)
Interracial contact	.09	(.06)	.12	(.06)[a]
Age	.002	(.003)	.005	(.004)
Sex	.05	(.10)	-.02	(.10)
Education	-.06	(.02)[a]	.01	(.02)
Financial status	.02	(.07)	-.18	(.07)[a]
Constant	.98	(.44)[a]	-.25	(.34)
R squared	.04		.10	

Note: b is the unstandardized regression coefficient, derived from an ordinary least squares regression analysis, and s.e. is the standard error of the coefficient.
[a] $p < .05$.

ceived much discrimination against whites, the incidences we were trying to predict were quite infrequent. Among African Americans, only level of education registered a significant impact; those with more education were less likely to see whites as discriminated against in the Detroit area. Among whites, it was not education but financial status that mattered; whites in more problematic economic circumstances were significantly more likely to believe that whites, in general, were discriminated against. Again, too, whites who had more contact with African Americans perceived more discrimination against whites, as did whites living in the city of Detroit.

CONCLUSIONS

Before concluding this analysis, we should acknowledge what has been called the Achilles heel of contextual research, namely, the problem of self-selection (Huckfeldt, 1986: 61). Perhaps contexts are related to perceptions about race because people choose to place themselves in contexts where their attitudes are most compatible rather than having their attitudes shaped by the contexts in which they find themselves.

Although we will address the problem of self-selection in more detail in the chapters that follow, insofar as this chapter is concerned it seems highly unlikely that self-selection is biasing our findings. It would make no sense for either blacks or whites to move to the very neighborhoods where they see discrimination against themselves, that is, racially mixed city neighborhoods. If anything, one would expect people to move away from areas where they perceive greater discrimination.

In this chapter we have examined the extent to which blacks and whites saw the two races as victims of discrimination. We have been particularly concerned with the manner in which these perceptions were affected by where our interviewees lived. Because the environment of the city of Detroit differs so radically from that of the Detroit suburbs, we expected to find a sizable gap between perceptions in the city and the suburbs. Detroit has long been a hotbed of racial antagonism, where intergroup conflicts are played out daily. Moreover, blacks are numerically and politically dominant in Detroit, potentially leaving white residents of the city feeling outnumbered, powerless, and discriminated against. On the other hand, whites dominate the city's economy, with the majority of African Americans living in poverty. We are not surprised, then, that city versus suburban residence was related to a heightened sense of racial discrimination. Blacks in the city perceived more discrimination against themselves and against blacks in general than did suburban blacks, and whites in the city perceived more discrimination against whites than did suburban whites. However, city whites perceived more discrimination against blacks as well as against whites. Thus, living in Detroit seems to have heightened the salience of race and to have engendered a city-based feeling of victimization that transcended race.

We have also explored the effect of neighborhood racial composition on perceptions of discrimination. This factor, we have discovered, had a greater effect on perceptions of discrimination against blacks than against whites. As is consistent with the history of Detroit's neighborhoods as contested turfs, as whites sought to hang on to their old neighborhoods and blacks sought new and better housing alternatives, racial hostility was perceived as greater in neighborhoods with sizable proportions of both blacks and whites. That is, both black and white residents of racially mixed neighborhoods acknowledged more antiblack discrimination than did blacks and whites living in mostly black or mostly white neighborhoods. On the other hand, residential context had little to do with perceptions of discrimination against whites, perhaps because housing and housing discrimination were not pressing issues for whites.[6] In addition, as some indication that living in mixed-race neighborhoods does foster a more common set of views of the world, blacks living in the city and in mixed-race neighborhoods were more likely to acknowledge discrimination against blacks as well as whites.

The findings reported in this chapter provide new evidence of the impact of residential context on racial attitudes. That context, as these findings have made clear, has the potential to shape not only whites' attitudes about African Americans and African Americans' attitudes about whites but also the attitudes of each about their own group and, indeed, their own personal situation. In short, in the Detroit area, the extent to which one felt like a victim or a member of a victimized group and the extent to which one perceived members of the other race as victims of discrimination depended on one's place as well as one's race.

6 Only 2% of whites perceived that whites were discriminated against in housing in the Detroit area.

5

Black Racial Solidarity

"Detroit has helped nurture a new black mentality. More than any other city, blacks here make an issue of where you live. If you're with us, you'll find a place in the city" (Arthur Johnson, a former president of the Detroit NAACP, quoted by Chafets, 1990: 28). This statement captures the centrality of place in race relations in Detroit, the tendency of many black Detroiters to judge both blacks and whites by where they choose to live. The distinction between city and suburb separates those who live in an overwhelmingly black central city that has been run by blacks for several decades from those who live in smaller suburban communities, some of which have large proportions of African Americans but none of which possess the highly visible black political leadership of the city.

In this chapter, we probe the impact of residence on African Americans' sense of solidarity with other African Americans. If blacks are more likely to feel ties of solidarity with other blacks when they live in more segregated settings, then such ties will be loosened by the movement of blacks to the suburbs. But perhaps feelings of solidarity are more intense among blacks who live in *less* segregated settings. Many black college students at majority-white colleges, for example, seem to feel a strong sense of racial solidarity. If less segregation promotes solidarity, then black solidarity should, if anything, be enhanced by suburbanization.

We explore these alternatives in this chapter. We assume that mixed-race residential neighborhoods change interracial relations. They facilitate interracial contact and they promote an awareness of discrimination by both blacks and whites, an outcome suggestive of both heightened racial empathy and heightened racial tension.

The neighborhood context certainly has the same potential to shape intraracial dynamics as interracial ones. Neighborhoods offer opportunities for casual and intimate contact with people of one's own race as well as with those of the other race, as well as opportunities to participate in community groups. In single-race neighborhoods, almost all of these

94

interactions are necessarily with people of one's own race. In mixed-race neighborhoods, opportunities for interacting with members of one's own race decline and opportunities for interracial interaction increase. Does this dynamic mean that individuals will have a greater sense of identity with members of their own race in one setting or another? Does spatial concentration promote a sense of solidarity among blacks?

BLACK RACIAL SOLIDARITY

Group solidarity is an especially important aspect of the social attitudes of any ethnically or racially defined group. Those who feel a stronger sense of group identity, consciousness, or solidarity have higher rates of political participation (Olsen, 1970; Shingles, 1981; Verba and Nie, 1972), at least under certain conditions (Gurin, Miller, and Gurin, 1980; Miller, Gurin, Gurin, and Malanchuk, 1981). For blacks, group solidarity structures vote choice in local elections, even when the opposing candidates are African Americans (Chesley, 1993; but see Jackson, 1987), and in some national elections. Blacks with unusually high levels of racial consciousness were among Jesse Jackson's most enthusiastic supporters in his 1984 and 1988 campaigns for the Democratic presidential nomination (Gurin, Hatchett, and Jackson, 1989; Jackson, 1987). Moreover, they are more likely to be liberal and Democratic than those with a weaker sense of racial identification (Tate, 1993). Blacks with a stronger sense of racial solidarity are also more likely to see themselves as victims of discrimination, to perceive widespread discrimination against blacks as a group, to belong to organizations intended to improve the status of blacks, to favor government aid to assist blacks, and to prefer developing the black community rather than pursuing black integration into the broader society (Bledsoe, Welch, Sigelman, and Combs, 1994; Tate, 1993).

Most African Americans feel some sense of solidarity with other African Americans (Dillingham, 1981).[1] What we have chosen to call racial solidarity – and others have referred to as black identity, black separatism, black autonomy, or even black nationalism – was the subject of research long before our study (e.g., Clark and Clark, 1939; Hraba and Grant, 1970; London and Hearn, 1977; Sampson and Milan, 1975; Carter and Helms, 1988). Most prior research has been conducted since the 1960s, when the civil rights movement, with its "Black Power" and "Black Is Beautiful" slogans, altered the ways in which African Ameri-

---

[1] We prefer the term *solidarity*, which refers to a union or community of interests, responsibilities, objectives, or standards, because it reflects an attachment deeper than *identification* or *consciousness*. A person may identify with a certain group or be conscious of his or her membership in the group but feel little attachment to it and be unwilling to sacrifice individual interest and prerogatives for it.

cans perceived themselves, one another, and their collective situation. Several studies have focused on the conditions that encourage feelings of racial solidarity, other studies have attempted to identify various consequences of these feelings, and still other studies have done both. Little of that research, however, has focused on the impact of residential context.

Racial solidarity has been linked to socioeconomic status, but not in consistent ways. Allen, Dawson, and Brown (1989), analyzing data from the 1979–1980 National Survey of Black Americans, observed that solidarity was less intense among more affluent blacks. Tate (1993: 28, 158) found that more highly educated African Americans were likely to identify with other blacks but less likely to support black political parties. In an analysis of data from the 1984 National Black Election Study, Gurin et al. (1989) found black nationalism more widespread among more highly educated blacks and among black males. However, Dillingham (1981) observed only a weak relationship between race consciousness and social class among black adults in the Chicago area: The overwhelming majority in all social classes scored high on a scale of race consciousness, although (contrary to the pattern observed by Allen et al., 1989) race consciousness was somewhat more pronounced among blacks who were better off economically (see also Jaynes and Williams, 1989).

Several studies have explored the possibility that the development of black racial solidarity or identity is rooted in the black church (Allen et al., 1989; Demo and Hughes, 1990; Ellison, 1991; Wilcox and Gomez, 1990; Harris, 1994; Reese and Brown, 1995). The leadership and emotional stamina that sustained the civil rights movement were supplied, in large degree, by the black church (Lincoln and Mamiya, 1990), which underwent a metamorphosis during the movement years, replacing its traditional theology of resignation and accommodation with a call for collective racial mobilization. The church played a significant role in black consciousness in the 1960s, provided an organizational foundation for many black candidates for elected office, and was a key factor in Jesse Jackson's campaigns for the presidency (Harris, 1994; Reese and Brown, 1995; Morris, 1984; Tate, 1993). In the 1990s, the church continued to embrace and nurture racial solidarity among African Americans. Prior to our study, though, no substantial evidence had been found of a church-based link to individual differences in black solidarity.

Similarly, little was known about how black solidarity is shaped by segregated housing patterns or by the decline of such patterns, although Demo and Hughes (1990) reported that both preadult and adult contacts with whites shape feelings of solidarity. In a study of a small group of African American schoolchildren in predominantly white suburbs, Banks (1984) observed that increased assimilation was associated with less positive attitudes toward blacks. From the work of Lau (1989), though, we

Black Racial Solidarity

extracted the first of three competing hypotheses about the impact of place of residence on black solidarity. Lau explored the relationship between the racial composition of the census tract in which black interviewees in the 1972 and 1976 American National Election Studies resided and their sense of racial identification. The tendency of blacks to identify with blacks as a group increased, he found, as the black share of the population increased, although this positive impact topped out in tracts with approximately 70% black residents, after which the probability of identifying with blacks as a group declined somewhat.

From Lau's research we extracted a *social density* hypothesis, which posited that blacks' sense of racial solidarity should increase as a function of the black share of the population in the area where they live (although we had to remain alert to the possibility of a tipping point). For a ghetto black, the boundaries between oneself and outsiders are formidable, as one experiences an overwhelming amount of contact with other blacks in all aspects of social, economic, and political life but relatively little contact with nonblacks (Shibutani, 1987: 131; Sigelman, Welch, Bledsoe, and Combs, 1996). This saturation of intraracial contact could precipitate a high degree of group awareness and cohesiveness. By contrast, for an African American residing in a predominantly white area, the relative infrequency of interaction with other African Americans could diminish the saliency of race.

The social density hypothesis, usually applied to ethnic or nationality groups, is based on the simple but compelling idea that for a social group to become significant on an individual's perceptual horizon, the group must be a highly visible and regular feature of the individual's perceptual universe. Visibility and regularity are both enhanced by spatial concentration, which encourages the development of institutions that reinforce and perpetuate the group. Several studies (e.g., Lieberson, 1963; Yancey, Ericksen, and Juliani, 1976) have made a strong case that residential context plays a key role in maintaining ethnic solidarity in American cities, and similar arguments have been made specifically for Slavic Americans (Pavalko, 1981), German Americans (Conzen, 1979), French Canadians (Driedger, 1979), and Jewish Canadians (Driedger, 1980). Spatial concentration can also be important in warding off marriages outside the group, which can undermine group solidarity (Pavalko, 1981).

Of course, the social density hypothesis might well be an example of reverse causality. Where one lives would, for many people, be a matter of choice, and one's sense of solidarity with a social group could well be among the factors shaping that residential choice. For example, in Northern Ireland, religious identification exercises a "major influence" on residential preferences (Stringer, Cornish, and Finlay, 1991). We will address this self-selection effect in more detail later.

97

Social salience offered an alternative hypothesis, to the effect that blacks living in suburban and mixed-race neighborhoods would feel a greater sense of solidarity with other blacks. The idea underlying this interpretation is that race takes on special importance for blacks in mixed-race communities (Lau, 1989; Tajfel, 1981).[2] These would be the group members who virtually every day are reminded by their (sometimes unpleasant) contact with nonblacks that they are different from most of the people around them and that they share a common identity and common destiny with other blacks.

The social salience hypothesis, too, has had a long, although less fully documented, history. The tendency of group members to unite and engage in collective action when faced with another group of threatening size was certainly borne out in the case of white Southerners during the pre–civil rights era. White southerners who lived in areas with the largest number of blacks, often areas where whites were in the minority, were the most single-minded in their opposition to the civil rights movement and exhibited great unity of purpose in combating it (see chapter 4). The race issue was far more salient for them than it was for whites who lived in parts of the South that had relatively few black residents, and this greater salience produced greater cohesiveness among them.

We labeled the third hypothesis *identity supremacy*. This hypothesis is one of no difference, the idea being that group identity and loyalty are so important and enduring that group solidarity should not be expected to vary as a function of spatial concentration. That is, group members would be aware of their identity and would support collective efforts on behalf of the group regardless of how frequently they came into contact with other group members. The underlying assumption here is that the historic experiences that African Americans share are of such tragic proportions that their sense of collective identification would be unaffected by the character of the neighborhoods in which they lived. Blacks living in the suburbs would not necessarily live close to, or have close contact with, whites, and living in the suburbs would not spare them from experiencing racial distinctions and discrimination. If racism and discrimination know no geographic bounds, then their psychological effects on blacks seem unlikely to have been eradicated by a move to the suburbs or by having grown up apart from a large concentration of other blacks.

In sum, the social density, social salience, and identity supremacy hypotheses equipped us with three different interpretations of the relationship between where blacks live and their sense of solidarity with

2 Tajfel explains that identification with a particular group, especially a minority group, depends on the perceived clarity of the differences between the group and the rest of society.

other blacks. According to the social density hypothesis, blacks living in more racially segregated settings should feel greater solidarity with other blacks. Given what we have learned about the impact of neighborhood context on attitudes about race thus far, we expect that the social density explanation will find the largest support. We expect that, on balance, interracial contact facilitated by mixed-race neighborhoods will erode rather than build racial barriers.

The social salience hypothesis, by contrast, makes exactly the opposite prediction. The identity supremacy hypothesis rejects both of these ideas, viewing residential context as of little consequence in shaping the sense of racial solidarity.

MEASURES

Our 1992 Detroit survey contained the same six items that Allen et al. (1989) used as indicators of black autonomy, and from our black interviewee's responses to these questions we constructed a measure of racial solidarity.[3] Listed in the order in which they appeared in our survey, the six items were as follows:

Blacks should always vote for black candidates when they run.
Black people should choose to shop in black-owned stores whenever possible.
Black parents should give their children African names.
Black children should study black history.
Black children should study an African language.
Blacks should marry other blacks.

As can be seen in Table 5.1, agreement with these statements varied widely from item to item. Only 16% of the black interviewees agreed that blacks should always vote for black candidates, and only half that many agreed that black children should be given African names. However, about four blacks in ten agreed that blacks should marry other blacks, and more than half agreed that black children should study an African language and that blacks should try to patronize black-owned businesses. Almost everyone thought that black children should study black history. The proportion of blacks favoring study of an African lan-

---

3 There are almost as many conceptualizations of black autonomy or solidarity as there are researchers on the topic. We choose to focus on solidarity rather than on, for example, the concept of "linked fate," how closely the individual feels to other blacks and how closely the individual believes that other blacks' fates are aligned with their own (Tate, 1993).

Table 5.1. *Responses to questions about black solidarity*

Blacks should...	Strongly agree	Agree	Neither agree nor disagree	Disagree	Strongly disagree
Have children study black history	54	43	1	2	0
Marry other blacks	16	24	40	17	3
Shop in black-owned stores	16	45	17	20	3
Have children study an African language	12	42	23	22	2
Vote for black candidates	4	12	18	55	11
Give children African names	1	7	35	47	10

guage was strangely high in light of minimal support for African names.[4] The biggest differences between whites and blacks are on the items on shopping in black-owned stores, which only 16% of whites approved of, and having children study an African language, which only 18% approved of.

Tate (1993: 156) has presented national comparison data from 1984 for three of the items. Of a national sample of African Americans, 56% agreed that African Americans should shop in black-owned stores wherever possible, about the same proportion as in our Detroit sample (61%); 36% of the national sample agreed that black children should learn an African language, considerably below the 54% in our Detroit sample; and 19% of the national sample compared with 16% of our interviewees agreed that blacks should always vote for black candidates when they run. Thus, on two of the three items, our 1992 Detroit sample closely resembled a 1984 national sample of African Americans. On the remaining item, our Detroit-area interviewees were considerably more likely to express racial solidarity.

We summed each of our Detroit black interviewee's responses to these six questions to form a composite scale of black solidarity, on which scores could range from a low of 0, for those who strongly disagreed with all six statements, to a high of 24, for those who strongly agreed with all six statements. The mean scale score of 13.6 meant that on these six items

---

4 It is of some interest that the rank order of responses by whites to these items was the same as that of blacks. Whites generally approve very much of having children study black history, are evenly divided about blacks marrying other blacks, and are unenthusiastic about the other indicators.

the typical response was slightly above the midpoint of the scale, that is, it leaned somewhat in the direction of agreement, and the standard deviation of 3.3 indicated that most scores fell between 10 and 17.

As in chapters 3 and 4, our analysis focused on whether our interviewees lived in the city or the suburbs and on the racial composition of their neighborhood. We also took into account a number of other factors that seemed to have the potential to affect our interviewees' standing on the racial solidarity scale. We included ten such factors in the model, most of which were the same as those we employed in chapters 3 and 4 and for which we have already referred interested readers to Appendix B for detailed measurement information. Seven of these were individual traits and three were measures of childhood socialization experiences. Two of the individual traits were place-related: whether the interviewee worked in the city and whether the interviewee worked in the suburbs. The other five were age, sex, education, financial status, and religiosity; of these, only religiosity was not used in chapters 3 and 4, where we considered churchgoing per se rather than religiosity to be the pertinent factor.

We expected blacks who worked in the suburbs to express less and those who worked in the city more racial solidarity. In prior studies, older blacks were observed to be more supportive of symbolic acts reaffirming racial identity (Gurin et al., 1989; Jaynes and Williams, 1989; but see Tate, 1993: 28, 158, for mixed findings), perhaps because many of them have experienced first hand the blatant racism of an earlier era and lived through the civil rights movement era as well; for these reasons, we expected to find a positive connection between age and racial solidarity. Similarly, black men have been shown to exhibit deeper "nationalist" sentiments than black women (Gurin et al., 1989; again, Tate, 1993: 28, presents more mixed findings). Previous studies have failed to document a consistent link between socioeconomic status or its various components, such as level of education, income, or financial stringency, and racial identity or solidarity, but we controlled for these factors nonetheless because, as we have seen, they were strongly related to suburban residence. Finally, there has been little evidence linking racial solidarity to religiosity (Allen et al., 1989; Demo and Hughes, 1990; Ellison, 1991; Wilcox and Gomez, 1990), but, like others before us, we wanted to explore the possibility that black churches, which tend to be highly politicized, are catalysts promoting higher levels of group consciousness, just as when they were in the forefront of the civil rights movement.[5]

---

5 On the measurement of religiosity (and of having grown up in the South), see Appendix B.

Race and Place

The three childhood socialization experience factors in the model all related to the racial environment in which an interviewee had been raised: whether he or she grew up in the South (the other new predictor in the model), the racial mix of the neighborhood in which he or she grew up, and the racial mix of the schools he or she attended.

FINDINGS

Unfortunately, these racial solidarity items were not employed in earlier surveys in the Detroit area, so we have no longitudinal comparisons to offer. We can, of course, compare our respondents on our key residential variables. Scores on the index of racial solidarity did not vary as a function of living in the city or in a suburb. The mean score was 13.5 for city residents and 13.9 for suburbanites, essentially identical. Neither did these scores vary significantly among those who lived in all-black neighborhoods (where the mean was 13.7), nearly all-white neighborhoods (14.2), or mixed neighborhoods (13.5). However, these simple comparisons could mask real differences, for feelings of solidarity with other African Americans seem likely to be related to many of the socioeconomic and other factors we just described. Accordingly, holding those factors constant could reveal some significant effects of race.

Indeed, that is what we found. The two columns headed (1) in Table 5.2 summarize the results of our initial analysis of racial solidarity, in which the predictors were the African American percentage of the interviewee's neighborhood[6] and whether the interviewee lived in the city of Detroit or the suburbs, along with the 10 control variables just listed.

Four of the control variables and one of the two residential context variables registered statistically significant impacts on racial solidarity. As expected, men scored higher than women; controlling for the effects of the other variables in the model, we found a male–female differential of approximately 1.3 points on the 0 to 24 scale. Those who worked in the city of Detroit, as opposed to those working in the suburbs or not working outside the home, also scored higher, by almost 1 point. Similarly, those who grew up near white families scored two-thirds of a point lower than those who grew up in an all-black neighborhood. Religiosity also affected racial solidarity: Between two blacks, one of whom was perfectly average in terms of religiosity whereas the other's religiosity score was a full standard deviation above the mean, the latter would be

---

6 To determine whether, as Lau (1989) had concluded, the density of the group might have a tipping point, we experimented with including a squared term in the model. This produced no evidence whatsoever of a tipping point, so in light of the complexities that the polynomial term introduced into our presentation of results, we did not retain it in the version of the model shown in Table 5.2.

Black Racial Solidarity

Table 5.2. *Predicting black racial solidarity*

Predictor	(1) b	(1) (s.e.)	(2) b	(2) (s.e.)	(3) b	(3) (s.e.)
Detroit residence	−.40	(.35)	−2.36	(.88)[a]	−1.99	(.88)[a]
Percent black in neighborhood	.02	(.01)[a]	.02	(.01)[a]	.01	(.006)[a]
Work in the city	.94	(.45)[a]	.92	(.45)[a]	.88	(.45)[a]
Work in the suburbs	.27	(.43)	.17	(.43)	.31	(.43)
Age	−.01	(.01)	−.03	(.01)[a]	−.03	(.01)[a]
Sex	−1.32	(.34)[a]	−1.34	(.33)[a]	−1.15	(.33)[a]
Education	−.01	(.06)	.0002	(.06)	.01	(.06)
Financial status	.06	(.18)	.03	(.18)	.17	(.17)
Religiosity	.51	(.19)[a]	.53	(.19)[a]	.61	(.19)[a]
Early life neighborhood composition	−.67	(.34)[a]	−.58	(.34)[a]	−.38	(.35)
Early life school composition	.14	(.08)	.12	(.08)	.14	(.09)
Southern upbringing	−.37	(.42)	−.50	(.42)	−.58	(.42)
Interaction between age and Detroit residence			.04	(.02)[a]	.04	(.02)[a]
Contact with whites					−.47	(.18)[a]
Preferred neighborhood racial mix					−.95	(.27)[a]
Constant	13.67	(1.17)[a]	14.45	(1.20)[a]	17.14	(1.44)[a]
R squared	.07		.08		.13	

Note. *b* is the unstandardized regression coefficient, derived from an ordinary–least squares regression analysis, followed in parentheses by the standard error of the coefficient.
[a]$p < .05$.

expected to outscore the former by 0.5 point on the black solidarity scale. Because most blacks presumably attend all-black or nearly all-black churches, being a part of the church and taking one's membership seriously seem to have intensified the sense of community with other blacks. Thus, religiosity affected racial solidarity in the manner that had often been predicted but had rarely been observed. Neither the remaining control variables, including age, education, and economic status, nor two of the three childhood socialization measures displayed any independent impact on racial solidarity, although we shall presently have more to say about age.

This brings us back to the two variables of central interest, residence in the city or the suburbs and the racial composition of one's neighborhood. (See also Bledsoe, Welch, Sigelman, and Combs, 1994, for an earlier explanation of these data.) The nonsignificant coefficient for the city versus suburbs term in the first model suggested that whether one lived in the city of Detroit or the suburbs did not significantly affect one's sense of racial solidarity, at least once the proportion blacks in the neighborhood is accounted for. Initial appearances proved deceptive, however, when we pursued this point further.

Prior to undertaking the first analysis summarized in Table 5.2, we fitted separate models for residents of the city and the suburbs. Comparing the results of these separate models, we noted that every predictor except age had essentially the same effect on city dwellers as on suburbanites. In the city, the age coefficient was positive, though not significantly so, but in the suburbs it was significant and negative. In light of this difference, it seemed likely that we could learn more about the effects of both age and urban or suburban residence if we added an interactive age–place of residence term to the model summarized in the first two columns of Table 5.2. As can be seen by comparing the coefficients in the next two columns, designated (2), in the table, this refitting did affect the estimated impacts of age and city or suburban residence.

The significant coefficient for the age–place of residence interaction term means that the effect of where someone lived depended on how old he or she was. The easiest way to grasp this interactive effect is to imagine a perfectly typical interviewee in our survey, that is, someone who had a mean score on every variable in the model except age and place of residence. For purposes of illustration, let us assume that this individual was either 28 or 64 years old, that is, one standard deviation below or one standard deviation above the mean age of 46, and lived in either the city of Detroit or the suburbs, that is, had a score of either 1 or 0 on the place of residence variable. Some simple mathematics revealed that a 28-year-old black suburbanite would be expected to have outscored an otherwise identical resident of the city by more than a full point on the racial solidarity scale. By contrast, a 64-year-old black suburbanite would be expected to have had a slightly lower racial solidarity score than an otherwise identical resident of the city. Thus, incorporating the interactive impact of age and place of residence into the model led us to rethink the link between racial solidarity and living in the city or the suburbs. The older the individual, the less living in the city versus the suburbs affected his or her sense of racial solidarity. Among younger blacks, racial solidarity was significantly higher in the suburbs, which is consistent with the social salience hypothesis, but among older blacks, there was at most a slight urban–suburban differential in racial solidarity, which is consistent with the identity supremacy hypothesis.

One possible interpretation of these results is that age interacts with the length of time one has lived in the neighborhood. (Age and time lived in the neighborhood are correlated at .37.) If the social density argument is true, it would make sense, for example, that the longer African Americans had lived in the suburbs, the less solidarity they would feel with other African Americans, and the longer they had lived in the inner city, the greater solidarity they would feel.

Unfortunately, we could not fully test this interpretation because, although we know how long respondents lived in their current neighborhood, we do not know the kind of neighborhood they had lived in before. Many people move from one neighborhood to another within the same community or between similar types of communities. Therefore, we cannot assume that time lived in the neighborhood equals time lived in the particular racial mix of the current neighborhood. Moreover, the correlation between time lived in the neighborhood and racial solidarity is weak and nonsignificant and does not hold up in a multivariate context. Thus, we can only suggest that the interactive effect of age, to the extent that it is a real age effect and not a time in residence effect, may be less a generational than a life cycle effect. The racial mix in the residential context in which one ages affects one's degree of racial solidarity.

Controlling for the effects of the remaining predictors in the model, we found that those who lived in neighborhoods with more blacks had significantly higher racial solidarity scores, which is consistent with the social density hypothesis. However, this effect was modest. The regression coefficient of .02 meant that for every 1-point increase in the percentage of one's neighbors who were African Americans, one's score on the racial solidarity scale would increase by only .02; thus a 10-point difference in the racial composition of one's neighborhood would translate into only a difference of .2 in one's racial solidarity score. Though hardly a fundamental difference, this was more than could be attributed to chance, and it was independent of any differences in socioeconomic status.

Why did blacks who lived in mixed-race neighborhoods express less solidarity than those who lived in more heavily black neighborhoods? Earlier we mentioned two possible ways in which living in a mixed-race neighborhood could undermine racial solidarity. The first followed directly from the social density interpretation. Blacks who lived in mixed-race neighborhoods were more likely to have close white friends (see Table 3.2), which in turn could lead them to feel less intensely about solidarity with other blacks. With close white friends as well as white acquaintances, neighbors, merchants, and service providers, blacks in racially integrated areas may have been less motivated than those whose interactions were more confined to other African Americans to see themselves as part of the black community.

Alternatively, the decision to live in a mixed-race neighborhood may itself have been shaped, in part at least, by a relatively weak sense of group solidarity. Decisions about where to live are complex, guided by a combination of economic considerations, employment conditions, and life-style preferences. It seems reasonable to suppose that racial considerations play a role in African Americans' residential location decisions, as such considerations clearly do for whites.[7] Presumably, blacks who feel less need to maintain group solidarity would be less likely to have located in a predominantly black neighborhood in the first place. Thus, in contrast to the social density interpretation, which focuses on the neighborhood racial mix as an explanation of racial solidarity, this residential preference interpretation focuses on racial solidarity as a key to sorting out blacks who preferred to reside in a predominantly black neighborhood from those who preferred to reside in a racially integrated neighborhood.

However, the strength of the self-selection effect is mitigated to a considerable extent by the fact that blacks do not have the same range of housing choice as whites; that is, housing segregation still drives blacks to mostly black neighborhoods no matter what their levels of racial solidarity. Moreover, when they have a choice, as we have seen in chapter 2, most blacks prefer to live in mixed-race neighborhoods, not those with only black neighbors. Thus, if given a choice, the distribution of blacks among different types of neighborhoods would look very different from that in Detroit. We conclude that self-selection can account for little of the variation in racial solidarity.[8]

Of course, there is no logical reason why solidarity cannot influence neighborhood choice while neighborhood choice simultaneously influences solidarity, adding separate pieces to solving the puzzle of neighborhood differences in racial solidarity. Clearly, African Americans who are the most hostile to whites are not going to locate in a nearly all-white suburb, where they would come into contact mostly with whites and be governed by a white mayor and council. Even so, in the suburbs the decline of solidarity as one ages suggests the relevance of the social density explanation to the extent that age and length of time in the community are related. The longer one lives in the suburbs, the weaker the solidarity. Similarly, and using the same logic, the increase of solidarity with age among central city dwellers also suggests the overall relevance

---

7 In our survey of whites in the Detroit area, over 20% said they felt they "had to move from a neighborhood because blacks were moving in and it was causing problems for their family."
8 Blacks who preferred mixed-race neighborhoods had slightly lower levels of solidarity ($r = .19$) than those who preferred mostly black or all-black neighborhoods.

of the social density explanation. The longer a person lives in a primarily black neighborhood, the stronger the solidarity.

To isolate the underlying causal linkages, we would need data from a multiwave survey conducted while the interviewees were deciding whether to move to a new neighborhood or longitudinal data collected over several years before and after a move to a neighborhood with a different racial mix. We do not have data of this sort. However, we do have, for each interviewee in our survey, measures of frequency of contact with whites and of the preferred racial mix of the neighborhood.[9] The question then becomes whether adding these two measures to the model of racial solidarity would have any effect on the observed impact of neighborhood racial composition.

The answer is that when one's contact with whites and one's preferred neighborhood racial mix were added to the model, as in columns (3) of Table 5.2, the estimated effect of neighborhood racial composition faded considerably, although it remained marginally statistically significant. The lesson we extracted from this result was that the impact of neighborhood racial composition on racial solidarity was mediated, although not entirely, by a combination of interracial contact and the preference to live in a racially integrated setting. More specifically, those whose personal interactions were more focused on blacks expressed greater solidarity with other African Americans, and this was part of the reason why those who lived in racially mixed neighborhoods had lower racial solidarity scores. Another part of the explanation seemed to be that some blacks preferred to live in a predominantly black area and others in a racially mixed neighborhood, these preferences reflecting, among other things, their differing senses of black solidarity. To this extent, it should occasion no great surprise that blacks who lived in more integrated neighborhoods felt less solidarity with other blacks than did those who lived in predominantly black neighborhoods, for that was one of the reasons they lived in such neighborhoods in the first place.

RESIDENTIAL CONTEXT AND BLACK SOLIDARITY

We have examined three possible links between racial solidarity and neighborhood context. One, the social density hypothesis, posited that blacks living in largely black neighborhoods would express the highest degree of solidarity. The second, the social salience explanation, suggested that blacks living as minorities in their neighborhood would express higher degrees of solidarity. The third, the identity supremacy

---

9 See Appendix B for a detailed description of these measures.

argument, hypothesized that residential context would make no difference at all.

In testing these three interpretations, we uncovered empirical support for an interpretation based on the concept of social density. As we expected, blacks living in predominantly black neighborhoods displayed greater solidarity than those living in mixed neighborhoods. Moreover, the fact that older city residents expressed greater racial solidarity than younger ones whereas older suburbanites expressed less solidarity than their younger counterparts again provided support for the idea that social density is important not only in establishing but also in maintaining strong feelings of solidarity.

However, these findings are complex. In general, those living in racially mixed neighborhoods expressed less solidarity with other African Americans than did those living in predominantly black or all-black neighborhoods. When we went on to take interracial contacts and preferences concerning the racial composition of the neighborhood into account, we observed that the independent effect of living in a racially mixed neighborhood faded. We interpreted this as meaning that blacks' contacts with whites and their preferences for where to live could help explain why the racial composition of a neighborhood affected the racial solidarity of its residents. We certainly expected that blacks' contacts with whites would lead to decreased levels of solidarity, and that was true. We also speculated that blacks who felt greater racial solidarity would be more likely to select all-black neighborhoods and that living in an all-black neighborhood may in turn have increased their sense of racial solidarity. No matter which of these effects was more important, the link between neighborhood integration and diminished solidarity seemed clear.

The impact of living in the city of Detroit proved to be more ambiguous. Living in the city or the suburbs per se had no significant effect on racial solidarity. However, when we considered the joint effect of urban versus suburban residence and age, we discovered that living in Detroit had a positive effect on solidarity, which, if anything, increased with age, whereas living in the suburbs had a negative effect on solidarity, which increased significantly with age.

The extent to which African Americans feel bonds of solidarity with other African Americans may affect their pursuit of integrationist rather than separatist social, economic, cultural, and political strategies. The maintenance of solidarity with other African Americans would not preclude participation in nonblack aspects of American society, but an emphasis on making specifically African American connections could explicitly or implicitly diminish the importance of making connections with other groups in society. The idea of racial solidarity, then, is central to a variety of other beliefs and behaviors. It bears on how blacks see themselves as a group, and even on whether blacks see themselves as a group, and on how they approach white-dominated society.

Of course, the emphasis some blacks place on connections with other blacks and with black institutions may be driven primarily by their rejection by the institutions of white America. Black solidarity has been, in part, a reaction to that rejection, as well as an affirmation of blacks' own heritage, traditions, connections, and values. In fact, certain aspects of group solidarity have been evident in most American ethnic groups, and this has not deterred them from full integration into mainstream American society.

However, full integration into the larger society has long been denied to African Americans. Thus, the question becomes whether they can advance more readily by merging into mainstream, largely white, society or by practicing a racial solidarity that leads either to collective action to achieve group purposes or to a kind of racial separatism. In other words, is the road to advancement one on which individuals seek social and economic success within the context of the larger multiracial society? Or is success more likely to come through group cohesiveness? The latter route recognizes the social realities of prejudice and discrimination, which make it difficult for individuals to be genuinely integrated into the larger society. Carmichael and Hamilton (1967: 44) stated this point clearly more than three decades ago:

The concept of Black Power rests on a fundamental premise: before a group can enter the open society they must close ranks. By this we mean that group solidarity is necessary before a group can operate effectively from a bargaining position of strength in a pluralistic society.

The analyses reported above suggest that, regardless of whether the path of individual striving or group solidarity is the more successful, the increasing racial integration of America's large cities may well reduce black solidarity. Other factors may have the same effect. The development of a more genuinely multiracial society has blurred the line between black and white, and increasing income and life-style differences between poor and middle-income blacks also have the potential to undermine the sense of collective identity and fate. Despite the slow pace of integration, the findings reported here suggest that strategies of black advancement premised on the maintenance of strong bonds of racial solidarity are likely to face new challenges in the years to come, as more and more blacks leave the central cities and as new generations of black youngsters grow up in more racially heterogeneous settings.

6

White Racial Prejudice

"I was shocked by the vulgarity of their speech, their loudness and their inappropriate behavior. ... I ... came to resent them because their behavior wouldn't have been tolerated had they been anything but black... Now I consider myself a racist" (Baillie, 2000). Relatively few whites would admit to the kind of racial prejudice that would lead them to judge an African American as inferior biologically.[1] Like the white woman whose description of her co-workers is quoted above, though, many more do not hesitate to label black Americans as less hard working, less well behaved, less motivated, or falling short in other ways as compared with whites.

Of course, the degree of racial prejudice varies widely among whites. To what extent is this variability shaped by whites' residential context? In this chapter we examine whites' attitudes toward African Americans, and the impact of place of residence on these attitudes. We explore whether the heightened interracial contact brought about by integrated neighborhoods increases or reduces white prejudice.

RACIAL PREJUDICE

Previous chapters revealed that living in integrated neighborhoods significantly increases the number of contacts between blacks and whites. It also increases perceptions of discrimination as African Americans and whites come into closer contact with one another. For blacks, the expanded interracial contact decreases racial solidarity, other things being equal. These findings provided evidence for our social density

---

[1] The classic works documenting changes in white Americans' views of blacks are a series of articles in *Scientific American* (Hyman and Sheatsley, 1956; Hyman and Sheatsley, 1964; Greeley and Sheatsley, 1971; Taylor, Sheatsley, an Greeley, 1978). More recently, Schuman et al. (1997) have summarized a large variety of indicators of attitudes toward blacks.

interpretation (Lau, 1989).. Blacks living among other blacks tend to have a greater sense of affiliation with them.

These findings shape our expectations about the impact of residence on whites' attitudes. We expect that social density also will influence white attitudes toward blacks by creating higher levels of white solidarity. Others have shown that explanations of solidarity can apply to whites as well as to blacks, with particular focus on the role of social density in creating solidarity among white ethnic groups (e.g., Lieberson, 1963; Yancey et al., 1976; Pavalko, 1981; Conzen, 1979; Driedger, 1979, 1980).

We have noted the seeming contradictions in past research examining the impact on white attitudes of the presence of black populations. On the one hand, interracial contact and friendship can have positive effects on white attitudes, at least under the right conditions (Jackman and Crane, 1986; Meer and Freedman, 1966; Kinder and Mendelberg, 1995). We have argued that neighborhood integration, even if the numbers of blacks and whites are far from equal, gives blacks and whites an opportunity for casual interaction, for closer friendships, and for chances to work together in civic organizations and activities. These settings offer the opportunity to view members of the other race as individuals, thus perhaps offsetting previously held stereotypes.

Of course, as our opening quote from a white woman about her black co-workers indicates, close interaction can create negative attitudes as well. Moreover, although research suggests that close individual white–black interaction largely help to undermine racial antagonisms, larger overall proportions of blacks in these large demographic areas seem to exacerbate white racial antagonism. As we observed in chapter 4, large concentrations of African Americans in metropolitan areas and other major geographic areas are related to increased hate crimes against blacks, support for segregationist candidates, increased white prejudice, and lessened public support for public policies to ameliorate the status of blacks, among other indicators of white hostility (see Taylor, 1998; Orbell and Sherrill, 1969). Large black populations in neighborhoods are also associated with white flight, the tendency of whites to move away from such populations. However, Huckfeldt (1986) contends that it is not racial prejudice alone that has stimulated white flight but also proximity to higher rates of crime and (in the late 1960s) urban unrest and violence.

Just as the black social density theory predicts greater solidarity among African Americans, it also predicts greater white hostility. Social density tends to focus attention on the group to the exclusion of other groups. There is less opportunity to interact with those of another race and less opportunity to test the reality of racial stereotypes. If the idea that social density increases in-group solidarity is correct, then we would expect whites living in all-white tracts and those in the suburbs to be most likely to display racial prejudice. It is in these settings that whites are the most segregated from blacks.

AN OVERVIEW OF WHITE HOSTILITY TOWARD BLACKS OVER TIME

Although the 1969 DAS did not contain many measures of racial prejudice, it did include five items on whites' views of blacks as a group. One item, calling for assessments of the intelligence of African Americans, tapped traditional prejudice by questioning the innate capabilities of blacks. Three items assessed negative stereotyping of African Americans' behavior and motivation, as expressed in the views that blacks are more violent than whites, less likely to have high moral standards, and less likely to be ambitious.[2] The fifth item asked whether black–white differentials in jobs and income were mainly due to something about blacks themselves or to the way in which whites have treated blacks.

Most whites accepted negative stereotypes about black sloth and immorality, but only a minority (albeit a large one) accepted negative stereotypes about blacks' propensity to violence and only a small minority accepted the idea that blacks are less intelligent than whites (Table 6.1). In all, most whites attributed black–white socioeconomic inequalities to the shortcomings of blacks themselves but did not see these shortcomings as innate. These responses were consistent with whites' responses to national surveys of the time. In a 1968 Gallup poll, 58% of whites blamed blacks themselves for social inequalities, a proportion similar to the 54% in the DAS who expressed the same idea (Schuman et al., 1997).

In the 1980s, many researchers became interested in how whites explain racial inequality, so in designing this study we were able to draw on a fuller array of explanations and corresponding survey items than the simple dichotomy that was used in the 1969 DAS (Apostle, Glock, Piazza, and Suezele, 1983; Sniderman and Hagen, 1985; Kluegel and Bobo, 1993; Sigelman and Welch, 1991). We tapped a diverse set of white explanations of black–white socioeconomic inequalities by telling our interviewees: "Most people agree that, on the average, blacks have worse jobs, income, and housing than whites. I have a list of reasons that some people give for this difference. Let me know if each of the follow-

---

2 For the wordings of these items and the others referred to in the remainder of this chapter, see Appendix B.

Table 6.1. *Whites' agreement with negative*
stereotypes of blacks, 1969 (%)

Stereotype	Agreement
Blacks less ambitious	64
Blacks less moral	54
Blacks more violent	44
Blacks less intelligent	14
Black–white gap primarily due to black shortcomings	54

Note: The data are from the 1969 Detroit Area Survey.

ing is a major reason, a minor reason, or no reason at all for these differences." Several of the nine proposed reasons were factors attributable largely to white action: discrimination, lack of education, white conspiracies, white opposition, and the legacy of slavery. By contrast, three of the proposed reasons tapped directly into negative stereotypes about blacks: most blacks don't have the motivation or willpower to pull themselves out of poverty, most blacks have less in-born ability to learn, and black Americans teach their children values and skills different from those required to be successful in American society.[3]

Figure 6.1 shows our white interviewees' responses to the latter three items. As in 1969, only a small minority held in-born abilities largely responsible for racial inequality, with 9% declaring this a major reason and another 12% a minor reason. More agreed that different values held by blacks helped shape racial inequality, with 20% calling value differences a major reason and 30% a minor one. Still more agreed that racial inequality exists because blacks lack the motivation to pull themselves out of poverty, with 29% considering this factor major and 30% minor.

If we equate "motivation" and "values" in the 1992 items to "ambition" and "morals" in the 1969 items, then we see that the 1992 responses followed the same pattern as those of 1969, with deficient motivation viewed as the primary problem by the largest group of whites, followed by deficient values and then by deficient intelligence. These responses were also fairly consistent with responses to national surveys. For example, in a 1989 ABC/*Washington Post* survey, about

3 One item, "Because God made the races different as part of His divine plan," was ambiguous in its attribution of inequality to blacks themselves. Only 4% considered this a major reason for inequalities and another 4% a minor reason.

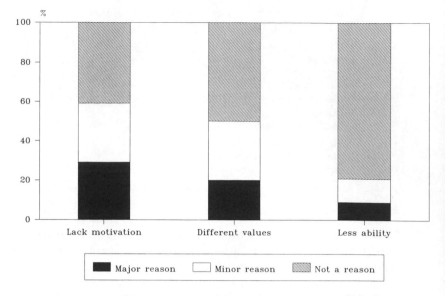

Figure 6.1. Whites' acceptance of negative stereotypes of blacks.

14% attributed black inequality to lack of in-born abilities and 43% to lack of motivation (Sigelman and Welch, 1991: 91; see also Kinder and Sanders, 1996: 97; Gillens, 1995)

Before branding a large proportion of our white sample as racist, though, it is worth pointing out that our African American respondents' answers to these same questions were nearly identical. Whereas 9% of whites considered blacks' ostensibly lesser in-born ability to learn to be a major reason for persisting black–white socioeconomic inequalities, 6% of black respondents' agreed. Moreover, 19% of black interviewees thought this lack of innate ability was at least a minor reason, as compared with only 12% of whites. Almost the same proportion of blacks (75%) as whites (79%) said differences in innate ability were not a reason for blacks' lower standing in American society. Although one might quibble with how the question is worded, the similarities between whites' and blacks' responses are striking (for similar findings see Sniderman and Piazza, 1993: 45–46).

We uncovered similarities between whites and blacks in their responses to each of the other stereotyping questions as well. About the same proportion of blacks as whites believed that blacks' status reflects blacks' lack of motivation or willpower to pull themselves out of poverty, and there was essentially no difference between blacks and whites in the

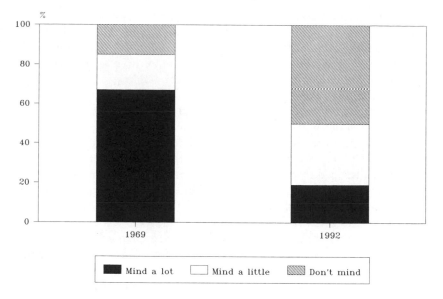

Figure 6.2. Whites' attitudes toward interracial marriage, 1969 and 1992.

proportion agreeing that black Americans teach their children values and skills different from those required to be successful.[4]

The reasons why many blacks accept these attributions are complex. We offer the African American responses to these items here only to point out that when it comes to race, it is easy to overgeneralize and, so to speak, to see in black and white issues that are really fuzzily gray. Nonetheless, we do believe that the items represent at least a blunt instrument for assessing whites' stereotypically negative attitudes toward blacks and we will use them in that way in the analyses reported below.

Figure 6.2 shows responses to the lone prejudice question that was asked in both the 1969 and 1992 surveys. In 1969, 67% of whites said they would mind a lot if a close relative married an African American, and the rest of the interviewees were divided about equally between those who said they would mind a little (18%) and those who said they would not mind (15%). By 1992, only 19% indicated that they would

---

4 However, in the same series of questions, blacks and whites strongly disagreed on other possible explanations for blacks' relatively poor standing in American society, with many more blacks than whites blaming powerful white people keeping blacks down, whites not wanting blacks to get ahead, and historical factors of slavery and discrimination.

mind a lot, a dramatic decrease; 50% said they would not mind at all, with the remaining 31% of our sample saying they would mind a little.[5]

Again, these responses were roughly consistent with national trends; Gallup surveys traced a rising trend, from only 4% in 1958 who approved of marriage between whites and nonwhites to 27% in 1972. Polls continued to show a steady increase in approval of interracial marriage through 1991, when it was 51%, and then a dramatic jump in the 1990s to 67% in 1997 (Schuman et al., 1997: 106–107).

Thus, despite the especially polarized racial climate in the Detroit area, whites there, like whites throughout the nation, became much less negatively disposed toward interracial marriage in the years between the late 1960s and the early 1990s. Given that the opposition to sexual contact between whites and blacks was at the very heart of opposition to integration and equality during the years of slavery and then segregation, these changes are remarkable, even if they are changes more in word than deed. However, as Schuman, Steeh, Bobo, and Krysan (1997) remind us, the original experiments measuring the difference between discriminatory attitudes and discriminatory behavior found that attitudes, not behavior, were discriminatory.[6] "That our concern today is with exactly the opposite problem indicates how great has been the change from the 1930s to the 1990s. ... We are dealing with a fundamental transformation of social norms..." (p. 306). Clearly these norms have changed in Detroit as well as in the rest of the country (see also Firebaugh and Davis, 1988).

RESIDENCE AND HOSTILITY TO BLACKS

In probing the effect of residence on whites' attitudes toward African Americans, we focused on two measures of racial prejudice: (1) responses to the item about marriage between an African American and a close relative of the interviewee and (2) a scale we created from responses to the three questions about agreement with negative stereotypes of blacks' motivation, values, and ability. Scores on the scale ranged from a low of 0, for those who did not endorse any of the three

---

5 We asked our respondents if they had any relatives of another race. To our surprise, 20% of whites (and 41% of blacks) said they did. This was a rather sweeping question; because we did not define "relative," all sorts of distant cousins may have been included. Nor did we confine the question to black relatives.

6 The earlier experiment was that of LaPiere (1934), who found that many hoteliers responded in a questionnaire that they would not provide accommodations for an interracial couple. However, when confronted with a nicely dressed, pleasant, middle-class, black couple with advance reservations, they registered them without protest.

White Racial Prejudice

Table 6.2. *Indicators of white prejudice by place of residence*

Indicator	City	Suburbs
Percent seeing a problem with interracial marriage	15	23
Mean stereotype scale score	1.1[a]	0.9[a]

Note: The stereotype scale was based on three items measuring whites' beliefs about African Americans'γ values, ambition, and morals.
[a] $p < .05$.

negative stereotypes, to a high of 3, for those who considered each a major reason for the black-white socioeconomic differential.[7]

Initial Analyses

Our survey revealed a complex pattern of responses. City residents were more likely to accept negative stereotypes of African Americans, scoring, on average, 1.1 on the 0–3 scale, compared with 0.9 for suburbanites (Table 6.2.) This difference, though not large, was consistent enough to be statistically significant ($p < .05$).

Because of the rather low reliability of the scale, we examined each item separately, but the item-by-item results proved to be very consistent with those for the overall scale. On each item, city residents were slightly more likely than suburbanites to hold negative stereotypes. This was least true for the item measuring motivation, where the differences were not statistically significant. However, the differences between suburbanites and city dwellers were significant on the other two items.

On the other hand, as expected, city residents were more likely than suburbanites to say that an interracial marriage involving one of their close relatives would not pose a problem. This difference (23% vs. 15%) was not particularly large, but it was consistent with our social density expectations. Thus, city residents appeared somewhat more personally tolerant in their willingness to accept an African American as an in-law, even as they were somewhat more likely to hold a variety of negative stereotypes of blacks.

Most prior research on the impact of black population size on whites' attitudes suggests that the most negative views of blacks should be expected to occur in all-white neighborhoods, a social density explanation. As Table 6.3 reveals, this expectation was borne out in Detroit:

---

7 Coefficient α for the scale was .50. The mean scale score for whites was .98, with a standard deviation of .77.

Table 6.3. *Indicators of white prejudice by neighborhood type*

Indicator	Largely white	Mixed	Largely black
Percent seeing a problem with interracial marriage	26	14	10[a]
Mean stereotype scale score	1.1	1.0	0.9

Note: The stereotype scale was based on three items measuring whites' beliefs about African Americans' values, ambition, and morals.
[a] $p < .05$.

Whites who resided in largely white areas were the most negative about blacks (the least likely to accept racial intermarriage and the most likely to express negative stereotypes). Of those living in mostly black neighborhoods, 10% said they would be troubled by the prospect of a black in-law, compared with 26% among whites living in largely white neighborhoods. Whites living in racially mixed areas fell in between these extremes but were closer to those living in largely black neighborhoods than to those living in largely white ones. This suggests that even a relatively small degree of integration might have positive effects on whites' attitudes.

Some indications of the same general pattern can be seen, although to a lesser (and statistically nonsignificant) degree, in whites' acceptance of negative stereotypes of African Americans. Whites living in white neighborhoods were slightly more likely to accept such stereotypes than those living in racially mixed neighborhoods, and those in mixed neighborhoods were slightly more likely to hold such views than those living in largely African American ones.

In sum, whites living among blacks, even where whites were in the minority, tended to display less rather than more hostility than those living in nearly all-white areas. In part, this may have been a result of self-selection; that is, those most hostile to blacks presumably would not, if given a choice, choose to live among blacks. We explored this question by asking whites whether they had ever moved to get away from blacks in their neighborhood. As we saw in chapter 2, 20% admitted that they had. This admission was related to levels of antiblack stereotyping, but the relationships were weak and nonsignificant; that is, whites who were more prejudiced were only slightly more likely to say they had moved for racial reasons. This is far from a perfect control for self-selection because not everyone who moved would admit to having done so, but it provides some indication that it is residential integration that affects favorable racial attitudes rather than vice versa.

White Racial Prejudice

Thus far, our results indicate that whites living in neighborhoods with greater opportunities for interracial contact tend to hold more positive attitudes about African Americans. These findings are quite consistent with the social density explanation, which posits that living with others of one's own group heightens an in-group–out-group distinctiveness.

Follow-up Analyses

To assess whether the relationships we have just glimpsed between residence and hostility toward blacks were spurious, we regressed the two hostility measures on a set of predictors drawn from our analysis of black solidarity. As in the preceding three chapters, our analysis here focused on whether our interviewees lived in the city or the suburbs and on the racial composition of their neighborhood. We also controlled for other conditions that we thought might affect expressions of racial prejudice. We included 10 such factors in the model, most of which were identical to those employed in chapters 3 through 5 and which are described in detail in Appendix B. Seven of these were individual traits and three were measures of childhood socialization experiences. Two of the individual traits were place-related: whether the interviewee worked in the city and whether the interviewee worked in the suburbs. The other five were age, sex, education, financial status, and religiosity.

In prior studies, older whites, those of lower educational and financial status, and men were observed to express more racial prejudice (Sigelman and Welch, 1991; Apostle et al., 1983; Kluegel and Smith, 1986; Sniderman and Hagen, 1985). We had no directional expectation about the impact of religiosity on white racial prejudice.

The three childhood socialization experience factors in the model all related to the racial environment in which an interviewee had been raised. We expected the most racial prejudice from whites who grew up in the South and in racially isolated neighborhoods and schools. We expected, among other things, that greater hostility toward blacks would be related to lower educational and financial status (Sigelman and Welch, 1991), greater age (Apostle et al., 1983; Kluegel and Smith, 1986; Sniderman and Hagen, 1985), less frequent interracial contact (Sigelman and Welch, 1993), living and working in the city rather than the suburbs, and living in nearly all-white areas.

These expectations were confirmed only in part (see column (1) in Table 6.4). As expected, less educated whites were substantially more likely to accept negative stereotypes of blacks, but the same relationship did not hold between financial status and stereotyping. Another factor shaping negative stereotypes of blacks was sex: White women were less likely than white men to endorse these stereotypes, although the

Table 6.4. *Predicting whites' attitudes toward African Americans*

| | Stereotypes[b] | | | | Interracial marriage | | | |
| | (1) | | (2) | | (3) | | (4) | |
Predictor	b	(s.e.)	b	(s.e.)	b	(s.e.)	b	(s.e.)
Detroit residence	.16	(.09)[a]	.18	(.09)[a]	-.17	(.13)	-.09	(.13)
Percent black in neighborhood	-.002	(.002)	-.0002	(.002)	-.008	(.003)[a]	-.004	(.003)
Work in the city	-.03	(.12)	.04	(.13)	.26	(.19)	.40	(.20)[a]
Work in the suburbs	.01	(.11)	.06	(.11)	.06	(.16)	.15	(.17)
Age	.004	(.003)	.002	(.003)	.02	(.004)[a]	.01	(.004)[a]
Gender	-.15	(.09)[a]	-.17	(.09)[a]	-.08	(.13)	-.10	(.13)
Education	-.03	(.02)[a]	-.02	(.02)	.01	(.02)	.01	(.02)
Financial status	-.05	(.05)	-.07	(.05)	.07	(.07)	.05	(.07)
Religiosity	-.01	(.04)	.03	(.04)	.09	(.06)	.17	(.07)[a]
Early life neighborhood composition	.13	(.10)	.11	(.10)	-.10	(.15)	-.16	(.15)
Early life school composition	-.05	(.03)	-.04	(.03)	.05	(.04)	.09	(.04)[a]
Southern upbringing	.23	(.26)	.26	(.26)	-.02	(.35)	.13	(.37)
Contact with blacks			-.14	(.05)[a]			-.34	(.08)[a]
Constant	1.26	(.30)[a]	1.28	(.30)[a]	-.70	(.42)[a]	-.81	(.44)[a]
R squared	.06		.09		.12		.16	

Note: Columns (1) and (2) show the results for two models of acceptance of negative stereotypes; (3) and (4) are for the models of opposition to racial intermarriage; *b* is the unstandardized regression coefficient, derived in (1) and (2) from ordinary–least squares regression analyses and in (3) and (4) from ordered probit regression analyses; s.e. is the standard error of the coefficient.
[a] *p* < .05.
[b] Higher values indicate acceptance of negative stereotypes and rejection of interracial marriage.

White Racial Prejudice

Table 6.5. *The impact of interracial proximity on whites'*
attitudes toward African Americans

	Stereotypes[b]		Interracial marriage	
Detroit residence	.12	(.09)	−.07	(.08)
Percent black in neighborhood	.001	(.002)	−.001	(.005)
Work in the city	.09	(.13)	.26	(.12)[a]
Work in the suburbs	.02	(.11)	.12	(.10)
Early-life neighborhood	.12	(.09)	.03	(.08)
Early-life school	−.22	(.11)[a]	.004	(.10)
Contact with blacks	−.14	(.05)[a]	−.19	(.04)[a]
Moved to get away from blacks	−.12	(.11)	−.25	(.10)[a]
R squared	.10		.17	

Note: These coefficients are calculated controlling for all other variables found in Table 6-4.
[a] $p < .05$.
[b] Higher values indicate acceptance of negative stereotypes and rejection of interracial marriage.

male–female differential was only .16 on the 0–3 scale. Residents of the city were slightly more likely than their suburban counterparts to accept negative stereotypes, but the proportion of whites in the neighborhood did not have the expected effect. However, whites who went to school with blacks were less accepting of negative stereotypes. Thus, controlling for all the other factors, it appears that early interracial contact has a greater effect on stereotyping than does current residential status.

These patterns persisted when we added interracial contact as a predictor (see column 2 in Table 6.4). Not surprisingly, interracial contact was the single best predictor in the augmented model, although here again the impact was not dramatic: For every 1-point increment on the interracial contact scale, scores on the negative stereotype scale fell by .12. In any event, familiarity with blacks clearly did not breed contempt, at least insofar as our interracial contact and negative stereotype scales tapped into familiarity and contempt, respectively.

We tested the stability of these relationships by holding constant whether respondents admitted to having moved because of black neighbors. Although this is an incomplete way of getting around the possibility that attitudes cause neighborhood choice rather than the reverse, by holding this effect constant, we can be more confident that we are looking at relationships in which residential choice is the antecedent. Table 6.5 shows the regression coefficients for the key residential variables, along with interracial contact and admission of a move in the face of

African American neighbors. Counter to our expectations, those who claimed to have moved for racial reasons were no more likely than others to hold negative sterotypes. Furthermore, even with this control interracial contact continued to have a positive effect of reducing acceptance of negative stereotypes.

Attitudes toward interracial marriage were only slightly more predictable (see column 3 in Table 6.4). Again, older whites were likely to voice more negative attitudes, as were more devout religious believers. Furthermore, the greater the proportion of African Americans in a neighborhood, the less likely white residents were to voice concerns about interracial marriage. However, residence in Detroit or in the suburbs seemed to make little difference. When we added interracial contact to the set of predictors (see column 4 in Table 6.4), these findings continued to hold. Moreover, once interracial contact was taken into account, those working in the city also emerged as significantly more accepting of interracial marriage. Thus, residence in neighborhoods with more blacks, working in the city, and interracial contact are predictive of positive attitudes toward interracial marriage. Of these effects, the strongest was again that of contact with blacks, although we should again note that this effect was not very strong, as the predicted probabilities shown at the bottom of the table indicate.

We again added a control for having moved because of the racial complexion of one's neighborhood, and it was significantly related to opposition to interracial marriage. As Table 6.5 indicates, working in the city and interracial contact continued to be significant. In any event, it was encouraging to find again that increased interracial contact on a personal, individual level reduced expressions of racial prejudice on the part of whites. That this increased contact was partly an effect of residential integration was clear on the basis of the data we considered in chapter 3.

CONCLUSIONS

Just as place of residence played an important role in shaping blacks' feelings of racial solidarity, it had a noticeable impact on whites' attitudes toward blacks. Earlier research indicated greater white hostility to blacks in large metropolitan areas and in counties with a larger proportion of African Americans, but less white hostility to blacks among those with more personal contact with African Americans. We have found that the direct effect of the spatial density of the black population was inconsistently related to whites' acceptance of negative stereotypes and their resistance to interracial marriage. Whites living in Detroit were somewhat more likely to accept negative stereotypes of blacks than were suburban whites, but also were somewhat less likely to oppose interracial marriage. Whites living in neighborhoods with greater proportions of blacks were significantly more accepting of interracial marriage, but neighborhood racial composition was unrelated to whites' acceptance of stereotypes of blacks.

We also found, however, that personal interracial contact lessened whites' hostility to blacks. Those with more interracial contact were significantly more likely to reject negative stereotypes and significantly more accepting of interracial marriage. These relationships continued to hold when we controlled for our respondents' admissions that they had moved to get away from black neighbors. Because increased interracial contact was strongly predicted by living in the city and in an integrated neighborhood, these residential factors had more influence on whites' racial attitudes than their direct links would suggest.

Just as the direction of the relationships we uncovered indicated that increased neighborhood integration would decrease black solidarity, so too did we find that increased neighborhood integration would decrease white hostility to blacks. The pace of integration has been accelerating, but the slow pace of this acceleration, combined with the rather small magnitude of the effects uncovered here, certainly cautions against too much optimism. Nonetheless, our findings suggest that trends in neighborhood integration do have the potential to bring about a slow improvement in interracial relationships.

7

Opinions on Urban Issues

THE SCHOOLS AND THE POLICE

Inadequate schools, drug addiction, crime, and poor housing have long been among the most familiar features of urban life in the United States. Unfortunately, our understanding of what the residents of urban areas think about these issues has been based largely on racial stereotypes – that blacks are dissatisfied with urban public services and consistently support more government spending to fix them and that whites are more satisfied and less favorable toward government spending.

In this chapter we explore blacks' and whites' attitudes about education and police protection, two of the most vexing problems in Detroit and across the nation. We expect the racial composition of the respondents' neighborhoods to emerge as important factors in shaping their views. Just as the neighborhood context influences attitudes about race, it also influences attitudes about how to deal with problems that are sometimes entangled with our views of race.

After exploring why we expect context to influence attitudes about these public services, we briefly examine national survey data on blacks' and whites' opinions on various urban policy issues and then probe more deeply into Detroit area residents' opinions about police and education.

THE IMPACT OF RESIDENCE ON ATTITUDES
ABOUT PUBLIC SERVICES

In prior chapters, we have stressed the importance of neighborhoods as settings to build personal contact between blacks and whites. In turn, these contacts have had a modest effect on breaking down feelings of hostility and promoting interracial empathy. These shared understandings may, in their turn, build more similar attitudes toward public services.

We have not seen research that illustrates this particular point. However, research on how neighborhood context affects partisan dispositions is quite relevant. Residential context affects partisan choices

Opinions on Urban Issues

(Tingsten, 1963; Segal and Meyer, 1974; Butler and Stokes, 1974; Cox, 1974) as well as friendship choices (Huckfeldt, 1986), both of which influence voting (Berelson, Lazarfeld, and McPhee, 1954; Fuchs, 1955; Putnam, 1966). To the extent that partisanship, too, is affected by attitudes about issues, we would expect that the dynamics swaying partisanship also shape issue positions.

Why Residence May Affect Attitudes on Public Services

Isolated from one another, it is not surprising that blacks and whites have different views. Thus, living in integrated neighborhoods, even those with relatively few of the other race, offers an opportunity to see the city's problems through a more common filter. Living in the same neighborhood, blacks and whites share the conditions of life that affect their attitudes. If crime in a neighborhood is high, it is probably high for people of both races. If schools are doing a good job, they lift up both black and white children. To the extent that people's attitudes toward local government services are shaped by the reality of the services they receive, and we think for the most part they are (Schuman and Gruenberg, 1972), sharing common services should bring about common attitudes.

Even black middle-class families live in neighborhoods with higher levels of social pathologies than their white counterparts (Massey and Denton, 1993: 152), a difference that would presumably contribute to a black–white differential in views of the need for and quality of urban services. Of course, poor blacks bear an even greater burden. Racial segregation has concentrated poverty and the attendant social ills in poor black communities (Hogan and Kitagawa, 1985; Massey and Denton, 1993: 118; see also Wilson, 1987, 1996). We have already noted that in 1980, the proportion of poor people in the neighborhood of the average poor black family in Detroit was almost three times as great as in neighborhoods of poor white Detroiters (32% to 12%, Massey and Denton, 1993: 129; for a discussion of social isolation, see Cohen and Dawson, 1993). Segregation does isolate poor blacks from the mainstream (Sucoff and Upchurch, 1998: 581).

Our research can illuminate whether the divisions between blacks and whites in their attitudes about policy issues are influenced by the conditions in which they live as well as by more general ideological concerns. Here, we think the social density effect will be strong, that blacks living only among blacks and whites living only among whites will have quite disparate attitudes. However, we expect whites and blacks living in the same neighborhoods to share views about education and police services. We expect not that the effects of race will be nonexistent, but only that they will be much more muted in integrated than in segregated neighborhoods.

Race and Place

Findings from Earlier Research

In the late 1960s, the National Advisory Commission on Civil Disorders (Kerner Commission) conducted a landmark survey of citizen attitudes toward urban public services. More than three decades later, the Commission's 15-city survey remains the most thorough study ever completed on this subject. The Commission's survey showed that African Americans were less satisfied than whites with all four of the city services about which they were asked (public schools, garbage collection, parks and playgrounds, and police protection), especially the latter two. Among both blacks and whites, dissatisfaction was most widespread for parks and playgrounds and least so for garbage collection. In Detroit, one of the 15 cities whose residents were polled, satisfaction among blacks ran slightly higher than in most other cities, whereas Detroit's whites were about at the 15-city average, as was Detroit's black–white gap in satisfaction with services (Schuman and Gruenberg, 1972: 374).

To what extent did the black–white gap in satisfaction with services reflect real differences in the quality of services blacks and whites received rather than the deeper alienation from government institutions among blacks? The Kerner Commission cited evidence that genuine differences in service quality were at work. Dissatisfaction with city services tended to be more widespread in cities with fewer parks and playgrounds, fewer police, higher crime rates, and fewer sanitation workers. In Detroit and Cleveland, where surveys of suburbanites were available for comparison, suburbanites voiced much greater satisfaction than city residents, again reflecting real differences in service quality.

Neighborhood racial composition also affected satisfaction with services. For both blacks and whites, the fewer the blacks in a neighborhood, the more satisfied residents were with the services they were receiving, especially with police protection. On the other hand, black–white differences in satisfaction with services were minimal among those living in areas of similar racial composition. Indeed, in such areas whites expressed greater dissatisfaction than blacks with some services. This spatial patterning of responses led Schuman and Gruenberg (1972) to conclude that overall service assessments reflected real differences in service quality and that blacks' greater dissatisfaction stemmed in large measure from living in largely black areas, which were less well served.

OPINIONS ABOUT SPENDING ON VARIOUS PROGRAMS, 1992 SURVEY

Let us now begin our explanation of how our Detroit-area interviewees assessed the government services they were receiving by focusing on

Opinions on Urban Issues

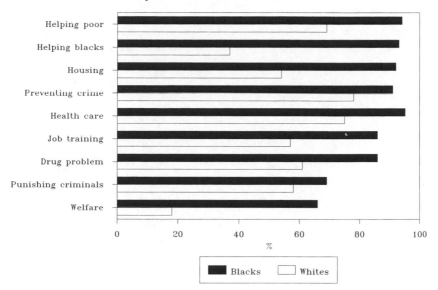

Figure 7.1. Support for more government spending.

national programs with a locus in urban problems: job training and retraining; helping low- and middle-income people buy housing; providing health care and health insurance; dealing with the drug problem; caring for the poor; welfare; improving the condition of blacks; punishing criminals; and preventing crime. Borrowing a question from the National Opinion Research Center's annual General Social Survey (GSS), we asked our Detroit interviewees: We are faced with many problems in this country. I'm going to name some of these problems and for each one I'd like you to tell me whether you think we're spending too much money on it, too little money, or about the right amount.

Racial differences stood out in the responses to these questions, as can be seen in Figure 7.1.[1] The smallest black–white differences in spending preferences were found for punishing criminals, preventing crime, and providing good health care and health insurance, with large majorities of both races favoring more spending on all those programs. Though fairly

---

1 In most cases these responses were very similar to those of interviewees in the 1993 GSS. The following are the proportions of GSS and Detroit interviewees, respectively, who said too little was being spent on each program. For whites, health, 73%, 75%; crime, 73%, 78%; drugs, 61%, 61%; race, 32%, 37%; welfare, 15%, 18%; caring for the poor, 61%, 69%. For African Americans, health, 82%, 90%; crime, 78%, 78%; drugs, 80%, 86%; race, 84%, 93%; welfare, 27%, 66%; caring for the poor, 86%, 94%. The GSS black sample had only 82 to 89 respondents per question, so those percentages should be treated with caution.

Table 7.1. *Predicting opinions on public spending*

		Significant impact of	
Spending target	Race	Neighborhood racial composition	City vs. suburban residence
Condition of blacks	Yes	No	No
Caring for poor	Yes	No	No
Dealing with drugs	Yes	No	No
Welfare	Yes	No	Yes
Health care	Yes	Yes	No
Jobs	Yes	Yes	No
Housing	Yes	Yes	No
Punishing criminals	Yes	Yes	No
Preventing crime	No	No	No

substantial, these black–white differences were not yawning chasms. At the other extreme, the largest black–white differences were for more spending to improve the condition of blacks, for which blacks' endorsements outran whites' by 56 percentage points. Moreover, 48% more blacks than whites favored increased welfare spending, even though blacks were less supportive of increased welfare spending than of any other proposal about which we asked them. Less extreme but still substantial black–white differences emerged on programs for the poor, dealing with the drug problem, job training and retraining, and helping low- and middle-income citizens buy housing. In all those instances most blacks and most whites, but many more blacks than whites, endorsed spending increases. Overall, then, blacks and whites were most closely aligned on what might be called middle-class issues and were most divided on issues that explicitly or stereotypically involved race.

To what extent did these racial differences stem from differences in where blacks and whites lived? To isolate differences attributable to living in the city or the suburbs and to the racial composition of a neighborhood, we statistically controlled for our interviewees' financial status, education, and sex. As shown in Table 7.1, significant differences in blacks' and whites' responses remained even after we imposed these controls. However, on five of the nine issues, responses were significantly affected by where interviewees lived, over and above whether they were black or white. The racial composition of their neighborhood significantly affected interviewees' opinions on four of the nine issues, and whether they lived in the city or the suburbs had such an effect on a fifth issue.

These residential effects were not especially consistent, then, nor upon closer examination did they prove to be especially strong. Still, it remained possible that stronger effects might come to the surface in responses to questions about less abstract, more concrete issues, and in particular about issues involving one's own city or neighborhood. That is, a greater commonality of views might well be produced by a greater commonality of experiences. Many of these issues were rather abstract and general. Urban schools and police protection, the subjects of the remainder of this chapter, are issues that specifically affect respondents in their neighborhoods.

ATTITUDES TOWARD PUBLIC SCHOOLS

In the 1990s, as had long been the case, America's schools were stratified by race, class, and residence. At the extremes, the typical educational opportunities and learning conditions available to children in upper middle-class white suburban schools were vastly superior to those available in poor, heavily minority city schools, as was the performance of the children in those schools (Feagin and Sykes, 1994). Schools in white or black middle- or working-class neighborhoods and in rural areas tended to fall between these extremes.[2]

Racial Inequalities in Schools

African Americans have long been concerned about racial inequalities in the schools (Henig et al., 1995). During the era of legal and sometimes mandatory segregation, blacks fought for improvements in their schools, even under segregated conditions (*To Secure These Rights,* 1947), and in the 1940s, 1950s, and 1960s the eradication of legal school segregation became a prime objective of the civil rights movement. That objective was partially achieved in the Supreme Court's 1954 *Brown v. Board of Education* decision, which outlawed state-mandated school segregation, and in later decisions dealing with implementation of this decision and resistance to it (Kluger, 1976; Chambers, 1993). However, proponents of integrated schools soon realized that the end of mandatory school segregation was not the end of actual school segregation. The "deliberate

---

2 Coleman (1966) established that most of the differences in achievement were a function of the socioeconomic status of the students rather than the condition of the buildings, training of the teachers, or spending on the schools. He also concluded that busing lower-income black children to predominantly white schools raised the achievement levels of the black students without affecting the achievement of the white students. These findings provided support for the idea of busing and, for that reason and others, were attacked from both right and left.

speed" with which the *Brown* decisions were supposed to be implemented proved much more deliberate than speedy. Year after year of delay dissipated the momentum toward integration, and demographic changes made school integration increasingly difficult to attain in any event, as whites fled from many central cities (McClendon, 1990; Mickelson and Ray, 1994; Orfield and Ashkimoze, 1991; Shapiro, 1990; Rossell, 1981). The structure of local government, especially in the North, also worked against school integration. After World War II, states ceded substantial authority to newly emerging suburbs in regulating education, as well as in law enforcement and zoning (Farley and Frey, 1994; *Milliken v. Bradley*, 418 U.S. 717, 1974). Many suburbs worked to keep their schools for whites only (Newman, 1993), and not surprisingly, African Americans, in particular, continued to be dissatisfied with the schools (Campbell and Schuman, 1968; Durand, 1976). In the late 1960s, after the nation exploded into racial violence, the Kerner Commission (National Commission on Civil Disorders, 1968: 143–150) found that lack of educational opportunity for black children ranked near the top of the list of black grievances in the nation's major cities.

New debates arose during the late 1960s and 1970s. White flight left center city schools largely filled with minority children in many cities (Farky, Richards, and Wurdock, 1979; Russell, 1981). If integrated schools could not be achieved by adhering to "natural" residential patterns, should students be bused to achieve school integration (Orfield, 1978, 1983)?[3] In light of the resistance to busing by both blacks and whites and the resistance of the courts to metropolitan area-based busing remedies,[4] should the goal of school integration be abandoned in favor of trying to improve the quality of education in segregated schools? Viewing school segregation as inevitable, African Americans in some areas deemphasized integration and fought instead for community control as a way to improve the schools their children attended.

During the 1980s and 1990s, discussions of school integration were overshadowed by a movement to reform public schools. It was widely reported that America's schools were falling behind those of other advanced nations in graduating employable young adults with competencies in reading, writing, computation, and an awareness of the world

---

3 The Supreme Court sanctioned intradistrict busing in *Swann v. Charlotte-Mecklenburg Board of Education*, 402 U.S. 1 (1973), *Keyes v. School District 1, Denver*, 413 U.S. 921 (1973), *Dayton Board of Education v. Brinkman* 443 U.S. 526 (1979), and *Columbus Board of Education v. Perick*, 443 U.S. 449 (1979).

4 See *Milliken v. Bradley*, 418 U.S. 717 (1974). The decision in this Detroit case greatly limited the ability of busing to reduce school segregation in major metropolitan areas where pupils in city schools were predominantly black and those in suburban schools predominantly white.

around them. Educational reform became a rallying cry, and several states introduced new standards for student achievements and outcomes. Middle-class Americans, including some middle-class blacks, came to view educational reform as a high priority (Mickelson and Ray, 1994; Shapiro, 1990), and inner-city schools continued to be singled out as examples of the worst American education had to offer. In integrated schools, attention turned to so-called second generation discrimination, tracking black students into remedial tracks and meting more severe discipline to them (Meier, Stewart, and England, 1989a; 1989b).

Public Attitudes

In the 1980s, pollsters stopped asking whether their respondents were in favor of school integration, because virtually everyone now expressed support for it. This marked a major change in white opinion over the years: The support shown on a survey question about whether whites and blacks should attend the same school rose steadily among whites from 1942 through 1982, culminating in 90% endorsement, while holding steady at nearly 100% among blacks. Support for busing to achieve racial integration was consistently much lower, with only about half of blacks and less than a quarter of whites favoring it (Bobo, 1988; Jaynes and Williams, 1989; Schuman et al., 1997; Sigelman and Welch, 1991).

In sum, at the time that we began this study, the attitudes of blacks and whites toward school integration were reasonably clear: The great majority of both blacks and whites consistently told the pollsters that they were in favor of integrated schools, but far fewer blacks and even fewer whites could agree on a means of achieving this goal. Far less was known, though, about public attitudes toward other means of improving the schools. We wondered how our Detroit-area interviewees felt about various strategies for improvement and how this related to the racial character of the neighborhoods in which they lived.

Detroit's Schools

In the 1990s, Detroit's schools reflected the sad condition of schools in many urban areas (Wong, 1990), although the Detroit school system was, by all accounts, far from the nation's worst. Governed by a school board on which seven of the nine members were African Americans, the Detroit city schools had a student population that was 90% black and less than 10% white (*Detroit Free Press*, 14 December 1993).

In 1994, a civic group graded the Detroit school district's performance as a C in overall student success, a B in fiscal integrity and managerial accountability, and a C+ in community confidence – mediocre grades, to be sure, but arguably better than would have been achieved by many other urban school systems (*Detroit Free Press,* 17 June 1994). Student achievement in the Detroit schools lagged far behind that found in the Detroit suburbs and the entire state. On one measure of student performance, scores on tests given to all students in Michigan in the fourth, seventh, and tenth grades in the Michigan Educational Assessment Program (MEAP), Detroit students' scores ranged from 86% of the statewide average for fourth grade science achievement down to 19% of the statewide average for tenth grade mathematics achievement. Detroit students' scores were worse in tenth grade than in fourth grade, indicating a growing deficit the longer students stayed in the Detroit school system.

By contrast, many schools in the Detroit suburbs had more than double the statewide proportion of high scores. Within the city, individual schools varied widely, with a few approaching the best in the state and others having hardly any students with satisfactory scores. The variation was also great in the suburbs, where some schools fell below the citywide average, although most far exceeded it.

Satisfaction with the Detroit area public schools had long been reported as higher among suburbanites than among city residents (Bledsoe, 1991), which is hardly surprising in light of the difference in student achievement scores and of the thousands of families, both blacks and whites, who fled to the suburbs in part to escape the city school system.

The gap in evaluations of city and suburban schools widened substantially during the post–World War II era. In 1954, among both suburbanites and city dwellers, more Detroit-area residents were satisfied than dissatisfied with the schools, but the ratio of satisfaction to dissatisfaction was 25 points higher in the suburbs than in the city (Bledsoe, 1991). In our survey, suburbanites were still more satisfied than dissatisfied (although less satisfied than in 1954), but dissatisfaction far outweighed satisfaction among both black and white city dwellers. The result was a huge city–suburb satisfaction gap of almost 70 percentage points.

Assessing Opinion on Educational Policy

We were primarily concerned with our interviewees' responses to a series of questions about the quality of the schools and strategies to improve them. The core question was: Do you think schools here in your community need lots of improvement, some improvement, or are they pretty good as is?

The 1968 and 1969 Detroit Area Surveys (DAS) offered little that we could directly contrast with our survey results. We noted in chapter 4 that in 1968 almost two-thirds of black Detroiters believed that blacks did not have as good schools as did whites in Detroit. When asked about the most important thing to do to improve the schools, about two-thirds of those who were dissatisfied with the schools said it was to improve the quality of the black schools rather than to focus on school integration.

In the 1969 DAS, whites were not asked to evaluate Detroit schools or the extent of discrimination faced by blacks in the schools. However, after being presented with the premise that "at present, some Negro neighborhoods have schools with rundown buildings and less trained teachers than in mainly white neighborhoods," they were asked whether the federal government should spend money to bring these schools "up to the standard of white schools." About 75% expressed support for this idea.

Thus, in both the 1968 and 1969 surveys, the focus of questions on local schools was very much on racial differences in schools and school quality. Our questions, on the other hand, focused on school quality without providing any racial cues.

To find out how our interviewees' assessments of their school system were influenced by where they lived, we looked for connections between these assessments and three residential factors. In addition to whether interviewees lived in the city or the suburbs and how many African Americans lived in their neighborhood, we analyzed the performance of students in the local schools, using district-by-district averages on the 1991–92 school year MEAP.

To isolate differences due to residential context, we included several other variables in the analysis: interviewees' age, sex, level of education, whether they had school-age children,[5] their early life school integration, and their current level of interracial contact – all measured as indicated in Appendix B. Because we assumed that those who were less familiar with the schools would rate them more highly, we expected older people and those with less education to express more favorable evaluations. Schuman and Gruenberg (1972) reported that, for both blacks and whites in the 15 communities they surveyed, the higher one's level of education, the greater one's dissatisfaction with the schools. However, on the basis of prior research, we also expected both city and suburban parents of school-age children to offer more positive evaluations than those without children (Bledsoe, 1990), largely because those with children who were doing well in school would be expected to have reasonably positive impressions of the schools. We anticipated no difference between men and women, but because of the segregation of the Detroit schools and of most suburban schools, we expected those who had

---

5 Unfortunately, we did not determine whether these children were attending public schools.

Race and Place

Table 7.2. *Evaluations of community schools, by race and residence*

Evaluation	Total		City		Suburbs	
	Blacks	Whites	Blacks	Whites	Blacks	Whites
Percent saying "pretty good as is"	20	38	9	22	28	53
Percent saying "need some improvement"	38	34	39	38	37	30
Percent saying "need lots of improvement"	42	29	52	40	35	17
Total	100	100	100	100	100	100
Number of interviewees	589	472	261	235	328	237

Note: Question wording: Do you think schools here in your community need lots of improvement, some improvement, or are they pretty good as is?

attended integrated schools and who had more frequent interracial contacts to have less positive opinions of the schools.

Evaluations of School Quality

African Americans were indeed more critical than whites of the performance of the schools in their community (Table 7.2.) Whereas the modal rating among African Americans was that the schools needed "lots of improvement" (the most negative response possible), the modal rating among whites was that the schools were "pretty good as is" (the most positive response possible). An 18 percentage point gap separated whites and blacks in ratings of "pretty good" – almost a two-to-one difference.

City dwellers and suburbanites expressed very different assessments of the schools in their community. In the city, whites were more likely than African Americans to rate the schools "pretty good," but by a margin of only 22% to 9%, and most blacks and the plurality of whites said the city schools needed considerable improvement. In the suburbs, the ratings were much higher and the racial differences were more pronounced: 53% of suburban whites and 28% of suburban blacks considered the schools "pretty good," and about 18% more blacks than whites saw their schools as needing "lots of improvement."

Some school districts in the Detroit area had a predominantly poor or working-class population, others a predominantly upper middle-class population. Some suburbs were almost all black, others almost all white. Of course, the city of Detroit also had black neighborhoods and white neighborhoods and poor and rich residents, but the school system was

Table 7.3. *Predicting evaluations of community schools*

Predictor	All		Blacks		Whites	
	b	(s.e.)	*b*	(s.e.)	*b*	(s.e.)
Detroit residence	−.34	(.09)[a]	−.39	(.10)[a]	−.33	(.19)[a]
Percent black in neighborhood	−.004	(.002)[a]	−.002	(.003)	−.003	(.003)
District MEAP score	.03	(.005)[a]	.03	(.008)	.03	(.009)[a]
Age	.01	(.002)[a]	.002	(.003)[a]	.02	(.004)[a]
Sex	.10	(.08)	.10	(.10)	.09	(.12)
Education	−.02	(.01)[a]	−.01	(.02)	−.05	(.02)[a]
Early-life school composition	−.01	(.02)	−.02	(.03)	−.02	(.04)
Interracial contact	−.06	(.04)	−.04	(.05)	−.08	(.06)
School-age children	.11	(.08)	.07	(.11)	.14	(.13)
Race	−.14	(.11)				
Pseudo-*R* squared	.16		.10		.21	

Predictor	Probability of rating the schools "pretty good"	
	Blacks	Whites
Detroit resident	.12	.29
Suburbanite	.22	.41
MEAP 1 s.d. below mean	.11	.23
MEAP 1 s.d. above mean	.25	.47

Note: b is the unstandardized regression coefficient, derived from an ordered probit regression analysis, followed in parentheses by the standard error of the coefficient (s.d. = standard deviation).
[a] $p < .05$.

unified. Accordingly, we expected the black–white difference in ratings of the schools to close, even in the suburbs, when school quality and socioeconomic factors were taken into account.

We confirmed that expectation in the analyses summarized in Table 7.3. As can be seen in the model for all interviewees, race had no significant impact on our interviewees' evaluations of the schools once we took place of residence, neighborhood composition, and the performance of district schools into account. That is, the fact that blacks' ratings of the schools were much lower than whites' was attributable to where blacks and whites lived and to the facts that the schools were worse in the city than in the suburbs and worse in mostly black neighborhoods than in mostly white neighborhoods.

Table 7.3 also summarizes analyses that we conducted for blacks and whites separately. In these models, place of residence was again a crucial factor. Without the school performance variable in the equations, the city–suburb distinction and the proportion of blacks in the neighborhood were both significant predictors of assessments of the schools; among blacks and whites alike, living in the city and living in a neighborhood with a higher proportion of blacks were negatively related to evaluations of the schools. When we took school performance into account, though, as indicated by district MEAP scores, a more complex picture emerged. Whether one lived in the city or the suburbs continued to matter strongly for both blacks and whites. Thus, even with the effects of all the other variables controlled, including school performance, suburbanites evaluated their schools more positively than did urbanites. Perhaps this is a reflection of the smaller bureaucracies in the suburban schools, which could lead to a greater sense of empowerment by the public (Ostrom, Bish, and Ostrom, 1988). On the other hand, perhaps the Detroit schools are perceived to be even worse than they are, based on "objective" evidence. Where the interviewees lived also affected their evaluations of the schools through the schools' performance, as measured by the MEAP scores, which themselves reflect the racial residential context. The impact of this factor was especially impressive in that the measure obscured intracity variation in the performance of the schools.

A clearer sense of the impact of living in the city and of school performance can be gleaned from the bottom section of Table 7.3. For a black city dweller who was average in all respects, the findings in the top part of the table implied a .12 probability of rating the schools as pretty good, as compared with a .22 probability for an identical black suburbanite. For an average white, the estimated probability would be .29 or .41, depending on whether his or her home was in the city or the suburbs.[6] The school performance scores also had a large direct impact. For an otherwise average African American living in a district whose MEAP score was 1 standard deviation above the average, the probability of offering a "pretty good" evaluation was .14 higher than for an identical African American living in a district where the average MEAP score was 1 standard deviation below the average. For an average white, the gap was even larger, at .24.

The proportion of neighborhood residents who were African Americans was unrelated to evaluations of schools for either blacks or whites after we took school performance into account. This implies that neigh-

---

6 The estimates for whites should be treated with greater caution than those for blacks because the standard errors for whites were higher, as reflected in the *t*-test ratios for the two groups.

borhood racial composition affected opinions about the schools only via its impact on the performance of the schools.

Among whites, older people gave the schools more favorable ratings. Also as expected, the higher one's own level of education, the lower one's assessment of the local schools. Among blacks, neither age nor level of education mattered. None of the other expected relationships materialized. Having school-age children did not substantially affect evaluations, nor did we observe the expected relationships with interracial contact or previous experience in integrated schools. In sum, the best predictors of our interviewees' evaluations of schools in their community were whether they lived in the city or the suburbs and how well their local schools were performing (which was closely linked to residence, especially for whites).

Thus, among our interviewees, residence did shape attitudes toward urban public policy, which is consistent with the idea that shared experiences of living in particular neighborhoods or communities are major factors affecting policy attitudes. In fact, once these were controlled, racial differences diminished to insignificance.

Strategies for Improving the Schools

We asked all those who perceived a need for improvement in the schools to answer the following question: Here are some ways which have been suggested for improving schools. Please give me the number of the three strategies you think would be most effective. The strategies we listed were: more or better teachers; more security for schools; better buildings; more or better classroom materials; more discipline for students; more programs for very good students; more programs for students who aren't doing too well; more school integration; and more programs to help parents cope with jobs and child-raising, such as before- and after-school day care, breakfast programs, and evening recreation programs for students. By limiting each interviewee to three choices, we hoped to avoid "motherhood and apple pie" responses; we feared that many interviewees would express support for most, if not all, of these options if we did not force them to focus on the options about which they were most enthusiastic.

Except for white suburbanites, most interviewees said their schools could use improvement, and even among white suburbanites, almost half shared that opinion. Opinions about the most promising strategies for improving the schools varied greatly. As the responses summarized in Table 7.4 indicate, among both blacks and whites the step mentioned most often was getting more or better teachers, an option selected by more than half of the black interviewees and two-thirds of the whites.

Table 7.4. *Support for strategies to improve community schools (%)*

| | Total | | City | | Suburbs | |
Strategy	Blacks	Whites	Blacks	Whites	Blacks	Whites
General academic						
More or better teachers	54	67	53	60	62	68
More or better materials	49	45	49	39	48	46
Physical arrangements and security						
More security for schools	39	17	41	34	25	14
Better buildings	12	6	11	13	15	5
More discipline for students	48	62	48	52	45	64
More programs						
For very good students	10	18	10	14	15	18
For students who aren't doing well	55	49	55	55	58	48
To help parents cope...	29	22	30	23	22	22
School integration	4	6	4	6	8	5

Note: Question wording: Here are some ways which have been suggested for improving schools. Please give me the number of the three strategies you think would be most effective. The options were: more or better teachers; more security for schools, better buildings; more or better classroom materials; more discipline for students, more programs for very good students; more programs for students who aren't doing too well; more school integration; and more programs to help parents cope with jobs and child-raising, such as before- and after-school day care, breakfast programs, and evening recreation programs for students. This question was asked only of those who had answered "need lots of improvement" or "need some improvement" when asked: Do you think schools here in your community need lots of improvement, some improvement, or are they pretty good as is?

The other strategies chosen most often were more discipline for students (which ranked second among whites, fourth among blacks) and more programs for students who aren't doing well (second for blacks, third for whites). Providing more or better classroom materials also won strong support from both blacks and whites.

Strikingly, the option selected least often by both blacks and whites was school integration, which ranked far below every other choice except better buildings. This did not mean that our interviewees were necessarily opposed to school integration; rather, it meant that when they compared integration with the other strategies, they did not see it as one of the best ways to improve the schools. Since Detroit's schools were 90% black and many suburban schools were nearly all white, schools in the city and many suburbs could be integrated only via busing to and from the suburbs – not a popular idea.

The most pronounced black–white differences in preferences emerged on the needs for more security for schools, seen as a high priority by nearly 40% of blacks but only 17% of whites, and for more programs for very good students, emphasized by one-third of whites but only one-tenth of the black interviewees.

When we distinguished between interviewees who lived in the city and those who lived in the suburbs, most of the racial differences shown in Table 7.4 disappeared, indicating that blacks' and whites' educational priorities reflected differences in their community schools rather than black–white differences in basic approaches to education. Residents of the city, black or white, were more concerned about security in the schools and programs to help parents cope than were residents of the suburbs, who were more concerned about hiring better teachers than were city residents. Within the city and within the suburbs, only minor differences emerged in the steps blacks and whites considered most urgent.

As a follow-up, we reexamined the impact of residence while statistically controlling for the same factors as in Table 7.3. We expected interviewees' own educational backgrounds to play an important role in shaping their priorities, with more highly educated interviewees being more likely to emphasize improvements in general academic quality rather than physical arrangements, security, or special programs. We also expected age to be positively related to giving priority to school security and discipline and expected experiences with integrated schools and current levels of interracial contact to be positively related to emphasizing school integration. As for residential factors, we thought city residents would express stronger preferences for security and discipline and for programs to help parents and to help students who were not doing well, and we expected interviewees from districts with lower MEAP scores to voice greater enthusiasm for providing more teachers and better materials and for supporting parents and students who were not doing well but less enthusiasm for programs for good students.

Few of these expectations were confirmed (see Table 7.5.) In light of the unpredictability of our interviewees' preferences for how to fix the schools and of the minimal impact of the residential and school context variables, we have presented these results only in brief overview.

Interviewees' educational backgrounds did conform to most of our predictions, but only for blacks. Age also displayed some of the expected relationships, being positively related to support for more student discipline among both black and white interviewees and among whites, being negatively associated with support for better buildings and for programs for students who were not doing well. In the latter two cases, older white interviewees seemed to be voicing more conservative attitudes against spending more for schools and "coddling" students. Interviewees who

Table 7.5. *Significant predictors of strategic priorities for improving the schools*

Strategy	Significant predictors for	
	Blacks	Whites
General academic		
More or better teachers	Education (+)	None
More or better materials	Education (+)	Contact with blacks (+)
Physical arrangements and security		
More security for schools	Education (–)	Education (–)
	City residence (+)	
Better buildings	Education (–)	Education (+)
		Age (–)
		Attended integrated schools (+)
More discipline for students	Age (+)	Age (+)
	Attended integrated schools (+)	Discrimination against self (+)
	Sex (–)	Percent black in neighborhood (–)
More programs		
For very good students	Education (–)	Age (+)
	School-age children (+)	
For students who aren't doing well	Sex (+)	Age (–)
To help parents cope…	None	Education (+)
School integration	None	Education (+)

had attended integrated schools assigned a higher priority to discipline for students, but, interestingly, not to school integration. In general, then, differences in support for these strategies for improving the schools were substantial but not very predictable.

Residence and Schools

Most interviewees found the schools in their community wanting. Only a minority considered the schools pretty good as is, and half of the blacks and nearly half of the whites said they needed lots of improvement. Suburbanites' ratings of the schools were much more favorable than those of city dwellers, but even in the suburbs one white in ten and one black in three said the schools needed lots of improvement.

We noted early in this chapter that blacks' and whites' attitudes on a variety of spending measures were inconsistently related to where they lived. In sharp contrast to that finding, blacks' less positive evaluations of their schools were almost totally explainable in terms of residential context, especially the performance of the schools in the areas where they lived. City dwellers' attitudes were firmly rooted in the realities of the Detroit schools. Blacks living in the suburbs expressed much more favorable evaluations of their schools than did black city residents. Thus, place of residence and the resulting quality of the schools in one's area overshadowed race per se as the primary determinants of evaluations of schools.

However, residential context had very little impact on the steps our interviewees endorsed for improving the schools. Instead of the contextually defined racial cleavage that we observed for assessments of the schools, blacks and whites expressed similar views about what should be done to improve the schools, views that transcended place of residence.

That neither blacks nor whites embraced school integration as a strategy for improving the schools in their community implies that an important change may have occurred in the views of blacks and some whites. During the 1950s and 1960s and into the 1970s, school integration was hailed as the major means by which the quality of education could be improved for African American children, but among our interviewees there was no widespread sense that racial integration held the key to improving the schools.

Our findings cast an interesting light on those of Henig, Hula, Orr, and Pedescleaux (1999), who, in their study of public education in four black-led cities, including Detroit, found that the issue of race is an impediment to school progress. They demonstrate that black civic leaders are reluctant to criticize black school leaders, hoping to show solidarity with them. White civic leaders are also reluctant to criticize because they do not want to be labeled racist. Hence, school problems are not dealt with head-on. Our findings reveal that underlying the tentativeness of these civic leaders, the public's views of the performance of the schools crosses racial boundaries. Individuals' views about their public schools are shaped much more by where they live than by the color of their skin. This suggests, yet again, that racial barriers are not impermeable and can be reduced when blacks and whites share common experiences (Sniderman and Carmines, 1997). Of course, it can never be forgotten that the color of an individual's skin in metropolitan Detroit has a great deal to do with where he or she lives.

URBAN JUSTICE

Just as we found that residence affected our respondents' views of their schools, so too did we expect residence to play a part in shaping their views of the police. Obviously, police services have a citywide scope, but police relations with residents can and do vary widely in different parts of a city. We expect residence to play a large role in attitudes toward the police, with blacks and whites who live in mostly black neighborhoods having a more negative view of the police than those in largely white neighborhoods, and with city dwellers being more negative than suburbanites.

Historical Context

American justice may be blind, but there is abundant evidence that it is not color-blind (Durand, 1976; Myrdal, 1944). Myrdal (1944) noted that disparities in the treatment of blacks and whites by the police and in the courts stemmed from racial attitudes, historical traditions, and the degree to which blacks held political power. Except in a few large cities, blacks had no voice in government and hence held no sway over the legal system. The legacies of slavery and of legalized segregation and discrimination gave law enforcement personnel life-and-death powers over African Americans, who perceived the police as agents of an oppressive, racist system rather than as enforcers of impartial justice. The beating that Rodney King suffered at the hands of Los Angeles police in 1991 and the belief of many blacks that O.J. Simpson was "framed" for murder exemplified ongoing episodes of mistreatment of blacks by the police and the deeply ingrained mistrust that grew out of decades of such mistreatment.

During the 1950s and 1960s, the American system of justice underwent major transformation, including the erosion of the legal foundations of segregation, Supreme Court decisions that empowered black defendants, and the enactment of civil rights legislation in 1964, 1965, and 1968. As profound as they were, these transformations did not bring about the demise of separate systems of justice for blacks and whites. Old patterns of race relations and the impact of centuries of racial injustice could not be overridden in just a few years or by words printed on paper, even words that were supposed to have the force of law.

In the 1960s, when racial tensions exploded into urban riots, the Kerner Commission characterized bitterness toward the police in black neighborhoods as the deepest source of resentment sparking these riots. Blacks resented the police for their brutality, harassment, and enforcement of two standards of justice. In white communities, rigorous standards of law enforcement were implemented, but in black communities, the authorities' laissez-faire attitude allowed drug addiction, prostitution, and street violence to flourish. Police response to black complaints was sluggish, and the police who responded were overwhelmingly white. The small numbers of black police officers and the even smaller numbers of African Americans in the police hierarchy reinforced the alienation of many blacks. According to the Kerner Commission, blacks' grievances against police practices, including verbal and physical abuse of blacks, discrimination against blacks who applied for jobs as police officers, lack of respect for black citizens, and the failure of the police to combat crime in black neighborhoods, were rivaled in seriousness only by their grievances about unemployment and inadequate housing (National Advisory Commission on Civil Disorders, 1968: 143–150). Most African Americans believed that police officers routinely harassed black suspects and that most police officers were prejudiced. The latter perception appeared to be accurate: According to one study, only 1% of the officers employed in predominantly black districts had attitudes that "could be described as sympathetic toward Negroes ... Close to half showed extreme prejudice" (National Advisory Commission on Civil Disorders, 1968: 306; see also Campbell, 1971; Widick, 1989). Blacks, especially younger blacks, continued to be very critical of the police (Durand, 1976; Peek, Alston, and Lowe, 1978; Scaglion and Condon, 1980).

By the 1990s, the racial composition of the police force in most big cities resembled that of the community much more closely than it had in the 1960s. Between 1970 and 1990, the number of black police officers nationwide nearly tripled (Hacker, 1992: 121). Even so, during the 1990s headline stories continued to publicize tensions between police and blacks, which surfaced regularly in allegations of police mistreatment of young black males, planting of incriminating evidence, and falsification of police testimony, along with beatings and verbal abuse (*Los Angeles Times*, March 10 1991: A1). African Americans were disproprotionately the victims when police killed civilians, although analysts disagreed about the extent to which racism was responsible (Jaynes and Williams, 1989: 478–479).[7] Toward the end of the decade, the issue of racial profiling and hostile treatment of African American drivers ("driving while black") became a national issue as well. Thus, images of police brutality and partiality continued to shape blacks' views of the police (Scaglion and Condon, 1980).

It was hardly surprising, then, that black distrust of the police persisted. In our survey, black interviewees were much less likely than whites to agree that it would be appropriate for a police officer to hit an adult male, although slightly over half (54%, as compared with 79% of our white interviewees) did say they could think of circumstances where this would be appropriate. The reluctance of blacks to endorse aggressive police behavior undoubtedly reflected a perception that when citizens are abused, blacks are likely to be the victims.

The Rodney King incident in Los Angeles revealed both the changes that had occurred in police–community relations and the underlying problems that remained. Most Americans, black and white, were outraged by the King beating. Nearly two-thirds of whites and 92% of blacks nationwide thought the officers who beat King should have been convicted, as two eventually were after first being acquitted. Yet, whereas 78% of blacks agreed immediately after the original acquittal that the verdict meant that "blacks cannot get justice in this country," 66% of the white public disagreed (Edsall, 11–17 May 1992: 10).

Changing Views of Justice in Detroit

Detroit was an especially appropriate setting for studying public attitudes toward the police and the justice system. Myrdal (1944) considered Detroit notable among Northern cities for its inhospitality to blacks, and it was an issue of police behavior that sparked Detroit's largest modern racial disturbance. In 1967, a police raid on an after-hours black nightclub set off several days of death and destruction, which were instrumental in the appointment of the Kerner Commission. In 1992, the bludgeoning death of Malice Green further intensified the already tense relations between the Detroit Police Department and the African American community.

---

7 Some research suggests that police are more likely to shoot blacks because blacks are more likely to be armed with guns or to be involved in criminal activities (Milton, Halleck, Lardner, and Abrecht, 1977; Fyfe, 1981) but also that the rate of police shootings of blacks is much lower where police departments have stringent policies on the use of firearms and conduct stringent reviews whenever guns are used (Fyfe, 1982; Sherman, 1980; see also Sherman, 1979).

Opinions on Urban Issues

At the time of the Kerner Commission report, whites controlled Detroit. The city had a white mayor, a white city council, and a white police force. In a city where 39% of the residents were African Americans, the police force was only 5% black.[8] By the 1990s, though, blacks occupied the mayor's office, controlled the city council, and accounted for 55% of the police force.

Evaluations of the Police

How did the facts that Detroit was run by an African American–dominated local government and that the police force was heavily African American influence black residents' assessments of the police in our 1992 survey (see Welch, Combs Bledsoe, and Sigelman, 1996 in another examination of these data)? Of course, any evaluation of the effectiveness of police services depends not only on the services themselves, but also on the frequency and seriousness of crime. Even so, assessments of police effectiveness reflect a perception of fair treatment and responsiveness as well as crime solving.

We asked our interviewees how satisfied they were with police protection in their neighborhood, whether they thought the police would respond as quickly to their own call for police assistance as to a call from a person of the other race, and whether police officers, if given the right to stop and search people who looked suspicious, would use this power against blacks. In all three cases, blacks voiced greater distrust of the police than did whites (Figure 7.2). More than half of our white interviewees (55%) described themselves as well satisfied with police protection in their neighborhood, but only 17% of our black interviewees agreed. Five blacks in ten (49%), but only one white in ten (11%) were apprehensive that the police would not respond as quickly to their call for help as to a call from a member of the other race. In addition, 89% of blacks but only 61% of whites suspected that police officers would use the right to stop and search against blacks.

Detroiters' reactions to the killing of Malice Green by Detroit police officers in November, 1992 (see chapter 2) provided additional evidence of black–white differences in views of the police. As it happened, the Green killing occurred while our survey was underway. Although 90%

---

8 Black police were more representative of the community population in several other cities with large black populations, although none approached proportionality. Philadelphia, for example, with 29% black population, had a 20% black police force; St Louis, 37% and 11%, respectively; Atlanta, 38% and 10%; and Chicago, 27% and 17%. Detroit was more similar in this respect to Baltimore (41% and 7%); Cleveland (34% and 7%); Memphis (38% and 5%); and New Orleans (41% and 4%).

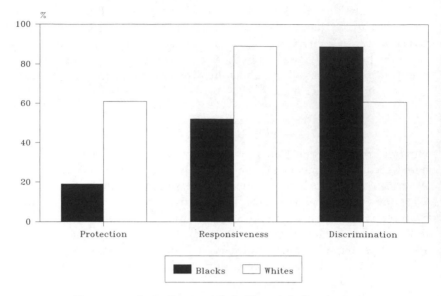

Figure 7.2. Attitudes toward the Detroit police, by race.

of our interviews had already been completed, nearly 100 were carried out afterwards, allowing us to examine the impact of the incident on our interviewees' views of the police (see Sigelman, Welch, Combs and Bledsoe, 1997, for a more comprehensive account).

Before the Green incident, 80% of the African Americans we interviewed agreed that a "Rodney King–like incident could happen here," reflecting distrust of the police and the justice system. Only 24% of whites agreed. After the Green killing, nearly every black (99%) interviewee agreed, and the proportion of whites who agreed rose dramatically, to 63%. Thus, even before the Green incident, black Detroiters' distrust of the police was very widespread. Afterwards it was nearly universal.

Surveys conducted in Detroit in 1959, 1971, and 1990 enabled us to provide greater historical context for these sentiments (Bledsoe, 1990). Based on those surveys, it would appear that African Americans' satisfaction with the police declined dramatically after 1959.[9] In 1959, about 20% more blacks said they were very satisfied with police service than said they were dissatisfied (Figure 7.3). By 1971, about 20% more were dissatisfied than very satisfied, and by 1990, about 25% more were dissatisfied. Thus, most of the decrease in satisfaction occurred between

9 The question was: Are you well satisfied, more or less satisfied, or not at all satisfied with the protection provided for your neighborhood by the police?

Opinions on Urban Issues

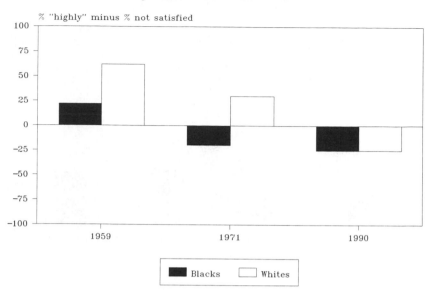

Figure 7.3. Satisfaction with police, Detroit, 1959, 1971, and 1990.

1959 and 1971, when the police department was still dominated by whites. The election of a black mayor and the transformation of the police into a majority-black force slowed the downward trend in blacks' satisfaction, but obviously did not reverse it.

In 1959, white Detroiters were much more satisfied than blacks with the police, with satisfaction among whites outrunning dissatisfaction by more than 60%. Over the next 12 years, satisfaction declined somewhat, but whites were still very positively disposed. After 1971, whites' satisfaction with the police plummeted, falling to the level expressed by blacks. Thus, the dramatic change in the racial composition of Detroit's police force did not enhance blacks' satisfaction and may have reduced whites' satisfaction. Racial equality was finally achieved in public assessments of the police. Both blacks and whites were massively dissatisfied.

What has not come through in these comparisons of the assessments of blacks and whites is the dramatic importance of location. Black Detroit residents' evaluations of the police dropped noticeably, but over the same period white Detroit residents' evaluations of police protection dropped by more than twice as much. Indeed, in sharp contrast to the situation in 1968, by the 1990s there was no black–white gap in Detroit residents' evaluations of the quality of the police services that they were receiving: Blacks and whites offered identical, and extremely negative, evaluations of the police.

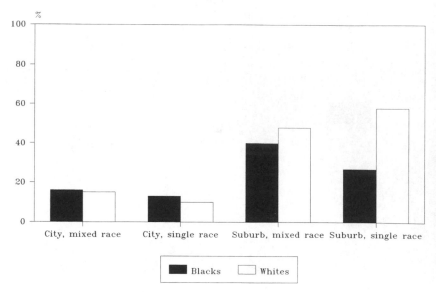

Figure 7.4. Satisfaction with police protection, by race and place.

Figure 7.4 focuses on blacks and whites who expressed satisfaction with the protection the police were providing for their neighborhood. If by equal justice we mean a sense of equal protection under the law, then these responses indicate that blacks and whites in metropolitan Detroit did not enjoy equal justice.

Blacks and whites residing in mixed-race neighborhoods of the city voiced very similar views, nor was there much difference between the views expressed by whites in white neighborhoods in Detroit and blacks in black neighborhoods in Detroit. As noted above, the vast majority of both blacks and whites living in the city expressed negative views about the police. If anything, blacks were slightly more positive than whites.

Black and white suburbanites living in mixed-race neighborhoods also expressed very similar views of police protection, views that were much more positive than those of city residents. Thus, as we expected, residence is a key factor in shaping attitudes toward police services and police fairness. It appears to be more important than race per se. This is further confirmed by the fact that it was only blacks and whites living in single-race suburban neighborhoods who differed substantially in their satisfaction with police services. Whites in white neighborhoods were more than twice as likely to be satisfied with the police as blacks in black neighborhoods (59% vs. 25%).

Opinions on Urban Issues

To gain a clearer understanding of the racial patterning of attitudes toward the police, we broadened the analysis to encompass all three measures of our interviewees' attitudes toward the police: the question about overall satisfaction with police protection that we have just been examining, the question about whether the police would respond as quickly to their call for help as to a call from a person of the other race, and the question about whether the police would use the power to stop and search unfairly against African Americans.

We assessed the impact of the respondent's race on attitudes toward the police while controlling for many of the same personal and contextual factors that we used in earlier analyses. Here we included the interviewee's age, sex, level of education, financial status, and degree of interracial contact, along with the variables of central interest, residence in the city of Detroit or the suburbs, and the black percentage of the residents of an interviewee's neighborhood. Previous research indicated that personal and neighborhood factors were predictive of attitudes such as fear of crime as well as actual victimization. For example, women and older people had been shown to be more likely to be victims of crimes and to fear crime, and levels of education were known to be inconsistently related to fear of crime (Houts and Kassab, 1997; Moeller, 1989; Skogan and Maxfield, 1981; Stafford and Galle, 1984).

The results of these analyses indicated, first, that when other personal and contextual factors were taken into account, African Americans were no less satisfied than whites with the protection the police were providing for their neighborhood, although "no more dissatisfied" might be a more appropriate description (Table 7.6.) However, black–white differences emerged when we asked whether the police would be as responsive to the interviewee's call as to that of a caller of another race and whether the police would use stop-and-search powers against blacks. Blacks were less likely than whites to believe that the police would respond with equal alacrity when called by an African American; controlling for all the other variables in the model, a black interviewee had about 6 chances in 10 of believing this (.62), a white interviewee about 3 chances in 4 (.78). By a wider margin, African Americans were also more likely than whites to doubt that the police would use stop-and-search powers in a nondiscriminatory way. The "average" African American in the lower portion of Table 7.6 had only a .09 probability of expecting the police to wield such powers evenhandedly, less than one-third of the probability (.38) we calculated for an otherwise identical white.

Where our interviewees lived was a crucial factor structuring their responses to our questions about the police. On two of the three questions (the exception being the one about stop-and-search powers), whether an interviewee lived in the city or the suburbs was the best pre-

Table 7.6. *Predicting attitudes toward the police*

Predictor	Satisfaction		Responsiveness		Fairness	
	b	(s.e.)	*b*	(s.e.)	*b*	(s.e.)
Detroit residence	–.89	(.08)^a	–.49	(.09)^a	.08	(.10)
Percent black in neighborhood	–.004	(.001)^a	–.002	(.002)	–.001	(.002)
Age	.01	(.002)^a	.01	(.003)^a	.01	(.003)^a
Sex	.22	(.07)^a	.19	(.09)^a	–.006	(.10)
Financial status	.16	(.05)^a	.18	(.06)^a	–.04	(.07)
Education	.01	(.01)	.05	(.02)^a	–.03	(.02)
Interracial contact	–.02	(.04)	.02	(.05)	–.03	(.05)
Race	.02	(.11)	–.46	(.13)^a	–1.05	(.14)^a
Constant	.38	(.21)	–.25	(.28)	–.33	(.29)
Pseudo-*R* squared	.19		.14		.13	

	Predicted probability of responding:		
	"Well satisfied" with police protection	Police would respond as quickly	Police would be fair
Detroit resident	.12	.60	.20
Suburbanite	.39	.77	.18
Percent black 1 s.d. below mean	.29	.73	.20
Percent black 1 s.d. above mean	.20	.66	.18
White	.24	.78	.38
Black	.25	.62	.09

Note: b is the unstandardized regression coefficient, derived from a binomial or ordered probit regression analysis (depending on the number of categories in the dependent variable), followed in parentheses by the standard error of the coefficient (s.d. = standard deviation).
$^a p < .05$.

dictor of these responses. Other factors being equal, suburbanites were more than three times as likely as residents of Detroit to be "well satisfied" with police protection (.39 versus .12) and were more confident, by a .77 to .60 margin, that their call would be handled as quickly as one from someone of the other race.

Living in a predominantly black neighborhood also led to negative evaluations of police performance. The larger the proportion of blacks in a neighborhood, the less likely an interviewee, black or white, was to be satisfied with the protection the police were providing for the neighborhood. Thus, the racial composition of the interviewee's neighborhood rather than the race of the interviewee appeared to shape satisfaction with police protection. On the other hand, it was the race of the interviewee rather than the racial composition of the neighborhood that shaped responses to the other two questions.

Of the remaining variables in the model, age displayed the most consistent relationship with assessments of the police. Older interviewees were more likely to believe that the police were providing adequate protection, that their calls would be answered as quickly as those of someone of the other race, and that the police would act in a nondiscriminatory manner. Women also were more satisfied with police services, as were wealthier interviewees, but level of education and interracial contact had few consistent effects on these attitudes.

The null effect of interracial contact is worth noting because interracial contact has been significantly related to many of the attitudes we have explored in previous chapters. Interracial contact tends to breed more positive feelings and empathy toward those of the other race. Here we are asking individuals to evaluate public services; interracial contact has little effect. Blacks and whites obviously are judging police performance from their own experience and do not rely on their acquaintances of other races to help interpret that performance.

In general, then, when we took city versus suburban residence into account, we observed negligible black–white differences in satisfaction with the police, although blacks were skeptical that their calls for assistance would produce as rapid a response as calls from a white person and that the police would use stop-and-search powers in a nondiscriminatory fashion.

As we have done throughout this work, we also looked at whites and blacks separately. Does residence account for within-race differences in views of the police? As before, we assumed that both blacks and whites would have more positive attitudes toward the police in largely white areas and in the suburbs. Table 7.7 suggests that this is true some of the time. Both blacks and whites in Detroit are less likely to be satisfied with police protection in their neighborhood. This is highly significant for both races. City residents are also less likely to believe that the police would respond to blacks as quickly as to whites. There is no difference between central-city and suburban residents in their belief that police would use stop-and-search procedures unfairly against blacks.

These individual race analyses are consistent with our findings in Table 7.6 for our sample as a whole. City residence does make a big difference on two of the three items.

Our findings concerning the proportion of blacks in the neighborhood are also consistent with the combined race analysis of Table 7.6. The

Table 7.7. *Predicting attitudes toward the police, by race*

	Satisfaction		Responsiveness		Fairness	
Predictor	Black	White	Black	White	Black	White
Detroit residence	−.19[a]	−.36[a]	−.14[a]	−.18[a]	−.03	−.03
	(.04)	(.04)	(.06)	(.06)	(.03)	(.05)
Percent black in neighborhood	−.002	−.001	−.002[a]	−.001	−.000	.001
	(.001)[a]	(.001)	(.001)	(.001)	(.001)	(.001)
Age	.003[a]	.004[a]	.007[a]	−.001	−.002	−.003[a]
	(.001)	(.001)	(.001)	(.001)	(.001)	(.001)
Sex	.07[a]	.03[a]	.14[a]	.05[a]	−.03	.03
	(.03)	(.03)	(.04)	(.02)	(.03)	(.05)
Financial status	.002[a]	.001[a]	−.07[a]	.01	.001	.001
	(.001)	(.001)	(.03)	(.03)	(.001)	(.001)
Education	.001	.01[a]	.05	.02	.01	.01
	(.006)	(.006)	(−.01)	(.01)	(.01)	(.01)
Interracial contact	−.001	.01	.02	.001	−.02	.04
	(.02)	(.02)	(.02)	(.02)	.01	.03
Constant	.41	.29	−.26	.72	.94	−.39
Pseudo-R squared	.15	.31	.12	.08	.04	.04

Note: Coefficients are *b* values with standard errors in brackets.
[a] *p* < .05.

proportion of blacks in the neighborhood matters for blacks. Those living in neighborhoods with greater proportions of blacks are less satisfied with police protection and less likely to believe that police would respond as quickly as they do for whites. Blacks' responses on the third item, using stop-and-search procedures against blacks, are not affected by the proportion of blacks in their neighborhoods, and whites' responses are not affected on any of the three items by the proportion of blacks in their neighborhoods.

Of course, our survey measured public perceptions of police practices, not necessarily the reality of these practices. That the police would use stop-and-search powers in a discriminatory manner against blacks hardly seemed far-fetched, as many law-abiding blacks who have been stopped for "driving while black" would have had reason to understand. On the other hand, the idea that the police would actually respond more promptly to white than to black requests for service has not fared well when put to the test; research has indicated that police response times tend to be about the same for white and black calls (Brandl, Frank, Worden, and Bynum, 1993; Worden, 1981, 1993).

More generally, our conclusion that the race of the individual mattered little in understanding public satisfaction with police protection, while correct, could be misleading, because it did not reflect the proportion of blacks and whites living in a given type of location. For example, although whites living in predominantly white neighborhoods in the city of Detroit were as dissatisfied with police protection as were blacks living in black Detroit neighborhoods, it was also the case that whites living in predominantly white neighborhoods in Detroit constituted only 3% of the white population of the metropolitan area, whereas blacks living in predominantly black neighborhoods in the city of Detroit accounted for 54% of the black population of the metropolitan area. Similarly, although suburban blacks living in mixed-race neighborhoods were relatively satisfied with police protection in their neighborhoods, only 10% of metropolitan area blacks lived in these neighborhoods.

The racial contrast in satisfaction with police services can be well illustrated by the fact that whites in the most highly satisfied group, those living in white suburban neighborhoods, were 84% of all whites in the Detroit metropolitan area. Those blacks in the least satisfied group, central-city blacks in black neighborhoods, constituted 54% of all metropolitan blacks. By controlling for our interviewees' place of residence, then, we clarified the source of public frustration with police services but camouflaged the real differences in attitudes toward the police between most blacks and most whites in the metropolitan area.

The complexity of these patterns becomes even more obvious when we consider who was in control of the local governments in the Detroit area when our survey was conducted. It was in the black-controlled city that blacks were least satisfied with police protection, and it was in the white-controlled suburbs that they were least dissatisfied. Thus, unlike earlier eras, when police brutality and neglect of African Americans' needs could plausibly be attributed to white control of government in general and of the police force in particular, that explanation obviously would not hold for Detroit in the past decade.

DISCUSSION

By the 1990s, African Americans possessed considerably more political power than they had ever before wielded in the United States in general and in Detroit in particular, where they controlled the apparatus of city government. Yet even in Detroit, they were profoundly dissatisfied with the services they were receiving from local government.

Residues of segregation and discrimination continued to affect vital urban services. Segregation, whether de facto or de jure, produced schools in black neighborhoods that were generally inferior to those in white areas in terms of physical facilities, curricula, and pupil outcomes. Exacerbating these problems were family structures and resources in parts of the black community that were not highly supportive of academic achievement. Poverty-level incomes were manifestations of historical patterns of discrimination compounded by the poor quality of education provided for black children. The prevalence of single-parent families in black neighborhoods was a residue of segregation interacting in a complex manner with poor employment opportunities for black men and with contemporary mores whose impact was most corrosive for low-income families.

Residues of historical patterns of discrimination also remained in the actions of police officers who violated the rights of African Americans and in public attitudes about the police. Most of our black interviewees distrusted the police, even when the person wearing the uniform was an African American, and in retrospect it hardly seems surprising that people, black or white, who perceived their homes and neighborhoods as unsafe would not support the police. The continuing lack of support for the police among African Americans in Detroit suggests, among other things, the limitations of acquiring political power as a step toward erasing bitterness and alienation. National surveys have portrayed African Americans as far more likely than whites to want to place limits on police discretion. When more details of the context for police action have been provided in these surveys, blacks' attitudes more closely resemble those of whites, which suggests that blacks probably expect the same sort of law enforcement as do whites but view the police suspiciously, as symbols of oppression.

Black Detroiters were dissatisfied with both the schools and the police during the 1960s, and their dissatisfaction grew after the city passed to black control. Thus, although blacks' ascension to political power may have eroded the most blatant racial injustices of the past, it was not sufficient to provide what was widely seen as a high-quality school system for educating the city's children or an impartial system of justice for protecting the city's residents.

Of course, neither city governments nor school boards are autonomous units with clear-cut powers to change decades of inequitable treatment. Both school boards and city governments have limited powers and resources. They are restricted by national and state governments, often much less interested in urban problems than in other issues, and also financially pressed with demands for other services, such as health care and prisons. Urban education and the issues of urban police performance are not at the very top of either the national or the state agenda. Therefore, the failure of the black-led government in Detroit to make dramatic changes in the opinions that black citizens hold of the police and the schools should not necessarily be attributed to that government's lack of interest in or commitment to these issues. What it does illustrate is that the problems of race are much more complex than in the days of Myrdal, when it was clear that a white-led police force and a white-led school board were quite comfortable with unequal justice and education.

A central finding of this chapter is that where African Americans lived shaped their perceptions and assessments of the schools and the police in their community. Blacks living the Detroit suburbs had very different views of both the schools and the police than did those living in the city. These attitudinal differences reflected, in large measure, the differential performance of the neighborhood schools and differences in neighborhood crime and safety. Within the city of Detroit, blacks and whites expressed similar views of the schools and the police, and the same was true in mixed-race suburban neighborhoods. Only in single-race suburban communities did blacks and whites differ in their views of the schools and the police. Nonetheless, even though blacks and whites living in similar circumstances had similar views of the police, relatively few Detroit-area blacks lived in the sorts of circumstances that produced more positive views of the police. Thus, the hypersegregation of the Detroit area – the confinement of African Americans to the central city and the dispersion of whites to the suburbs – was instrumental in maintaining the differential quality of justice that blacks and whites perceived, even though the control of the police in the city had passed into the hands of African Americans.

8

Conclusions

We began this book by asking whether the decline in residential segregation in major metropolitan areas affects the way blacks and whites think about themselves and each other. We begin this concluding chapter by stating that it does matter. Whites' attitudes about blacks and blacks' attitudes about whites are indeed affected by where blacks and whites live in relationship to each other. The views of both blacks and whites about urban public policies are also strongly shaped by where they live.

Of course, residential segregation shapes much about urban life, including the quality of schools that children attend, the crime rates and the social pathology of the neighborhood in which families live, and the availability of opportunities for job seekers. On the whole, life chances are strongly influenced by the neighborhood in which one resides, so it is not surprising that where one lives affects attitudes too. Directly and indirectly, residential patterns have the potential to influence many key attitudes and behaviors, including those about race, opportunity, politics, and policy.

The influence does not run exclusively in one direction, however. People choose their neighborhoods, and some do so to escape living with people of another race. However, to acknowledge this important reality is not to deny the significance of the findings that neighborhoods influence individuals' choice of friends, casual contacts, views about public policies, and many other attributes relevant to interracial relationships.

These findings flow from a long and distinguished tradition of research on the impact of context on the political and social lives of individuals. Beginning in the presurvey research era of the 1940 election, political scientists and sociologists have explored the influence of friendship circles and residential context on electoral behavior (see, e.g., Berelson, Lazarsfeld, and McPhee, 1954), ethnic identity (Huckfeldt, 1983), political attitudes (Cox, 1974), and white flight (Orbell and Sherrill, 1969; Huckfeldt, 1986, chapter 6), among other things. The key finding of this stream of research is that social groups are not important just because their members share some characteristic such as race, religion, residential locale, or income, but because of the interaction of members of the group in a variety of social experiences. That interaction can promote intragroup cohesion, as when Polish American immigrants associate only with other Polish Americans or African Americans with other African Americans. To the extent that residential proximity promotes social interaction with other groups, residential context can help in the process of assimilating so-called minority groups into a broader mainstream. Moreover, social interaction can affect the dominant group by exposing its members to the perspectives and life experiences of the minority group.

Interaction can also promote conflict between groups. Contact can create friction and misunderstanding, reinforce group identities, and widen the gap between groups. Although we acknowledge the opportunities for increased conflict that interaction brings, on the basis of previous findings about interracial friendship and its positive effects we expected neighborhood racial integration to lead to many more positive than negative outcomes. In fact, we did find that on balance, residential integration and the greater social contact it produced served to break down rather than exacerbate racial barriers.

Detroit, the focus of our study, is one of America's most racist areas, as measured by a long history of racial tension and violence, extreme housing segregation, and massive white flight from the city. For this reason, Detroit provides a hard test of our expectation that declines in residential segregation positively affect attitudes about race. If residence makes a difference in the Detroit area, it can make a difference anywhere. We also chose Detroit as our research site because of the wealth of previous survey data that has been accumulated there. Although no previous studies had carefully examined black suburbanites as we did, excellent data on black and white city dwellers and some data on white suburbanites provided historical benchmarks for the racial attitudes that we probed.

RACE RELATIONS IN DETROIT SINCE THE 1960S

Much has changed in Detroit since the 1960s: A majority-white city has become a majority-black city surrounded by largely white suburbs; a city government controlled by whites has become a city government dominated by blacks; a city school system controlled by whites and with a majority of white students has become a city school system controlled by blacks and with a majority of black students; and a police force that systematically underrepresented blacks as officers and frequently abused black citizens has become a police force led by and largely composed of African Americans.

Despite these sea changes in demographics and politics in the quarter-century since the Detroit riots, our study showed that changes in public attitudes about race have been less consistent. Our black and white inter-viewees perceived different realities on a number of racial and race-related issues. Blacks detected little evidence of progress in reducing discrimina-tion against themselves. They seemed to believe that there was almost as much discrimination in 1992 as there had been in the late 1960s, although we must take care in reaching that conclusion, given differences in the questions to which they responded in different surveys. Blacks recognized the limitations of civil rights laws and Supreme Court cases in their experi-ences. That is, while black interviewees did not dismiss the importance of changes brought by laws and public policy on race, they still perceived evi-dence of racism in their own day-to-day experiences and encounters with whites and institutions. Thus, blacks insisted that progress is more a change in manifestations of discrimination than an overall reduction in the impact of racism on their lives.

On the other hand, our white interviewees tended to believe that much progress in racial relations has been made, pointing to changes in the legal and legislative arenas and the decrease in overt discrimination and overt symbols of discrimination and racism. They noted the greatly decreased amount of violence against blacks, the disappearance of racially targeted zoning laws and restrictive covenants, and laws against discrimination in housing and lending. Although few could cite the details, whites can point to laws and court cases guaranteeing civil rights.[1] Finally, whites can emphasize the names of blacks who have "made it" in sports, entertain-ment, and other highly visible pursuits, including politics, education, and business. Thus, whites see the great progress in America's legal framework for race relations and they know about certain African Americans who have succeeded. They are less likely to see the all too frequent daily exam-ples of racism that their black counterparts see and experience. Thus, the gap between the races in perceiving discrimination against African Ameri-cans was probably wider in 1992 than it had been in 1968.

What this says is that whites and blacks have different lived experi-ences even in an era of progress. These different perspectives on the issue of progress are extremely important because they shape many other atti-tudes about race, about public policy, about life chances, and at the most fundamental level, about American society.

---

1 These include the Civil Rights Act of 1964, the Fair Housing Act of 1968, the Civil Rights Act of 1991, and the Supreme Court cases *Griggs v. Duke Power Company, Milliken v. Bradley,* and *Regents of the University of California v. Bakke.*

Conclusions

Segregation in neighborhoods as well as in the organizations and activities rooted in neighborhoods is a key factor in maintaining that diversity of perspectives. With limited opportunities to interact with blacks, whites are sheltered from the realities of life as many, perhaps most, African Americans experience it. Likewise, with opportunities to interact with whites restricted, blacks often base their views of American society on a selective and limited set of individuals and institutions.

Despite the gulf in perceptions of racism in America, Detroit whites' own attitudes about blacks showed signs of softening somewhat. Whites became more likely to approve of blacks as neighbors and less likely to express racist attitudes. Moreover, compared with the situation a quarter of a century earlier, blacks and whites in the 1990s saw more of one another. Just as national trends have shown increased racial intermingling as evidenced by, at its closest, interracial marriage and mixed-race children, so too has contact increased between blacks and whites in Detroit. Casual interracial contact increased considerably. On the job, in venues for children's activities, in shopping, and even in residential patterns, blacks and whites were having more contact with each other than they used to. In our 1992 survey, a quarter of the white interviewees and 40% of blacks claimed to have a friend of the other race (a black or a white friend, respectively), and over 12% of whites and nearly 40% of blacks claimed to have a relative of the other race.

Beyond mere contact, we have seen that increased interaction between blacks and whites affects their attitudes on racial issues as well as their perceptions of one another. Our Detroit respondents often came into contact under just those conditions that stimulate a positive effect: voluntary interaction between those of more or less equal status.

For the most part, however, blacks found themselves interacting with whites where whites were in the majority. Most blacks who attended school with whites had numerous white classmates, whereas whites who went to an integrated school had only a few black classmates. The same can be said of interracial contact in the workplace. As early as 1968, most blacks had some contact with whites on the job, and the trend continued apace in 1992. In the late 1960s, contact with blacks was still the exception for whites. By 1992, however, more than two whites in three had job-related contact with blacks.

Most blacks continued to register a preference for living in integrated neighborhoods, and whites expressed greater acceptance of integrated housing then they had earlier. Even so, 20% of our white interviewees admitted to having moved to escape black neighbors.

Blacks and whites do not see eye to eye on ideal levels of integration. In school and residential settings, integration is often still at a token level. Although most blacks prefer to live in neighborhoods that are about half black, few neighborhoods fit that pattern. Rather, either blacks or whites are small minorities in neighborhoods overwhelmingly of the other race. When whites are a vast majority in a neighborhood, integration approximates what most whites see as ideal; they want integration, but only where whites continue to be overwhelmingly dominant. When blacks become a significant minority, this often touches off white flight, turning a once segregated and then integrated neighborhood into a resegregated one (Schelling, 1973).

This has been true of schools as well, for an integrated school often means a few blacks in an overwhelmingly white school. When the number of black students becomes significant, then often the school resegregates, with few whites left behind in a school that other whites have deserted. Of course, in American society, it is easier to sustain the white ideal of integration (a small number of blacks in an overwhelmingly white setting) than the black (a more even mixture of black and white). This white ideal balance is much more reflective of the overall societal balance of blacks and whites, but it is not reflective of the racial balance in most of the nation's big cities, including Detroit.

The black–white gap in evaluations of urban public services narrowed in the quarter century preceding our survey. In the late 1960s, Detroit's whites were much more satisfied with local public services, such as police and education, than were blacks, but by the 1990s both blacks and whites were dissatisfied. Satisfaction declined even more precipitously among whites than among blacks, and blacks' assessments of city services fell rather than rose under a black-majority city government. Ironically, blacks' satisfaction with urban services was significantly higher in white-controlled suburbs than in black-controlled Detroit.

Thus, the overall response patterns we observed defied easy summary. It would be misleading to say, on the one hand, that attitudes did not change, that the racial gap was as large as it had been 25 years earlier. On the other hand, it would be equally erroneous to claim that all signs were pointing toward increased racial harmony and tolerance. The fact is that the patterns of interracial tolerance were extremely complex and were not all moving in the same direction. Those who want to believe that nothing changed and those who want to believe that almost everything changed for the better can both find some evidence to support their point of view. However, neither perspective takes into account the whole picture.

In *Facing up to the American Dream*, Jennifer Hochschild (1995) argued that although the status of African Americans has improved over the past 30 years, not only are well-off and poor blacks living in different worlds from each other, but many well-off blacks are discouraged about ever getting their fair share of what America has to offer (see also Cose,

Conclusions

1993; Hochschild, 1993). At the same time, whites are becoming ever more convinced that blacks are in fact sharing in the American dream. Our findings are consistent with Hochschild's interpretation. In spite of many concrete signs of progress, we uncovered numerous signs that many blacks did not feel that conditions for themselves and for blacks in general were getting better. They remained discouraged and in some ways were as likely to find discrimination as in the past. Yet we also saw that whites were quite optimistic about the treatment that blacks were receiving, being willing to believe that discrimination is largely a thing of the past and that blacks were sharing fully in the American dream.

Given that so many whites consider racial discrimination a thing of the past, it is not surprising that our white interviewees were not especially supportive of various proposed remedies to racial inequities (Sigelman and Welch, 1991). Kinder and Sanders (1996) make a related point in their examination of what they call racial resentment. In their view, white opinions about whether blacks have gotten more than they deserve, whether blacks can overcome prejudice without special favors, and whether blacks would do better if they would try harder are good predictors of other attitudes about race and public policy. Those who score high on a measure of racial resentment are quite unsupportive of policies designed to improve the status of blacks. Our white interviewees' beliefs that blacks are not victims of prejudice suggest that white support for policies to ameliorate the effects of racial discrimination will be hard to garner.

From another perspective, Sniderman and Hagen (1983), Sniderman and Piazza (1993), and Sniderman and Carmines (1997) have argued that white racism is no longer all that salient, that racial attitudes are highly susceptible to change if the right information is presented, and that much of what is often mistaken for prejudice against blacks is really more class prejudice than race prejudice. Although we find ample evidence of white racism in our data, we find support as well for Sniderman's idea that other factors also shape the fate of black Americans. In particular, where one lives and the resources one has are important influences on one's attitudes and the quality of one's life. The fact that suburban blacks were more satisfied with schools and police than were blacks living in the city has little to do with the race of those who control local government and much to do with the quality of and the resources provided for these services.

ASSESSING THE EFFECT OF RESIDENCE
ON RACE RELATIONS

In probing the link between opinions and interracial contact, we analyzed contextual data in ways that previous examinations of the link between attitudes and contact have not. Some previous studies had assessed individual-level indicators of interracial contact (friendship and association at work or elsewhere) without regard to residential patterns that might affect contact or conflict. Other studies had assessed individual attitudes about race in light of macrolevel residential patterns (the proportion of blacks at the county or metropolitan level). We combined these two perspectives by relating attitudes to neighborhood residential patterns.

We focused on two key measures of residential context. We expected attitudes in the city and suburbs to differ in a variety of ways, so we looked closely for urban–suburban differences. We expected that interracial contact would be higher in the city because of the greater racial heterogeneity there. In addition, we expected to uncover more signs of interracial friction in the city, in part because of the tremendous salience there of the race issue, which underlines and provides a steady flow of examples of prejudice and discrimination.

Because we also anticipated that the level of racial integration in neighborhoods would affect attitudes, we examined the proportion of blacks in an interviewee's neighborhood at the level of the census tract. Here our expectations were shaped by somewhat contradictory past research findings. At the macrolevel, the presence of significant numbers of black residents has often been found to be associated with greater white hostility toward African Americans, perhaps because whites feel threatened by large concentrations of blacks. However, at the individual level, interracial contact is generally thought to promote amity, not hostility, at least under some conditions. Our overall expectation was more in line with the latter idea, in that we thought neighborhood integration would likely promote better understanding and less prejudice between the races.

Using measures of city versus suburban residence and of the racial composition of the census tract, we did find evidence suggesting that residential integration was helping to modify public attitudes about race. This evidence was largely indirect, being based on significant differences between suburbanites and central city dwellers and between those living in nearly all-white or all-black neighborhoods and those in mixed-race neighborhoods. Many of these differences held, even after we controlled for a variety of demographic factors and for experience with racial integration. Living in the city and in mixed-race areas led, not surprisingly, to increased interracial contact. Even in hypersegregated Detroit, mixed-race neighborhoods do exist, and most of our interviewees reported that there were at least some members of the other race living in their neighborhood. Among whites, interracial contact was increased by living in the city and working in the city as well as by living in a mixed-race neighborhood. Among blacks, living in the city and living in a mixed-

Conclusions

race neighborhood did not affect interracial contact, but working in the suburbs did.

We observed a widening racial gap in perceptions of discrimination against African Americans, with blacks perceiving much more discrimination than did whites. In general, city dwellers, both blacks and whites, were more attuned to discrimination than were suburbanites, and both blacks and whites were more aware of antiblack discrimination if they lived in mixed-race neighborhoods.

We also found residence to be linked to African Americans' feelings of closeness to others of their race and to whites' feelings about blacks. In the case of blacks' racial solidarity, we found, as expected, that living in mixed-race neighborhoods decreased racial solidarity. In the suburbs, solidarity decreased with age, as older suburban blacks expressed less solidarity than did younger blacks. In general, solidarity seemed to decrease as contact with whites increased. These findings are in accord with those reported by Tate (1993), who found that higher-income blacks expressed less support than their lower-income counterparts for black candidates and black political parties.

Some commentators seem to find it unlikely that black solidarity can be eroded by environmental conditions of various sorts. In American politics, blacks are often discussed as if they were always a unified group with a single interest, race. However, without discounting at all the over-riding issue of race in America, we need to recognize that, like any other group, African Americans differ one from another, with differing emphases, needs, and interests in their lives. Cohen (1999) has sketched a sophisticated portrait of schisms within the black community, specifically schisms brought about by the onset of AIDS among black homosexuals and drug users. These conflicts produced new alliances and networks and fragmented some old networks. Although the processes of residential integration that we have discussed are far less striking forms of social change than the AIDS epidemic, they too have the potential to change ongoing structures and patterns of behavior and thought among both blacks and whites.

Just as blacks in mixed-race neighborhoods were less likely to feel a sense of solidarity with others of their race, whites in mixed-race neighborhoods were less likely to express prejudiced attitudes about blacks. Living in mixed-race areas seems to have reduced whites' reliance on negative stereotypes about blacks and their opposition to racial intermarriage. However, when we controlled for the racial composition of the neighborhood, we observed that city whites were more prejudiced than suburban whites in terms of accepting negative stereotypes of blacks, but they were also more accepting of interracial marriage. Thus, the effect of city residence on racial prejudice was mixed.

Race and Place

We acknowledge that residential context can be both a cause and an effect of racial attitudes. We tested the expectation that where one lives influences one's attitudes, but racial attitudes obviously have some influence over where one chooses to live. The whites who are most hostile to racial integration would presumably be the first to flee when their neighborhood begins to be integrated, and would be the last to think about moving into a mixed-race neighborhood. Nonetheless, to the extent that residential integration has the power to change people's racial views, it will promote further residential integration, which in turn will positively influence attitudes about race.

ASSESSING THE EFFECT OF RESIDENCE ON POLICY ATTITUDES

Just as place of residence shapes attitudes about race, so too does it influence how they think about the services they are receiving from their local government. Real differences in the quality of services provided in the suburbs and the central city are, of course, a major reason for the link between place of residence and perceptions of the quality of services. Students in suburban schools perform better on standardized tests, and residents of the suburbs are less likely to be victims of crime. Thus, it is not surprising that when black suburbanites are compared with white suburbanites and with black and white city dwellers, suburbanites, no matter what their race, turn out to be more satisfied than city dwellers with educational and police services. Blacks and whites in the city are united in their dissatisfaction with both of these local services.

Ironically, in Detroit the replacement of a white-led city government with a black-led one led to a similarity of attitudes among blacks and whites toward the police, not by increasing the satisfaction of blacks but by decreasing the satisfaction of whites. Although we do not have similar information about racial trends over time in attitudes toward schools, the lack of racial differences in satisfaction observable in our survey probably stems from increasing white dissatisfaction along with widespread dissatisfaction among African Americans.

To say that the advent of black elected officials in Detroit was coincident with decreased satisfaction with public services on the part of both blacks and whites does not imply that these African American officials have done a poorer job than their white predecessors. Like their white counterparts, black elected officials do not control the resources necessary to improve service quality, let alone to boost quality of life indicators such as in-wedlock births or school retention ratios. In any community, urban officials are largely at the mercy of overall economic trends that are beyond their control and of state officials who do not

Conclusions

answer to them. What the increasing black–white convergence of opinion about urban services does suggest is that inadequate or unfair police and education services are not just a matter of race and of racial discrimination by unsympathetic or prejudiced white officials. Widespread dissatisfaction reflects complex conditions that make even sympathetic officials ineffective.

We do not intend to discount the key factor of race when we say that place is more important than race in predicting attitudes toward local services or when we point out that African Americans are more satisfied with public services in white-led suburban communities than in Detroit. As we have seen, relatively few blacks in the Detroit metropolitan area live in the mixed-race suburban neighborhoods, where satisfaction with services is high, and relatively few whites live in central-city areas, where satisfaction is low. Rather, segregated residential patterns have led most blacks to be clustered in areas where services are poor and where satisfaction with services is consequently very low and most whites live in areas where services are much better and satisfaction is consequently much higher. Nonetheless, our findings illustrate that, when they live in the same type of environment, blacks and whites react similarly to the performance of their local government.

DETROIT AND THE FUTURE OF RACE RELATIONS

During the quarter century that led up to our 1992 survey, Detroit's economy changed for the worse. The city's population plummeted, its median family income fell, its housing stock aged, and its industrial base withered. In the face of that almost unrelievedly bad news, however, not every indicator of racial harmony declined. Some things about race relations improved.

Having reviewed these decidedly mixed signals about race relations in Detroit, we will end on an optimistic note. Despite continuing perceptions of serious discrimination against blacks and despite eroding confidence by both blacks and whites in the efficacy of local public policies, both blacks and whites seemed to judge the racial situation in Detroit as improving. This is remarkable, given the overall pattern of responses by African Americans to our questions about discrimination and by both blacks and whites to our questions about local educational and police services. Nonetheless, as Table 8.1 shows, not only were blacks more upbeat in evaluating local than national government, but, amazingly, they were also more upbeat than were whites.

For example, 39% of blacks, compared with 30% of whites, perceived less antiblack sentiment than 4 or 5 years earlier in the area where they were living, and only 9% and 15%, respectively, perceived more. Over-

Race and Place

Table 8.1. *Perceived antiblack feeling among whites compared with four or five years ago*

	Locally		Nationally	
Perception	Blacks	Whites	Blacks	Whites
Less	39	30	21	30
About the same	52	55	47	47
More	9	15	31	23

Note: Question wording: On a national basis, do you think today there is more, less, or about the same amount of antiblack feeling among whites as compared with four or five years ago? What about the area where you live? Do you think today there is...

all, of course, the modal response was that things had not changed much at either the national or the local level. Still, two to four times as many at the local level believed that things were getting better than believed that things were getting worse. What is especially surprising about these data is that both African Americans and whites were more optimistic about their local situation than about the national one. Despite Detroit's image as a bastion of Northern racism, more people, both black and white, saw progress than deterioration.

We have argued that residential integration and integration in the workplace have been promoting changes in how blacks and whites see one another. The good news is that the changes brought about by residential integration are largely in the hoped-for direction: Residential integration has increased interracial contact, and integration and contact have helped bring about more positive views of the other race and greater congruence in attitudes toward local public policies.

These trends are illustrated by the fact that it was blacks in largely white sections of the metropolitan area and whites in the largely black sections who saw the most positive change in race relations. Among blacks, 47% in largely white areas and 44% in the mixed-race areas but only 33% living in mostly black areas perceived less racism in 1992 than 5 years earlier. Among whites, 40% living in mostly black areas and 36% in mixed-race areas but only 26% in mostly white areas perceived less racism. Thus, having neighbors of the other race seemed to lessen perceived racial tensions.[2]

---

2 The proportions perceiving worse race relations did not differ significantly among the groups, being 8, 11, and 8%, respectively for blacks and 15, 15, and 12%, respectively, for whites in largely white, mixed, and largely black neighborhoods.

Conclusions

However, the bad news is that, despite progress in residential integration, most blacks and most whites in the Detroit area still live in neighborhoods where representation of the other race is minimal at best. As long as that continues to be the case, the ability of residential integration to facilitate further easing of racial tensions will obviously be limited.

Our study underscores the influence of interracial contact and place of residence in shaping attitudes among both blacks and whites. At the same time, we are aware that the maintenance of black communities can have important implications for the empowerment of blacks. The vast majority of black elected officials come from majority-black areas, and most black-owned businesses are located in majority-black areas (Barker, Jones and Tate, 1999). These political and economic power bases would be eroded by racially integrated neighborhoods. At the same time, interracial contact might increase the propensity of whites to vote for black candidates,[3] to support black-owned businesses, and even to attend black-led churches.

THE FUTURE OF RACE AND PLACE IN AMERICA'S MULTIETHNIC COMMUNITIES

The patterns we have uncovered bode well for race relations because of the slow trend toward greater racial integration in America's large cities. Moreover, Detroit is one of the most segregated cities in America and one of the cities not yet changed dramatically by immigration. These are other indications that the small changes we observed in Detroit will have larger societal implications.

Of U.S. cities with populations over 100,000, 55% have populations that are at least 10% black and at least 10% white (U.S. Census, 1998). Cities with black and white population combinations dominate the East, South, and Midwest (Frey and Farley, 1996:41).[4] Thus, the gradual movement toward black–white residential integration is an immensely important development in urban life.

However, another, more visible, demographic shift also bears on the patterns we have noted. With the increase in the number of Asians, Hispanics, Arabs, and other racial and ethnic groups from all over the world, American cities are becoming more pluralistic. The nation's political and social mosaic is significantly different from what it was at the height of the civil rights movement during the 1960s. These changes are

---

3 For an optimistic reading of this likelihood see Swain (1993); see also Whitby (1998).

4 In the Southwest, the predominant ethnic groups are, of course, non-Hispanic whites and Hispanics.

Race and Place

Table 8.2. *Changes in residential segregation in areas with large black populations[a]*

	North		South	
	1970	1990	1970	1990
Mean, all designated areas[b]	85	78	75	67
Mean, cities with largest Asian and Latino population	86	70	81	65
Detroit	88	88		

[a] These are 30 metropolitan areas with the largest black populations, 18 in the North, 12 in the South (see Massey, forthcoming). The dissimilarity index is used, which is a measure of the proportion of the population that would have to move for each group to equal in each census tract its overall proportion in the city's population. The most segregated city would score 100 and the least 0.

[b] Data are derived from Massey (forthcoming) and the *Statistical Abstract of the United States, 1999*, Table 45. The cities with the largest Asian and Latino populations are Los Angeles and San Francisco among the Northern cities (50% and 37%, respectively) and Miami and Houston in the South (37% and 29%, respectively).

muting the focus on black–white conflict that for so long has been the core of America's racial consciousness.

We expect movements toward residential integration, which in turn lessen tension in race relations, to happen faster in these more multicultural cities. Walls between ethnic groups are less rigid, as Asians and Hispanic communities develop beside and within those of blacks and whites (see Frey and Farley, 1996; Denton and Massey, 1991; Lee and Wood, 1991). Such communities may be a mediating force in black–white relationships because of difficulties in maintaining black and white barriers in cities where large groups of residents are neither white nor black. Latinos and Asians, though residentially segregated, are significantly less so than blacks (Massey, 2000).

One illustration of the potential mediating effect of Asian and Latino populations on black and white racial segregation is that black and white residential segregation decreased most between 1970 and 1990 in metropolitan areas with significant proportions of Asian and Latino residents (Table 8.2). (For a broader illustration, see Frey and Farley, 1996: Table 4.) In the two Northern and two Southern cities with the largest Asian and Latino populations, black–white residential segregation dropped significantly between 1970 and 1990, much more steeply than in other cities. This occurred even though these cities' initial (1970) levels of black–white residential segregation were slightly higher than those of other cities.

Although rates of decline in residential segregation are lower in cities that are predominantly black and white, mostly older cities of the North and Midwest, we have shown that even in one of the most segregated of those cities, neighborhood racial integration has had a modest salutary effect on race relations. This itself is a hopeful sign. That many of America's cities are changing their racial composition much faster than Detroit gives even more hope that these positive effects will make a real difference in America's race relations.

Appendix A: The Detroit Surveys

Between mid-July and mid-November, 1992, representatives of the Center for Urban Studies, Wayne State University, conducted in-home interviews with 1,124 residents of the Detroit metropolitan area. Funding for the survey was provided by National Science Foundation Grant SES-9112799.

Every household in the tricounty area was eligible for inclusion in the sample, but the stratification scheme made use of higher sampling fractions for African Americans, city residents, and residents of mixed-race neighborhoods than for whites, suburbanites, and residents of single-race neighborhoods. In mixed-race neighborhoods, interviewers engaged in doorstep screening to adjust for the overrepresentation of members of the predominant race (African Americans in the city, whites in the suburbs). In mixed-race neighborhoods in Detroit, interviews were conducted in every white household that was contacted but in only one out of every three black households. In mixed-race neighborhoods in the suburbs, interviews were conducted in every black household that was contacted but in only one out of every four white households. After interviewers established that an interview should be conducted in a given household, they used a "Kish table" to determine who within the household should be interviewed, and made as many as 10 call-backs to contact the designated respondent. In every instance, the race of the interviewer was matched to that of the respondent.

The response rate for the survey was approximately 56%. It was higher for African Americans than for whites and for city residents than for suburbanites. The sample has been weighted to adjust for differences in response rates and, where appropriate, in sampling fractions.

In the 1968 Detroit Area Study, which was directed by Howard Schuman, 619 African American residents of the city of Detroit were interviewed; all interviewees were adults below the age of 70. For further information about that survey and a summary of its major findings, see

Appendix A

Schuman and Hatchett (1974). The 1969 Detroit Area Survey, directed by Irwin Katz and Howard Schuman, sampled 640 white adult residents of the Detroit metropolitan area. We obtained the 1968 and 1969 Detroit Area Study data sets from the Inter-University Consortium for Political and Social Research.

The National Science Foundation, the Inter-University Consortium for Political and Social Research, and the original collectors of the 1968 and 1969 Detroit Area Study data bear no responsibility for our analyses and interpretations.

Appendix B: 1992 Detroit Survey Items and Measures

In this appendix we describe the items from our 1992 survey and the composite measures based on responses to those items that we employed in the figures and tables in this book, listed in the order in which the figures and tables appear. Each item or measure is described in conjunction with the figure or table in which it was introduced. Thus, any figure or table in which no "new" items or measures were introduced is not included here.

Figure 2.3:
Based on responses to: If you could find housing you would want and like, would you rather live in a neighborhood that is all-black, mostly black, half black–half white, mostly white, or all white?

Figure 2.4:
Based on responses to: Some civil rights leaders say that blacks should be more concerned with developing the black community than with working for integration. Do you mostly agree or mostly disagree with this?

Figure 2.5:
Based on responses to: On the whole, do you think most white people in the Detroit area want to see blacks get a better break, or do they want to keep blacks down, or don't they care one way or the other?

Figure 2.6:
Based on responses to: If two or three black families move into a white neighborhood do you see any sorts of problems as likely to arise?; Some people in the Detroit area have felt they had to move from a neighborhood because blacks were moving in and it was causing problems for their family. Have you ever moved from a neighborhood

partly for this reason?; and In this city or community, are blacks in general discriminated against or not in getting decent housing?

Figure 3.1:
Based on responses to two questions: How many [other race] students were in your elementary school?; and How many [other race] students were in your junior high and high schools? Allowed responses to both questions were: None, few, less than half, and half or more.

Figure 3.2:
Based on responses to: On your job do [did] you work with only blacks, only whites, or with both blacks and whites?

Figure 3.3:
Based on responses to: In the two or three blocks right around here, how many of the families, if any, are [other race]: none, only a few, many but less than half, or more than half?

Figure 3.4:
Based on responses to: Do you and any of the white families that live around here visit in each other's home, or do you only see and talk to each other on the street, or do you hardly know each other?

Figure 3.5:
Based on responses to: How often do you have conversations with [members of the other race] ... on the job?; ... at places where you shop?; ... at events involving your children (day care, school, youth sports, etc.)?; ... at church or religious activities?; ... at sports events or other entertainment? Allowed responses were: Never, sometimes, and frequently.

Table 3.1:
Casual interracial contact: A composite measure based on responses to the five questions displayed in Figure 3.5. Responses to each question were z-scored (standardized such that, for each item, mean=0, s.d.=1) and then summed. We then standard-scored the composite scale. Coefficient α for the scale was .62.

Place of residence: Coded 0 for those who lived in the suburbs and 1 for those who lived in the city of Detroit.

Neighborhood racial composition: The black percentage of the population of the census tract in which an interviewee resided.

Place of work: Represented by two dummy variables, one coded 1 for those who worked in the city of Detroit, o for all others, and the other coded 1 for those who worked in the suburbs, o for all others. The excluded or reference category consisted of those who did not work outside the home.

Church attendance: Based on responses to: How often do you usually attend religious services? Would you say nearly every day, at least once a week, a few times a month, a few times a year, or less than once a year?

Early life neighborhood composition: Coded 1 for those who answered Yes and o for those who answered No when asked: When you were growing up, were there any [other race] families living in or near your neighborhood?

Early life school composition: A composite scale based on responses to the two questions displayed in Figure 3.1. The responses were assigned integer scores from o through 3, and the two scores were summed for each interviewee. Coefficient α for the scale was .79.

Age: The interviewee's age, in years.

Sex: Coded o for men, 1 for women.

Education: The number of years of school the interviewee had completed.

Financial status: A composite scale based on four items: total household income, on a scale ranging from less than $10,000 per year through more than $120,000 per year, in 14 steps; receipt of government aid, as indicated by responses (yes or no) to the question: Do you or anyone in your household receive food stamps or aid for dependent children or some other government welfare assistance other than Social Security benefits?; financial stringency, as indicated by responses to the question: How difficult is it for you to meet your monthly household expenses: ... not difficult at all? ... somewhat difficult? ... very difficult? ... or are there some months when you cannot meet your monthly household expenses?; and home ownership, coded 1 for those who owned their home, whether free and clear or with a mortgage, and o for all others. On each item, we ordered responses from the one signifying the lowest status to the one signifying the highest status, and then z-scored the items. The z-scores were summed, and the resulting composite was z-scored. Coefficient α for the scale was .67.

Table 3.2:

Close interracial friendships: Based on responses to the following question: I would like to ask you some questions about the people you consider your good friends. By good friends, I mean adults you enjoy getting together with at least once a month and any other adults who live elsewhere that you try to keep in close touch with by calling or writing. Are any of these good friends [members of the other race]?" [If Yes]: Would you say that only a few, about half, or most of your friends are white? Responses ranged from None through Most in four steps.

Figure 4.1:
Based on responses to: In this city or community, are blacks in general discriminated against or not … in getting a job? Responses were Yes or No.

Figure 4.3:
Based on responses to: Have you yourself ever been discriminated against or not, on the basis of your race, … in getting a quality education?; … in getting decent housing?; … in getting a job?; … in getting equal wages for a job?; … in getting promoted to better positions? During the past year, has your boss or a co-worker ever used racial slurs or told derogatory jokes against [interviewee's race] that you felt showed prejudice? How often have you felt that other people at your workplace treat you worse because of your race? Do you often feel that way, sometimes, rarely, or never feel that way? Because of your racial background, do you ever feel that you will be treated worse than others when you do business at: … stores where you shop daily or weekly?; … stores where you shop occasionally?; … government offices?; … other places where you go for services, such as dentists, doctors, and so forth? If the interviewee had children attending school: Do your children report that they are treated worse by teachers or staff because of their ethnic or racial background? Do your children report that they are treated badly by other children because of their ethnic or racial background? Allowed responses to the latter two questions were Often, Sometimes, and Never.

Table 4.1:
Based on responses to: In this city or community, are blacks in general discriminated against or not, … in getting a quality education?; … in getting decent housing?; … in getting a job?; in getting equal wages for a job?; in getting promoted to better positions? We totaled the number of Yes responses to form a 0–5 scale. Coefficient α was .87 and .80, respectively, for African American and white interviewees. The Blacks … Against Themselves column was based on responses to the questions described in conjunction with Figure 4.3; Yes responses were summed, and coefficient α was .85 for African American interviewees.

Appendix B

Table 4.2:

Based on responses to: In this city or community, are whites in general discriminated against or not, ... in getting a quality education?; ... in getting decent housing?; ... in getting a job?; ... in getting equal wages for a job?; ... in getting promoted to better positions? We totaled the number of Yes responses to form a 0–5 scale. Coefficient α was .92 and .78, respectively, for African American and white interviewees. The Whites ... Against Themselves column was based on responses to the questions described in conjunction with Figure 4.3; Yes responses were summed, and coefficient α was .73 for white interviewees.

Table 5.1:

Based on responses to six items: Blacks should always vote for black candidates when they run; Black people should choose to shop in black-owned stores whenever possible; Black parents should give their children African names; Black children should study black history; Black children should study an African language; and Blacks should marry other blacks. The allowed responses to each item were strongly agree (scored 4); agree (scored 3); neither agree nor disagree (scored 2); disagree (scored 1); and strongly disagree (scored 0). Responses were summed across the six items to form a composite racial solidarity score for each interviewee. Coefficient α for the scale was .61, indicative of marginally acceptable internal consistency.

Table 5.2:

Religiosity: A composite scale based on responses to six items: church attendance, ranging from Never through Nearly every day, in five steps; salience of church services, as indicated by responses to the question: How important is going to church or a place of worship to you?, with responses ranging from Not important at all through Very important, in four steps; religious reading, as indicated by the frequency with which the interviewee read religious books or other religious materials, ranging from Never through Nearly every day, in five steps; religious viewing, as indicated by the frequency with which the interviewee watched or listened to religious programs on television or radio, with responses ranging from Never through Nearly every day, in five steps; frequency of prayer, ranging from Never through Nearly every day, in five steps; and biblical literalism, on a four-point scale ranging from The Bible is God's word and all it says is true through The Bible was written by men who lived so long ago that it is worth very little today. The six components, with responses on each ordered so that higher scores signified greater religiosity, were summed after being z-scored, and the composite scale was itself z-scored. Coefficient α for the scale was .88.

Southern upbringing: Coded 1 for those who had lived in the South at age 16, otherwise 0.

Interracial contact: This was a more inclusive measure than the casual interracial contact and close interracial friendship measures that we employed in chapter 3. The scale had eight components: responses to the close interracial friendship item introduced in conjunction with Table 3.2; to the interracial visitation item introduced in conjunction with Figure 3.4; to the five interracial conversation items introduced in conjunction with Figure 3.5; and responses (Yes or No) to: Are there any other acquaintances or casual friends you keep in touch with or get together with occasionally who are [other race]? Each component was z-scored, the z scores were summed, and the sum was z-scored. Coefficient α for the scale was .70 for African Americans and .72 for whites. Preferred neighborhood racial mix: Based on responses to: If you could find housing you would want and like, would you rather live in a neighborhood that is all-black, mostly black, half black–half white, mostly white, or all-white?

Table 6.1:

Based on responses to five questions: Here are some characteristics sometimes mentioned about people. For each one, would you tell me whether it is more true of whites, about equally true of blacks and whites, or more true of blacks: ...Being inclined toward violence; having high ambition, having high morals; In general, do you think Negroes are just as intelligent as white people, that is, can they learn just as well if they are given the same education? (The response options were Yes or No); and Where Negroes are behind whites in such things as jobs or income or housing, do you think this is mainly due to something about Negroes themselves, or mainly due to the way whites have treated Negroes in the past?

Figure 6.1:

Based on responses to three items: Most people agree that, on the average, blacks have worse jobs, income, and housing than whites. I have a list of reasons that some people give for this difference. Let me know if each of the following is a major reason, a minor reason, or no reason at all for these differences: .. Because most blacks don't have the motivation or willpower to pull themselves out of poverty; .. Because most blacks have less in-born ability to learn; and ... Because black Americans teach their children values and skills different from those required to be successful in American society.

Appendix B

Figure 6.2:
Based on responses to: If a very close relative married a black, would you mind it a lot, a little, or not at all?

Table 6.4:
Responses of Major reason to the three items on which Figure 5.1 was based were assigned a value of 1; responses of Minor reason a value of .5; and responses of No reason at all a value of 0. Scores were summed over the three items to form a scale with a minimum value of 0, a maximum value of 3, and values at half-point increments between the extremes. Coefficient α for the scale was a marginal .52.

Figure 7.1:
Based on responses to the following multipart question: We are faced with many problems in this country. I'm going to name some of these problems and for each one I'd like you to tell me whether you think we're spending too much money on it, too little money, or about the right amount: Providing good health care and health insurance for all who need it; Caring for the poor; Dealing with the drug problem; Improving conditions of blacks; Punishing criminals; Welfare; Job training and retraining; Helping low- and middle-income citizens buy housing; preventing crime.

Table 7.2:
Based on responses to: Do you think schools here in your community need lots of improvement, some improvement, or are they pretty good as is?

Table 7.3:
District MEAP score: Using data provided by the Michigan Department of Education, we assigned interviewees the mean Michigan Educational Assessment Program (MEAP) test score for their school district. This meant that all interviewees who were city residents were assigned the overall city average, because it was impossible to assign building-by-building scores for the Detroit school district.
School-age children: Coded 1=yes, 0=otherwise, based on responses to: Do you have children who are now attending elementary, middle, or high school?

Table 7.4:
Based on responses to the following multipart question: Here are some ways which have been suggested for improving schools. Please give me the number of the three strategies you think would be most effective.

The options were: More or better teachers; More security for schools; Better buildings; More or better classroom materials; More discipline for students; More programs for very good students; More programs for students who aren't doing too well; More school integration; and More programs to help parents cope with jobs and child-raising, such as before- and after-school day care, breakfast programs, and evening recreation programs for students. This question was asked only of those who had answered Need lots of improvement or Need some improvement when asked: Do you think schools here in your community need lots of improvement, some improvement, or are they pretty good as is?

Figure 7.2:

Based on responses to three questions: Are you satisfied with the police protection provided for your neighborhood?, with allowed responses of Well satisfied, More or less satisfied, or Not satisfied at all; Do you think that the police here in [city name] would respond as quickly to your call for help as they would if a [other race] person called for help?, with allowed responses of Yes or No; and Do you think many police officers would use [the right to stop and search people they just think look suspicious] unfairly against blacks?, with allowed responses of Yes or No.

References

Aberbach, Joel, and Jack Walker. 1973. *Race in the City*. Boston: Little, Brown.

Abrams, Charles. 1965. The Housing Problem and the Negro. In Talcott Parsons and Kenneth Clark (eds.), *The Negro American*. Boston: Beacon Press, pp. 512–24.

Alba, Richard D., and John R. Logan. 1991. Variations on Two Themes: Racial and Ethnic Patterns in the Attainment of Suburban Residence. *Demography* 28:431–53.

Alba, Richard D., and John R. Logan. 1993. Minority Proximity to Whites in Suburbs: An Individual-Level Analysis of Segregation. *American Journal of Sociology* 98:1388–1427.

Allen, Richard, Michael C. Dawson, and Ronald Brown. 1989. A Schema-Based Approach to Modeling an African-American Racial Belief System. *American Political Science Review* 83:421–42.

Amir, Yehuda. 1976. The Role of Intergroup Contact in Change of Prejudice and Ethnic Relations. In Phyllis A. Katz (ed.), *Toward the Elimination of Racism*. New York: Pergamon, pp. 245–308.

Apostle, Richard, Charles Glock, Thomas Piazza, and Marijean Suezele. 1983. *The Anatomy of Racial Attitudes*. Berkeley: University of California Press.

Baillie, Cathryn. 2000. Letter to the Editor. *New York Times Magazine*. July 16:6.

Baker, Ray Stannard. [1908] 1964. *Following the Color Line*. New York: Harper.

Banks, James A. 1984. Black Youths in Predominantly White Suburbs: An Exploratory Study of Their Attitudes and Self-Concepts. *Journal of Negro Education* 53:3–17.

Barker, Lucius J., Mack H. Jones, and Katherine Tate. 1999. *African Americans and the Political System*. Upper Saddle River, NJ: Prentice-Hall.

Barker, Lucius J., and Jesse J. McCorry, Jr. 1980. *Black Americans and the Political System*, 2nd edition. Cambridge, MA: Winthrop.

Berelson, Bernard, Paul Lazarsfeld, and William McPhee. 1954. *Voting: A Study of Opinion Formation in a Presidential Election*. Chicago: University of Chicago Press.

Berscheid, Ellen, and Elaine Hatfield Walster. 1969. *Interpersonal Attraction*. Reading, MA: Addison-Wesley.

References

Blackwell, James E., and Philip S. Hart. 1982. *Cities, Suburbs and Blacks*. Bayside, NY: General-Hall.

Blalock, Hubert M., Jr. 1957. Percent Non-White and Discrimination in the South. *American Sociological Review* 22:677–82.

Blalock, Hubert M., Jr. 1967. *Toward a Theory of Minority Group Relations*. New York: John Wiley.

Blau, Peter. 1977. *Inequality and Heterogeneity*. New York: Free Press.

Bledsoe, Timothy. 1991. *From One World, Three: Political Change in Metropolitan Detroit*. Working paper. Center for Urban Studies, Wayne State University.

Bledsoe, Timothy, Susan Welch, Lee Sigelman, and Michael Combs. 1994. Suburbanization, Residential Integration, and Racial Solidarity Among African Americans. Paper prepared for delivery at the annual meeting of the Midwest Political Science Association, Chicago, April 14–16.

Bledsoe, Timothy, Michael Combs, Lee Sigelman, and Susan Welch. Trends in Racial Attitudes in Detroit, *Urban Affairs Review* 31 (March, 1996): 508–528.

Bledsoe, Timothy, Susan Welch, Lee Sigelman, and Michael Combs. 1995. Residential Context and Racial Solidarity among African Americans. *American Journal of Political Science* 39:434–58.

Blossom, Teresa, David Everett, and John Gallagher. 1988. The Race for Money. *Detroit Free Press* 24 July, p. 1A.

Bobo, Lawrence. 1988. Group Conflict, Prejudice, and the Paradox of Contemporary Racial Attitudes. In P. Katz and D. Taylor (eds.), *Eliminating Racism: Profiles in Controversy*. New York: Plenum.

Bobo, Lawrence. 1989. Keeping the Linchpin in Place: Testing the Multiple Sources of Opposition to Residential Integration. *Revue Internationale de Psychologie Sociale* 2:306–23.

Bobo, Lawrence, and Franklin D. Gilliam, Jr. 1990. Race, Sociopolitical Participation, and Black Empowerment. *American Political Science Review* 84:377–393.

Bornstein, Robert F. 1989. Exposure and Affect: Overview and Meta-Analysis of Research, 1969–1987. *Psychological Bulletin* 106:265–89.

Bornstein, Robert F. 1993. Mere Exposure Effects with Outgroup Stimuli. In David L. Hamilton and Diane M. Mackie (eds.), *Affect, Cognition, and Stereotyping: Interactive Processes in Group Perception*. New York: Academic Press.

Bradburn, Norman, Seymour Sudman, Galen L. Goekel, and Joseph Noel. 1971. *Side by Side: Integrated Neighborhoods in America*. Chicago: Quadrangle Books.

Brink, William, and Louis Harris. 1966. *Black and White: A Study of U.S. Racial Attitudes Today*. New York: Simon & Schuster.

Brooks-Gunn, Jeanne, Greg Duncan, Pamela Klebanov, and Naomi Sealand. 1993. Do Neighborhoods Influence Child and Adolescent Development? *American Journal of Sociology* 99:353–95.

Burr, Jeffrey A., Omer Galle, and Mark Fossett. 1991. Racial Occupational Inequality in Southern Metropolitan Areas. *Social Forces* 69:831–50.

Butler, David and Donald Stokes. 1974. *Political Change in Britain*. New York: St. Martin's.

References

Campbell, Angus. 1971. *White Attitudes Toward Black People*. Ann Arbor: University of Michigan, Institute for Social Research.

Campbell, Angus, and Howard Schuman. 1968. *Racial Attitudes in Fifteen American Cities*. Ann Arbor: University of Michigan, Institute for Social Research.

Carmichael, Stokely, and Charles V. Hamilton. 1967. *Black Power: The Politics of Liberation in America*. New York: Random House.

Carsey, Thomas. 1995. The Contextual Effects of Race on White Voter Behavior. *Journal of Politics* 57:221–28.

Carter, Robert T., and Janet E. Helms. 1988. The Relationship Between Racial Identity Attitudes and Social Class. *Journal of Negro Education* 57:22–30.

Chafets, Ze'ev. 1990. *Devil's Night and Other True Tales of Detroit*. New York: Random House.

Chesley, Roger. 1993. Group Is Small But Dedicated, and Risky to Court. *Detroit Free Press* (August 8): 4F.

Clark, Kenneth B., and M.P. Clark. 1939. The Development of Consciousness of Self and the Emergence of Racial Identification in Negro Pre-School Children. *Journal of Social Psychology* 10:591–99.

Clay, Philip. 1979. The Process of Black Suburbanization. *Urban Affairs Quarterly* 14:405–24.

Cohen, Cathy J. 1999. *The Boundaries of Blackness*. Chicago: University of Chicago Press.

Cohen, Cathy J., and Michael C. Dawson. 1993. Neighborhood Poverty and African American Politics. *American Political Science Review* 87:286–302.

Coleman, James. 1966. *Equality of Educational Opportunity*. Washington DC: U.S. Government Printing Office.

Condran, J. G. 1979. Changes in White Attitudes toward Blacks: 1963–1977. *Public Opinion Quarterly* 43:463–76.

Connerly, Charles E. 1985. The Community Question: An Extension of Wellman and Leighton. *Urban Affairs Quarterly* 20:537–56.

Conzen, Kathleen Neils. 1979. Immigrants, Immigrant Neighborhoods, and Ethnic Identity: Historical Issues. *Journal of American History* 66:603–15.

Corzine, Jay, James Creech, and Lin Corzine. 1983. Black Concentration and Lynchings in the South: Testing Blalock's Power-Threat Hypothesis. *Social Forces* 67:774–96.

Cose, Ellis. 1993. *The Rage of a Privileged Class*. New York: Harper Collins.

Cox, Kevin. 1974. The Spatial Structuring of Information Flow and Partisan Attitudes. In Mattei Dogan and Stein Rokkan (eds.), *Social Ecology*. Cambridge: MIT Press, pp. 157–186.

Crosby, Faye J. 1982. *Relative Deprivation and Working Women*. New York: Oxford University Press.

Curry, Leonard P. 1981. *The Free Black in Urban America 1800–1850*. Chicago: University of Chicago Press.

Darden, J.T. 1990. Differential Access to Housing in the Suburbs. *Journal of Black Studies* 21:15–22.

Dedman, W. 1988. The Color of Money. *The Atlanta Journal-Constitution*. 1–4 May:1–6.

References

DeFrances, Carol. 1996. The Effects of Racial Ecological Segregation on Quality of Life. *Urban Affairs Review* 31:799–809.

Demo, David, and Michael Hughes. 1990. Socialization and Racial Identity among Black Americans. *Social Psychology Quarterly* 53:364–74.

Dent, David J. 1992. The New Black Suburbs. *New York Times Magazine*. June 14.

Denton, Nancy, and Douglas Massey. 1991. Patterns of Neighborhood Transition in a Multi-Ethnic World. *Demography* 28:41–46.

Desforges, Donna, Charles Lord, Shawna Ramsey, Julie Mason, Marilyn Van Leeuwen, Sylvia West, and Mark Lepper. 1991. Effects of Structured Cooperative Contact on Changing Negative Attitudes toward Stigmatized Groups, *Journal of Personality and Social Psychology* 60:531–44. Detroit Free Press, Various issues.

Deutsch, Morton, and Mary E. Collins. 1951. *Interracial Housing: A Psychological Evaluation of a Social Experiment*. New York: Russell and Russell.

Dillingham, Gerald L. 1981. The Emerging Black Middle Class: Class Conscious or Race Conscious? *Ethnic and Racial Studies* 4:432–51.

Driedger, Leo. 1979. Maintenance of Urban Ethnic Boundaries: The French in St. Boniface. *Sociological Quarterly* 20:89–108.

Driedger, Leo. 1980. Jewish Identity: The Maintenance of Urban Religious and Ethnic Boundaries. *Ethnic and Racial Studies* 3:67–88.

DuBois, David L., and Barton J. Hirsch. 1990. School and Neighborhood Friendship Patterns of Blacks and Whites in Early Adolescence. *Child Development* 61:524–36.

Edsall, Thomas B. 1992. Two Steps Forward, One Step Backlash. *Washington Post National Weekly Edition* 11–17 May:10.

Ellison, Christopher G. 1991. Identification and Separatism: Religious Involvement and Racial Orientations Among Black Americans. *Sociological Quarterly* 32:477–94.

Ellison, Christopher G., and Daniel A. Powers. 1994. The Contact Hypothesis and Racial Attitudes among Black Americans. *Social Science Quarterly* 75:385–400.

Eulau, Heinz, 1996. *Micro-Macro Dilemmas in Political Science*. Norman: University of Oklahoma Press.

Farley, John E. 1995. Race Still Matters: The Minimal Role of Income and Housing Cost as Causes of Housing Segregation in St. Louis, 1990. *Urban Affairs Review* 31:244–54.

Farley, Reynolds. 1970a. The Changing Distribution of Negroes within Metropolitan Areas: The Emergence of Black Suburbs. *American Journal of Sociology* 75:512–29.

Farley, Reynolds. 1984. *Black and White: Narrowing the Gap*. Cambridge; MA: Harvard University Press.

Farley, Reynolds, Suzanne Bianchi, and Diane Colasanto. 1978a. Barriers to the Racial Integration of Neighborhoods: The Detroit Case. *Annals of the American Academy of Political and Social Science* 441:97–113.

Farley, Reynolds and William H. Frey, 1994. Changes in the Segregation of Whites from Blacks During the 1980s: Small Steps Toward a More Integrated Society. *American Sociological Review* 59 (February):23–45.

References

Farley, Reynolds, Shirley Hatchett, and Howard Schuman. 1979. A Note on Changes in Black Racial Attitudes in Detroit. *Social Indicators Research* 6:439–43.

Farley, Reynolds, Toni Richards, and Clarence Wurdock. 1980. School Desegregation and White Flight: An Investigation of Competing Models and Their Discrepant Findings. *Sociology of Education* 53:123–39.

Farley, Reynolds, Howard Schuman, Suzanne Bianchi, Diane Colasanto, and Shirley Hatchett. 1978b. Chocolate City, Vanilla Suburbs: Will the Trend toward Racially Separate Communities Continue? *Social Science Research* 7:319–44.

Farley, Reynolds, Charlotte Steeh, Tara Jackson, Maria Krysan, and Keith Reeves. 1994. The Causes of Continued Racial Residential Segregation: Chocolate City, Vanilla Suburbs Revisited, *Journal of Housing Research* 4:1–38.

Feagin, Joe R. 1991. The Continuing Significance of Race: Antiblack Discrimination in Public Places. *American Sociological Review* 94:251–72.

Festinger, Leon, Stanley Schachter, and Kurt Back. 1950. *Social Pressures in Informal Groups: A Study of Human Factors in Housing*. New York: Harper.

Firebaugh, Glenn, and K.E. Davis. 1988. Trends in Anti-black Prejudice, 1972–1984: Region and Cohort Effects. *American Journal of Sociology* 94:251–72.

Fischer, Claude S. 1982. *To Dwell among Friends: Personal Networks in Town and City*. Chicago: University of Chicago Press.

Ford, W. Scott. 1973. Interracial Public Housing in a Border City. *American Journal of Sociology* 78:426–44.

Fossett, Mark, and Jill Kiecolt. 1989. The Relative Size of Minority Populations and White Racial Attitudes. *Social Science Quarterly* 70:820–35.

Franklin, John Hope. 1967. *From Slavery to Freedom*. New York: Alfred A. Knopf.

Frey, William. 1985. Mover Destination Selectivity and the Changing Suburbanization of Metropolitan Whites and Blacks, *Demography* 22:223–243.

Frey, William, and Reynolds Farley. 1996. Latino, Asian, and Black Segregation in the U.S. more Metropolitan Areas: Are Multiethnic Metros Different? *Demography* 33:35–50.

Frisbie, W. Parker, and Lisa Neidert. 1977. Inequality and the Relative Size of Minority Populations: A Comparative Analysis. *American Journal of Sociology* 82:412–17.

Fuchs, Lawrence. 1955. American Jews and the Presidential Vote. *American Political Science Review* 49:385–401.

Fyfe, James. 1981. Race and Extreme Police–Citizen Violence. In R.L. McNelley and Carl E. Pope (eds.), *Race, Crime, and Criminal Justice*. Beverly Hills: Sage, pp. 89–108.

Fyfe, James. 1982. Blind Justice: Police Shootings in Memphis. *Journal of Criminal Law and Criminology* 73:707–22.

Galster, George C. 1987. Residential Segregation and Interracial Economic Disparities: A Simultaneous Equations Approach. *Journal of Urban Economics* 21:87–117.

References

Galster, George C. 1991. Black Suburbanization: Has It Changed the Relative Location of the Races? *Urban Affairs Quarterly* 26:621–8.

Gilens, Martin. 1995. Racial Attitudes and Opposition to Welfare. *Journal of Politics* 57:994–1014.

Giles, Michael, and Melanie Buckner. 1993. David Duke and Black Threat: An Old Hypothesis Revisited. *Journal of Politics* 55:702–13.

Giles, Michael W., and Arthur S. Evans. 1985. External Threat, Perceived Threat, and Group Identity. *Social Science Quarterly* 66:50–66.

Giles, Michael W., and Arthur S. Evans. 1986. The Power Approach to Intergroup Hostility. *Journal of Conflict Resolution* 30:469–86.

Gillmor, Dan, and Constance Prater. 1991. Wayne County Segregation Up; Oakland Sees Integration. *Detroit Free Press,* 9 March: 1.

Glaser, James. 1994. Back to the Black Belt: Racial Environment and White Racial Attitudes in the South. *Journal of Politics* 56 (February): 21–41.

Gordon, G. 1993. Feds: Area Is Biased in Renting. *Detroit Free Press,* 20 June: 1 A, 6A.

Greeley, Andrew M., and Paul B. Sheatsley. 1971. Attitudes toward Racial Integration. *Scientific American* 225:13–9.

Grier, Eunice, and George Grier. 1966. Equality and Beyond: Housing Segregation in the Great Society. In Talcott Parsons and Kenneth Clark (eds.), *The Negro American.* Boston: Beacon Press, pp. 525–54.

Gurin, Patricia, Shirley Hatchett, and James Jackson. 1989. *Hope and Independence: Blacks' Response to Electoral and Party Politics.* New York: Russell Sage.

Gurin, Patricia, Arthur H. Miller, and Gerald Gurin. 1980. Stratum Identification and Consciousness. *Social Psychology Quarterly* 43:30–47.

Hacker, Andrew. 1992. *Two Nations: Black and White, Separate, Hostile, Unequal.* New York: Ballantine.

Hallinan, Maureen T. 1982. Classroom Racial Composition and Children's Friendships. *Social Forces* 61:56–72.

Hallinan, Maureen T., and Ruy A. Teixeira. 1987. Opportunities and Constraints: Black–White Differences in the Formation of Interracial Friendships. *Child Development* 58:1358–71.

Hallinan, Maureen T., and Richard A. Williams. 1989. Interracial Friendship Choices in Secondary Schools. *American Sociological Review* 54:67–78.

Hamilton, David L. 1981. Illusory Correlation as a Basis for Stereotyping. In David L. Hamilton (ed.), *Cognitive Processes in Stereotyping and Intergroup Behavior.* Hillsdale, NJ: Erlbaum.

Hamilton, David L., and George D. Bishop. 1976. Attitudinal and Behavioral Effects of Initial Integration of White Suburban Neighborhoods. *Journal of Social Issues* 32 (2):47–67.

Harris, Frederick C. 1994. Something Within: Religion as a Mobilizer of African-American Political Activism. *Journal of Politics* 56:42–68.

Harrison, A.A. 1977. Mere Exposure. In Leonard Berkowitz (ed.), *Advances in Experimental Social Psychology* Vol. 10. New York: Academic Press.

Henig, Jeffrey, Richard C. Hula, Marion Orr, and Desiree Pedescleaux. 1999. *The Color of School Reform: Race, Politics, and the Challenge of Urban Education.* Princeton: Princeton University Press.

References

Henig, Jeffrey, Desiree Pedescleaux, Marion Orr, Richard Hula, Carol Perannunzi, John Hutcheson, and Alan DiGaetano. 1995. The Politics of Education in Black-Led Cities. Paper presented at the 1995 Annual Meeting of the American Political Science Association, Chicago.

Hochschild, Jennifer. 1993. Middle-Class Blacks and the Ambiguities of Success. In Paul M. Sniderman, Philip E. Tetlock, and Edward. G. Carmines (eds.), *Prejudice, Politics, and the American Dilemma*. Stanford, CA: Stanford University Press, pp. 148–72.

Hochschild, Jennifer. 1995. *Facing Up to the American Dream*. Princeton, NJ: Princeton University Press.

Hogan, Dennis, and Evelyn Kitagawa. 1985. The Impact of Social Status, Family Structure, and Neighborhood on the Fertility of Black Adolescents. *American Journal of Sociology* 90:825–52.

Holmes, Steven. 2000. Which Man's Army. *New York Times*, 7 June.

Houts, Sandra, and Cathy Kassab. 1997. Rotter's Social Learning Theory and Fear of Crime: Differences by Race and Ethnicity. *Social Science Quarterly* 78:122–36.

Hraba, Joseph, and Geoffrey Grant. 1970. Black Is Beautiful: A Reexamination of Racial Preference and Identification. *Journal of Personality and Social Psychology* 16:398–402.

Huckfeldt, Robert. 1979. Political Participation and the Neighborhood Social Context. *American Journal of Political Science* 23:579–92.

Huckfeldt, Robert. 1983. The Social Contexts of Ethnic Politics: Ethnic Loyalties, Political Loyalties, and Social Support. *American Politics Quarterly* 99:91–123.

Huckfeldt, Robert. 1986. *Politics in Context*. New York: Agathon Press.

Hyman, Herbert H., and Paul B. Sheatsley. 1956. Attitudes on Integration. *Scientific American* 195:35.

Hyman, Herbert H., and Paul B. Sheatsley. 1964. Attitudes toward Desegregation. *Scientific American* 211:16–23.

Jackman, Mary R., and Marie Crane, 1986. Some of My Best Friends Are Black: Interracial Friendship and Whites' Racial Attitudes. *Public Opinion Quarterly* 50:459–86.

Jackson, Byran O. 1987. The Effects of Racial Group Consciousness on Political Mobilization in American Cities. *Western Political Quarterly* 40:631–646.

Jakubs, John. 1986. Recent Racial Segregation in the U.S. SMSAs, Urban Geography. 7:146–63.

Jaynes, Gerald D., and Robin Williams. 1989. *A Common Destiny: Blacks and American Society*. Washington DC: National Academy Press.

Jones, Charisse. 1994. Years on Integration Road: New Views on an Old Goal. *New York Times* April 10:1ff.

Jones, Jr. (eds.), Madison: University of Wisconsin Press, pp. 97–111.

Kalmijn, Mathijis 1993. Trends in Black/White Intermarriage. *Social Forces* 72 (September): 119–46.

Katzman, David M. 1973. *Before the Ghetto: Black Detroit in the Nineteenth Century*. Urbana: University of Illinois Press.

References

Key, V.O. 1949. *Southern Politics in State and Nation.* Knoxville: University of Tennessee Press.

Kinder, Donald, and Tali Mendelberg. 1995. Cracks in American Apartheid: The Political Impact of Prejudice among Desegregated Whites. *Journal of Politics* 57:402–24.

Kinder, Donald R., and Lynn M. Sanders. 1996. *Divided by Color: Racial Politics and Democratic Ideals.* Chicago: University of Chicago Press.

Kluegel, James R. 1990. Trends in Whites' Explanations of the Black–White Gap in Socioeconomic Status, 1977–1989. *American Sociological Review* 55:512–25.

Kluegel, James R. and Lawrence Bobo. 1993. Dimensions of Whites' Beliefs about the Black–White Socioeconomic Gap. In Paul Sniderman, Philip Tetlock, and Edward Carmines, (ed.). *Prejudice, Politics, and the American Dilemma.* Stanford: Stanford University Press, pp. 127–147.

Kluegel, James R., and Eliot R. Smith. 1986. *Beliefs about Equality: Americans' Views of What Is and What Ought to Be.* New York: Aldine De Gruyter.

Kluger, Richard. 1976. *Simple Justice: The History of Brown v. Board of Education and Black America's Struggle for Equality.* New York: Alfred A. Knopf.

Kornblum, William. 1974. *Blue Collar Community.* Chicago: University of Chicago Press.

Kornhauser, Arthur. 1951. *Detroit as the People See It.* Detroit: Wayne State University Press.

Krysan, Maria. 1999. Community Undesirability in Black and White: A New Look at Residential Preference and Segregation. Unpublished manuscript, Department of Sociology, Pennsylvania State University.

Landry, Bart. 1987. *The New Black Middle Class.* Berkeley: University of California Press.

LaPiere, R.T. 1934. Attitudes vs. Actions. *Social Forces* 13:230–37.

Lau, Richard R. 1989. Individual and Contextual Influences on Group Identification. *Social Psychology Quarterly* 42:220–31.

Lee, Barrett A. 1985. Racially Mixed Neighborhoods During the 1970s: Change or stability. *Social Science Quarterly.* 66:346–64.

Lee, Barrett A., Karen E. Campbell, and Oscar Miller. 1991. Racial Differences in Urban Neighboring. *Sociological Forum* 6:525–50.

Lee, Barrett A., and P.A. Wood. 1991. Is Neighborhood Racial Succession Place-Specific? *Demography* 28:21–40.

Lieberson, Stanley. 1963. *Ethnic Patterns in American Cities.* New York: Free Press.

Lieberson, Stanley. 1980. *A Piece of the Pie: Black and White Immigrants since 1880.* Berkeley: University of California Press.

Lincoln, C. Eric, and Lawrence Mamiya. 1990. *The Black Church in the African American Experience.* Durham, NC: Duke University Press.

Litvak, Stuart B. 1969. Attitude Change by Stimulus Exposure. *Psychological Reports* 25:391–6.

London, Bruce, and J. Hearn. 1977. The Ethnic Community Theory of Black Social and Political Participation: Additional Support. *Social Science Quarterly* 57:883–91.

References

Marchetti, D. 1990. Black Families Harassed in Waffen. *Detroit News* 22 May: 4A.

Massey, Douglas S. 2000. The Residential Segregation of Blacks, Hispanics, and Asians: 1970 to 1990. In Gerald D. Jaynes (ed.), *Immigration and Race: New Challenges to American Democracy.* New Haven: Yale University Press, pp. 44–73.

Long, L. and D. Deare. 1981. The Suburbanization of Blacks, *American Demographics.* 3:16–21.

Massey, Douglas S., and Nancy A. Denton. 1987. Trends in the Residential Segregation of Blacks, Hispanics, and Asians: 1970–1980. *American Sociological Review* 52:802–25.

Massey, Douglas S., and Nancy A. Denton. 1989. Hypersegregation in U.S. Metropolitan Areas: Black and Hispanic Segregation along Five Dimensions. *Demography* 26:373–93.

Massey, Douglas S., and Nancy A. Denton. 1993. *American Apartheid: Segregation and the Making of the Underclass.* Cambridge, MA: Harvard University Press.

Massey, Douglas S., and Andrew B. Gross. 1991. Explaining Trends in Racial Segregation, 1970–1980. *Urban Affairs Quarterly* 27 (September): 13–35.

Massey, Douglas, Andrew Gross, and Mitchell Eggers. 1991. Segregation, the Life Chances of Individuals, and the Geographic Concentration of Poverty. *Social Science Research* 20:397–420.

Matthews, Donald R., and James W. Prothro. 1966. *Negroes and the New Southern Politics.* New York: Harcourt, Brace and World.

McKinney, Scott. 1989. Change in Metropolitan Area Residential Integration, 1970–1980, *Population Research and Policy Review.* 8:193–64.

McRae, Norman. 1975. Early Blacks in Michigan. *Detroit in Perspective: A Journal of Regional History* 2:159–175.

Meer, Bernard, and Edward Freedman, 1966. The Impact of Negro Neighbors on White Homeowners. *Social Forces* 54:900–24.

Meier, Kenneth, Joseph Stewart, Jr., and Robert E. England. 1989a. *Race, Class, and Education: The Politics of Second-Generation Discrimination.* Madison: University of Wisconsin Press.

Meier, Kenneth, Joseph Stewart, Jr. and Robert E. England. 1989b. Second-Generation Educational Discrimination and White Flight from Public Schools. *National Journal of Political Science* 1:76–90.

Miller, Arthur H., Patricia Gurin, Gerald Gurin, and Oksana Malanchuk. 1981. Group Consciousness and Political Participation. *American Journal of Political Science* 25:494–511.

Miller, Warren. 1956. One Party Politics and the Voter. *American Political Science Review* 50:707–25.

Milton, Catherine, Jeanne Wahl Halleck, James Lardner, and Gary Abrecht. 1977. *Police Use of Deadly Force.* Washington, DC: Police Foundation.

Moeller, Gertrude. 1989. Fear of Criminal Victimization: The Effect of Neighborhood Racial Composition. *Sociological Inquiry* 59:208–21.

Morris, A.D. 1984. *The Origins of the Civil Rights Movement: Black Communities Organizing for Change.* New York: Free Press.

References

Myrdal, Gunnar. 1944 (1963). *An American Dilemma.* New York: McGraw-Hill.

National Advisory Commission on Civil Disorders [Kerner Commission]. 1968. *Report of the National Advisory Commission on Civil Disorders.* New York: Bantam Books.

National Opinion Research Center (1947, 1990, and various years). *General Social Surveys.*

Northwood, L.K., and Ernest A.T. Barth. 1965. *Urban Desegregation: Negro Pioneers and their White Neighbors.* Seattle: University of Washington Press.

O'Hare, William P., and William H. Frey. 1992. Booming, Suburban, and Black. *American Demographics* (September): 30–8.

O'Hare, William P., Kelvin M. Pollard, Taynia L. Mann, and Mary M. Kent. 1991. African Americans in the 1990s. *Population Bulletin* 46 (July): 1–39.

O'Hare, William P., and Margaret Usdansky. 1992. What the 1990 Census Tells Us About Segregation in 25 Large Metros. *Population Today* (September): 6–10.

Oliver, J. Eric, and Tali Mendelberg. 2000. Reconsidering the Environmental Determinants of Racial Attitudes. *American Journal of Political Science* 44 (July):574–89.

Oliver, Melvin L. 1988. The Urban Black Community as Network: Toward a Social Network Perspective. *Sociological Quarterly* 29:623–45.

Olsen, Marvin. 1970. Political Orientation and Riot Participation. *American Sociological Review* 35:682–97.

Olzak, Susan, Suzanne Shanahan, and Elizabeth H. McEneaney. 1996. Poverty, Segregation and Race Riots: 1960–1993. *American Sociological Review* 61:590–613.

Olzak, Susan, Suzanne Shanahan, and Elizabeth West. 1994. School Desegregation, Interracial Exposure, and Antibusing Activity in Contemporary Urban America. *American Journal of Sociology* 100:196–241.

Orbell, John, and Kenneth Sherrill. 1969. Racial Attitudes and the Metropolitan Context. *Public Opinion Quarterly* 33 (Spring): 46–54.

Orfield, Gary. 1978. *Must We Bus?* Washington DC: The Brookings Institution.

Orfield, Gary. 1983. *Public School Desegregation in the United States, 1968–1980.* Washington DC: Joint Center for Political Studies.

Orfield, Gary and Carole Ashkinaze. 1991. *The Closing Door.* University of Chicago Press.

Orfield, Gary. 1993. School Desegregation After Two Generations: Race, Schools and Opportunity in Urban Society. In Herbert Hill and James E. Jones (eds.), *Race in America: The Struggle for Equality* Madison: University of Wisconsin Press, pp. 234–62.

Ostrom, Vincent, Robert Bish, and Elinor Ostrom. 1988. *Local Government in the United States.* San Francisco: Institute for Contemporary Studies.

Pavalko, Ronald M. 1981. The Spatial Dimension of Ethnicity. *Ethnic Groups* 3:111–23.

Peek, Charles W., Jon P. Alston, and George D. Lowe. 1978. Comparative Evaluation of Local Police. *Public Opinion Quarterly* 42:370–379.

References

Perlman, David, and Stuart Oskamp. 1971. The Effects of Picture Content and Exposure Frequency on Evaluations of Negroes and Whites. *Journal of Experimental Social Psychology* 7:503–14.

Pettigrew, Thomas F. 1959. Regional Differences in Anti-Negro Prejudice. *Journal of Abnormal and Social Psychology* 59:28–36.

Phelan, Thomas J., and Mark Schneider. 1996. Race, Ethnicity, and Class in American Suburbs, *Urban Affairs Review* 31:659–80.

Piven, Francis Fox, and Richard A. Cloward. 1980. The Case Against Urban Desegregation. In Jon Pynoos, Robert Schafter, and Chester Hartman (eds.), *Housing Urban America*. New York: Aldine.

Pomper, Gerald. 1966. Ethnic and Group Voting in Nonpartisan Local Elections. *Public Opinion Quarterly* 30 (Spring): 79–97.

Price, Daniel O. 1969. *Changing Characteristics of the Negro Population* (A 1960 Census Monograph). U.S. Government Printing Office: Washington DC.

Putnam, Robert. 1966. Political Attitudes and the Local Community. *American Political Science Review* 60:640–654.

Quillian, Lincoln. 1996. Group Threat and Regional Change in Attitudes toward African-Americans. *American Journal of Sociology* 3:816–60.

Reese, Laura, and Ronald Brown. 1995. The Effects of Religious Messages on Racial Identity and System Blame Among African Americans. *Journal of Politics* 57:24–43.

Rich, Wilbur. 1989. *Coleman Young and Detroit Politics*. Detroit: Wayne State University Press.

Riley, Matilda White. 1985. Age Strata in Social Systems. In Robert Binstock and Ethel Shanas (eds.), *Aging and the Social Sciences*. New York: Van Nostrand-Reinhold, pp. 369–411.

Robinson, James L., Jr. 1980. Physical Distance and Racial Attitudes. *Phylon* 41:325–32.

Robinson, Jerry, and James Preston. 1976. Equal Status Contact and Modification of Racial Prejudice. *Social Forces* 90:900–24.

Rose, Harold M. 1976. *Black Suburbanization*. Cambridge, MA: Ballinger.

Rosenbaum, James E., Susan J. Popkin, Julie E. Kaufman, and Jennifer Rusin. 1991. Social Integration of Low-Income Black Adults in Middle-Class White Suburbs. *Social Problems* 38:448–59.

Rossell, Christine. 1981. Understanding White Flight and Doing Something About It. In Willis Hawley (ed.), *Effective School Desegregation*. Newbury Park, CA: Sage Publications.

Rothbart, Myron 1981. Memory Processes and Social Beliefs. In David L. Hamilton (ed.), *Cognitive Processes in Stereotyping and Intergroup Behavior*. Hillsdale, NJ: Erlbaum.

Russakoff, Dale. 1994. Can the Mayor Beat the Odds? *Washington Post National Weekly Edition* 28 March–3 April: 9.

Sampson, William, and Vera Milan. 1975. The Intra-racial Attitudes of the Black Middle Class: Have They Changed? *Social Problems* 23:153–65.

Scaglion, Richard, and Richard C. Condon. 1980. The Structure of Black and White Attitudes toward the Police. *Human Organization* 39:280–283.

References

Schelling, Thomas. 1973. Dynamic Models of Segregation. *Journal of Mathematical Sociology* 1:143–86.

Schneider, Mark, and Thomas Phelan. 1990. Blacks and Jobs: Never the Twain Shall Meet. *Urban Affairs Quarterly* 26:299–312.

Schneider, Mark, and Thomas Phelan. 1993. Black Suburbanization in the 1980s. *Demography* 30:269–79.

Schuman, Howard, and Barry Gruenberg. 1970. The Impact of City on Racial Attitudes. *American Journal of Sociology* 76:213–61.

Schuman, Howard, and Barry Gruenberg. 1972. Dissatisfaction with City Services: Is Race an Important Factor? In Harlan Hahn (ed.), *People and Politics in Urban Society*. Vol 6, *Urban Affairs Annual Reviews*. Beverly Hills, CA: Sage, pp. 369–92.

Schuman, Howard, and Shirley Hatchett. 1974. *Trends in Racial Attitudes*. Ann Arbor: University of Michigan, Institute for Social Research.

Schuman, Howard, and Maria Krysan. 1999. A Historical Note on Whites' Beliefs about Racial Inequality. *American Sociological Review* 64 (December): 1–9.

Schuman, Howard, Charlotte Steeh, and Lawrence Bobo. 1985. *Racial Attitudes in America*. Cambridge, MA: Harvard University Press.

Schuman, Howard, Charlotte Steeh, Lawrence Bobo, and Maria Krysan. 1997. *Racial Attitudes in America*. Cambridge, MA: Harvard University Press.

Segal, David, and Marshall Meyer, 1974. The Social Context of Political Partisanship. In Mattei Dogan and Stein Rokkan (eds.), *Social Ecology*. Cambridge, MA: MIT Press, pp. 217–32.

Sherman, Lawrence. 1979. Measuring Homicide by Police Officers. *Journal of Criminal Law and Criminology* 70:546–460.

Sherman, Lawrence. 1980. Execution Without Trial: Police Homicide and the Constitution. *Vanderbilt Law Review* 33:71–100.

Shibutani, Tamotsu. 1987. *Society and Personality: An Interactionist Approach to Social Psychology*. New Brunswick, NJ: Transaction Books.

Shingles, Richard D. 1981. Black Consciousness and Political Participation: The Missing Link. *American Political Science Review* 75:76–91.

Sigelman, Lee, and Susan Welch, 1991. *Black Americans' Views of Racial Inequality*. New York: Cambridge University Press.

Sigelman, Lee, and Susan Welch, 1993. The Contact Hypothesis Revisited: Interracial Contact and Positive Racial Attitudes. *Social Forces* 71:781–95.

Sigelman, Lee, Susan Welch, Timothy Bledsoe, and Michael Combs. 1994. The Impact of Police Brutality on Public Attitudes: A Tale of Two Beatings. *Political Research Quarterly*

Sigelman, Lee, Susan Welch, Timothy Bledsoe, and Michael W. Combs. 1996. Making Contact? Black–White Social Interaction in an Urban Setting. *American Journal of Sociology* 101:1306–332.

Simms, Margaret. 1987. Update on the Job Status of Blacks. *Focus* (April 6–7).

Singleton, Louise C., and Steven R. Asher. 1979. Racial Integration and Children's Peer Preferences: An Investigation of Developmental and Cohort Differences. *Child Development* 50:936–41.

Skogan, Wesley, and Michael Maxfield. 1981. *Coping with Crime*. Newbury Park, CA: Sage.

References

Smith, Richard A. 1991. The Measurement of Segregation Change through Integration and Deconcentration, 1970–1980. *Urban Affairs Quarterly* 26:477–96.

Sniderman, Paul, and Edward G. Carmines. 1997. *Reaching beyond Race*. Cambridge, MA: Harvard University Press.

Sniderman, Paul, and Michael Hagen. 1985. *Race and Inequality: A Study in American Values*. Chatham, NJ: Chatham House.

Sniderman, Paul, and Thomas Piazza. 1993. *The Scar of Race*. Cambridge: Harvard University Press.

Sorensen, Annemette, Karl E. Taeuber, and Leslie J. Hollingsworth, Jr. 1975. Indexes of Racial Residential Segregation for 109 Cities in the United States, 1940 to 1970, *Sociological Focus* 8:128–30.

South, Scott, and Kyle Crowder, 1999. Neighborhood Effects on Family Formation. *American Sociological Review* 64:113–32.

Spear, Allan. 1967. *Black Chicago*. Chicago: University of Chicago Press.

Sprague, John. 1982. Is There a Micro Theory Consistent with Contextual Analysis. In Eleanor Ostrom (ed.), *Strategies of Political Inquiry*. Beverly Hills: Sage.

Squires, Gregory D., Larry Bennett, Kathleen McCourt, and Philip Nyden. 1987. *Race, Class, and the Response to Urban Decline*. Philadelphia: Temple University Press.

Stafford, Marc C., and Omer R. Galle. 1984. Victimization Rates, Exposure to Risk, and Fear of Crime. *Criminology* 22:173–185.

Stahura, John M. 1986. Changing Patterns of Suburban Racial Composition, 1970–1980. *Urban Affairs Quarterly* 23:448–60.

Stang, David J. 1974. Methodological Factors in Mere Exposure Research. *Psychological Bulletin* 81:1014–25.

Stringer, Maurice, Ian M. Cornish, and Cathy Finlay. 1991. Strength of Group Identity and Locational Preference in Northern Ireland. *Journal of Social Psychology*. 131:743–45.

Sucoff, Clea, and Dawn M. Upchurch. 1998. Neighborhood Context and the Risk of Childbearing among Metropolitan-Area Black Adolescents. *American Sociological Review* 63:571–85.

Sugrue, Thomas J. 1996. *The Origins of the Urban Crisis: Race and Inequality in Postwar Detroit*. Princeton, NJ: Princeton University Press.

Swain, Carol. 1993. *Black Faces, Black Interests*. Cambridge, MA: Harvard University Press.

Taeuber, Karl, and Alma Taeuber. 1965. *Negroes in Cities: Residential Segregation and Neighborhood Change*. Chicago: Aldine.

Tajfel, Henri 1981. *Human Groups and Social Categories*. Cambridge, UK: Cambridge University Press.

Tate, Katherine. 1993. *From Protest to Politics*. New York: Russell Sage Foundation.

Taylor, D. Garth, Paul Sheatsley, and Andrew Greeley. 1978. Attitudes toward Racial Integration. *Scientific American* 238:42–9.

Taylor, Marylee. 1998. How White Attitudes Vary with the Racial Composition of Local Populations: Numbers Count. *American Sociological Review* 63:512–35.

Tienda, Marta, and Ding-Tzann Lii. 1987. Minority Concentration and Earnings Inequality: Blacks, Hispanics, and Asians Compared. *American Journal of Sociology* 93:141–65.

References

Tingsten, Herbert. 1963. *Political Behavior: Studies in Election Statistics* (translated by Vilgot Hammarling). Totowa, NJ: Bedminster Press.

Tsukashima, Ronald and Darrel Montero. 1976. The Contact Hypothesis: Social and Economic Contact and Generational Changes in the Study of Black anti-semitism, *Social Forces*. 55:149–65.

Turner, Marjorie Austin. 1992. Discrimination in Urban Housing Markets: Lessons from Fair Housing Audits. *Housing Policy Debate* 3:185–215.

U.S. Census, 1998. *Statistical Abstract of the United States 1997*. Washington, DC: US Department of Commerce.

U.S. Census, 2000. *Statistical Abstract of the United States 1999*. Washington, DC: US Department of Commerce.

Usui, Wayne M. 1984. Homogeneity of Friendship Networks of Elderly Blacks and Whites. *Journal of Gerontology* 39:350–6.

Vander Zanden, James W. 1984. *Social Psychology*. New York: Random House.

Verba, Sidney, and Norman H. Nie. 1972. *Participation in America*. New York: Harper & Row.

Verbrugge, Lois M. 1983. A Research Note on Adult Friendship Contact: A Dyadic Perspective. *Social Forces* 62:78–83.

Vose, Element. 1959. *Caucasians Only: The Supreme Court, the NAACP and the Restrictive Covenant Cases*. Berkeley: University of California Press.

Welch, Susan, and Michael Combs. 1985. Intra-racial Differences in the Attitudes of Blacks: Class Cleavages or Consensus. *Phylon* 46:91–7.

Welch, Susan, Michael Combs, Tim Bledsoe, and Lee Sigelman. 1996. Justice for All: Still an American Dilemma. In Obie Clayton (ed.), *An American Dilemma Revisited*. New York: Russell Sage Foundation, pp. 209–25.

Wellman, Barry. 1979. The Community Question: The Intimate Networks of East Yorkers. *American Journal of Sociology* 83:1202–31.

Whitby, Kenny. 1998. *The Color of Representation*. Ann Arbor: University of Michigan Press.

Widick, B.J. 1989. *Detroit: City of Race and Class Violence*. Detroit: Wayne State University Press, 1989.

Wiese, Andrew. 1993. Places of Our Own: Suburban Black Towns Before 1960. *Journal of Urban History* 19 (May): 30–54.

Wilcox, Clyde, and Leopoldo Gomez. 1990. Religion, Group Identification, and Politics among American Blacks. *Sociological Analysis* 51:271–85.

Wilcox, Jerry, and Wade Roof. 1978. Percent Black and Black–White Status Inequality. *Social Science Quarterly* 59:421–34.

Williams, Allen. 1964. Reduction of Tension through Intergroup Contact. *Pacific Sociological Review* 7:81–8.

Wilson, Robert. 1971. Anomie in the Ghetto: A Study of Neighborhood Type, People, and Anomie. *American Journal of Sociology* 77 (July): 66–68.

Wilson, William J. 1987. *The Truly Disadvantaged: The Inner City, the Underclass, and Public Policy*. Chicago: University of Chicago Press.

Wilson, William J. 1996. *When Work Disappears*. New York: Knopf.

Wong, Kenneth. 1990. *City Choices: Education and Housing*. Albany: State University of New York Press.

References

Wood, Robert C. 1959. *Suburbia: Its People and Their Politics.* Boston: Houghton Mifflin.

Wright, Gerald. 1977. Contextual Models of Electoral Behavior: The Wallace Vote in the South. *American Political Science Review* 74:497–508.

Yancey, William L., Eugene P. Ericksen, and Richard N. Juliani. 1976. Emergent Ethnicity: A Review and Reformulation. *American Sociological Review* 41:391–403.

Zajonc, Robert B. 1968. Attitudinal Effects of Mere Exposure. *Journal of Personality and Social Psychology* 9:1.

Author Index

Author Index

Author Index

Author Index

Subject Index

Subject Index

Other books in the series

Asher Arian, *Security Threatened: Surveying Israeli Opinion on Peace and War*

James DeNardo, *The Amateur Strategist: Intuitive Deterrence Theories and the Politics of the Nuclear Arms Race*

John Hibbing and Elizabeth Theiss-Morse, *What Is It About Government that Americans Dislike?*

Robert Huckfeldt and John Sprague, *Citizens, Politics, and Social Communication*

Mathew McCubbins and Samuel Popkin, *Elements of Reason: Cognition, Choice, and the Bounds of Rationality*

George E. Marcus, John L. Sullivan, Elizabeth Theiss-Morse, and Sandra L. Wood, *With Malice Toward Some: How People Make Civil Liberties Judgments*

Diana C. Mutz, *Impersonal Influence: How Perceptions of Mass Collectives Affect Political Attitudes*

Paul M. Sniderman, Richard A. Brody, and Philip E. Tetlock, *Reasoning and Choice: Explorations in Political Psychology*

John Zaller, *The Nature and Origins of Mass Opinion*